NO RUTS FOR ME!

NO RUTS FOR ME!

How to take the hard dirty jobs and turn them into rackets
How to have fun in the great outdoors without getting shot or drowned
How to survive (or not) as a newcomer in a small town
How to get rich, maybe, as a writer for periodical publications

NO RUTS FOR ME!

Outlandish Jobs, Outdoor Comrades, Outsider In A Small Town, Out To Get Rich As A Writer

Allan Ishmael Young

Writers Club Press

San Jose New York Lincoln Shanghai

NO RUTS FOR ME!
Outlandish Jobs, Outdoor Comrades,
Outsider In A Small Town, Out To Get Rich As A Writer

Writers Club Press
an imprint of iUniverse.com, Inc.

For information address:
iUniverse.com, Inc.
5220 S 16th, Ste. 200
Lincoln, NE 68512
www.iuniverse.com

ISBN: 0-595-19696-9

Printed in the United States of America

Dedication

To my wife, Rosemary, for all her support and understanding for over half a century, and for occasionally hiding her dismay, or mirth, at some of the things I do!

Epigraph

"While avoiding ruts, whatever you do has to meet three criteria, or maybe four. You have to like what you do, where and with whom you are doing it. The pay, enjoyment or other compensation has to be commensurate with similar activities in the area. You must never be made to feel that you are on the outside looking in. And it must look good on your next resume, or in the next chapter of your personal history."—Allan Young's Uncle Brigham

Contents

Foreword

By Mr. Galloway

"The only difference between a rut and a grave is the depth!" Allan Young is fond of saying, and it is true, at least for him.

By his own admission, Allan Young has performed over a hundred different types of work for pay, and, having known him all his life, I am here to confirm it. He has done everything from herding cattle to managing a large manufacturing plant, among other things. He has been a grocery produce clerk, a policeman, a farmer, a dog and horse breeder, and a truck driver. He served a hitch in the Navy. He is an educated engineer, a licensed marine pilot and engineer, and holds a masters license for inland lakes and rivers. He has been an editor and publisher of newspapers, magazines and books—and is currently a collegiate writing instructor. He makes many speeches and conducts seminars on a variety of writing, manufacturing and business subjects.

But Allan always envied Fred. Fred lived in the same small town all his life. Worked at the same job, driving a forklift in a paper mill, until he retired. His only sport was golf, which he played every Saturday morning, except in winter. His friends were the ones he grew up with—and this included his wife, the only girl he ever dated. There was absolutely no variety in Fred's life.

Allan envied him, but he would have gone nuts trying to live like him!

This book shows you the difference between Allan and Fred.

It is a compilation of humorous essays and stories about four different areas of life: where you work, how you play, where you live, and your ambition for the future. What else is there?

Fred never had any of these problems, but he had none of the excitement, enjoyment and satisfaction either.

Allan says this is meant to be a SEF HEP book, and Old Fred should have read it first!

Once when I asked him why he decided to captain riverboats, Allan replied, "Why not?"

When I asked him why he changed professions, he said, "Why the question?"

Well, I know he never missed any meals, and his family didn't want for anything, even though he and his wife of over half a century have had more than thirty residences, sometimes more than one at a time, including fourteen homes of their own.

He is an avid golfer, trout fisherman and duck hunter, having fished for everything that swims, and hunted many overabundant game animals and birds. He has played semi-pro baseball, and used to be a ping-pong and billiards shark, but has tried his hand at bowling, tennis, softball, basketball, croquet and badminton.

But, do you want to know what he really does for a living? He writes about all the other stuff he does, or at least includes it in his books and articles in some manner. He even writes his own training materials for teaching. He has had many books published, including novels, novellas, westerns, mysteries, humor, juvenile and children's stories, even some poems and cartoons—and, of course, his mainstay, non-fiction books.

This is one of them! A funny one!

I am Mr. Galloway—his lifelong friend, mentor, and sometime employer.

PART ONE
OUTLANDISH JOBS

TAKE THEM, AND TURN THEM INTO RACKETS
It pays to do the jobs no one else wants to do.

Hey, it's a dirty job but somebody has to do it!

How many times have you heard that? Or said it yourself?

Of course it's usually said in relation to an easy job, or when you take off to play golf, or go fishing, or some other equally delightful pastime. But never is it said bout a really dirty job.

And it should be! Especially if you know how to work it into a good deal for yourself. Just take the worst job to be done, whether you get it forced on you or have a choice, then ask yourself, "What's in it for me?"

Believe me, there is always something in it for you, if you just take a hard look at it.

When you are given a choice, always take the worst job.

Evaluate it for any side benefits it might give you—most of the time there are some, that have nothing whatsoever to do with doing the job.

Learn everything you can from the job, whether or not it is applicable to that particular activity.

Make every effort to see that it will look good on your next resume, and there always is a next resume.

Try to find out what part of his job the boss doesn't like to do, and do it yourself.

Find out when the boss just needs company and be there, without sucking up.

When others are assigned dirty jobs they don't want to do, jump right in and help.

There are always privileges to be gained in your other activities from doing the undesirable jobs.

Decide if it is really a dirty job, and if you can turn it to your advantage right up front—but be patient—sometimes the benefits appear later as you go along.

Herein are many varieties of outlandish job experiences that were turned into better situations—"rackets" is a better term—and they are all true!

Take heed, and apply them to your own situations. You will be all the better off for it!

CHAPTER 1

OUTLANDISH JOBS AS A WAY OF LIFE

There are at least a half dozen known ways to try to get out of doing a hard, dirty or just plain undesirable job or task—and none of them work!

The first is trying to convince others that it isn't necessary—that it really doesn't have to be done.

There is outright refusal to do it.

Then comes passing it off onto someone else.

The fourth way is wandering off somewhere to hide for a while and hoping it is forgotten, or, if it is time oriented, that the time for doing it will run out.

Then there is procrastinating on doing it as long as can be, thinking that maybe the idea will become obsolete. The time element plays in this one also.

And, finally, there is taking on the job but performing it so slowly, or haphazardly, that it is decided by those making the assignment originally that it will never get done, or at least not be finished on time—and some other action is required.

Rule number one in business is that no boss likes a hassle.

Rule number two says that if you think you can hassle the boss, reread rule number one!

And all of these methods of trying to get out of doing outlandish jobs add up to a half dozen ways to hassle the boss.

The danger in trying to convince others that a task doesn't have to be performed at all is that you might eventually become branded as a negative thinker, and that can be detrimental to your career.

Larry was a good manufacturing engineer, had much creative ability and was a good problem solver. He just didn't know what to do when given an undesirable assignment. When one was pointed his way, he would immediately start researching and telling his boss all the reasons why it should not be done.

"We never did that before."

"We don't do it that way here."

"Nobody has proven to me that we can't live without it."

"It looks like a lot of work to me. Is it worth it?"

"Can't it be subcontracted?"

And many more, until one day the chief engineer called Larry into his office and told him, "Larry, I'm getting afraid of you, and that is bad— not for me but for you."

When Larry asked him what he meant, he replied, "I'm afraid to give you an assignment, because you spend a lot of time hassling me about doing it. Sometimes the amount of time you and I spend discussing not doing it is greater than the time it would take you to do it in the first place. Here lately I've been looking right past you when I have a difficult assignment, to see who else might do it, even though it is more suited to your talents."

"I certainly don't object to that!" said Larry.

"But I do," replied his boss. "If any project which I give to you is automatically going to take up much of my time answering your objections to doing it, then I might as well take that time to do it myself in the first place. In that case, one of us is not needed. Can you guess which one it is?"

Larry's biggest problem was that he didn't know how to make an undesirable job work for him instead of against him, but he soon learned!

If you decide to simply refuse to do an undesirable job, you had better make sure you are on very stable ground—like being the offspring or in-law of the boss! Nothing else works.

Eldon would sit in the staff meetings of the vice president of the company and say repeatedly, "Naw, I'm not going to do that."

He felt that his twenty-seven years with the company, compared to the vice president's seven, gave him certain privileges such as choosing his own projects. What he failed to understand, in spite of his twenty-seven years of experience, (or was it one year's experience twenty-seven times?), was that his reaction to his boss' requests were sure to undermine that individual's authority with the rest of his staff. He wasn't always right, but he was always boss!

Eldon found a lower level position in a small competitive organization in which to finish out his working career.

In passing a job off to someone else, the danger is that you might be thought of as having not enough to do after that particular job is gone. There is no such thing as the indispensable person.

Dan was the manager of stock room for his company, but there were some things which he simply did not like to do, although they were part of his job description. One of these was checking receipts of new material as it arrived. So, he determined a way to slough it off on the incoming inspection people, since they had to look at it anyway.

He spent a considerable amount of time and maneuvering to accomplish this, finally convincing his boss that it should be done.

Of course, he was very much chagrined when, a short time later, in a consolidation move, the entire stockroom operation was placed under the direction of the supervisor of the incoming inspection department—and Dan was no longer needed!

The last three ways of trying to get out of an outlandish job can be linked together, since they are all time oriented—hoping that the time will run out in which to do the task, or that its scheduled completion date cannot be met.

Ben could get lost quicker than anybody, but he always went to the same place. His department in the company relied heavily on the data processing group for information. Since he was computer oriented and liked that type of work, he spent quite a bit of time in that area. This happened especially whenever he was given an undesirable assignment. He would simply wander over to the data processing department for days on end, presumably for the benefit of his own department, and never get his own job done.

One day, after noticing the lack of progress on one of Ben's assignments, his boss asked him what the trouble was.

"I've been helping data processing get a new program on line," he replied.

When his disturbed boss asked him why, he said, "It might be of help to us, and I wanted to see to it that it is done right."

A few days later he was surprised to be offered an entry-level position in the data processing department, since he spent so much time there anyway. Ben didn't have any problems at all taking on difficult assignments after that!

Louis was a tool and die maker who always hated to start a new job, whether it was difficult or not. Whenever the foreman gave him a project, usually right after he had completed a previous one, he would do everything he could think of to keep from starting in on it. He proceeded to carry the drawings all over the shop, discussing them with anybody who would listen, for at least one whole day, before he ever ordered the material and began cutting it.

This meant that many hours, all non-productive, were added to the cost of the tool. Louis wasn't lazy, and he was an expert at his craft—he was just a procrastinator.

Then one day the foreman, who didn't get to be boss by being stupid, said to Louis, when he was due for another job, "From now on you will work as part of a two-man team. I will assign a project to both of you, but the other guy will be in charge, and will direct your efforts. You will be expected to do what he says and when he wants it done. We'll start with Paul."

Louis liked Paul, but did not want to be a teammate of his, or anyone else. He didn't want to be one notch removed from getting orders directly from the boss. This subordinate position, even though it was not official, galled him.

Louis, also not having gotten to be a top tool and die maker by being a dummy, evaluated his situation, and after determining why he was assigned to work in this manner, became the starting member of whatever team he was assigned to, and soon was back working on his own.

(Of course, in the Navy, I've seen guys, who were supposed to be swabbing the decks, stand leaning on the handle of a mop, counting the strings in it until the day was over. But that's another story!)

Then there is the dragging out of a project as long as you can. If you get caught in this trap, you had better be sure it is one with a deadline, but that is really not very important in the long run. If not, you might be on it for the rest of your working life, and you had better find ways to always look busy at it.

John had taken on the job of providing engineering drawings to a small company, which had no engineering staff of its own. He worked at home, on an hourly rate, to invoice them upon completion of the job. As soon as he started the project, he knew he was in over his head. And besides, there was a deadline. He was happy to see that the shop was going ahead without him, and the deadline came and went without him

having a complete set of drawings.

Soon the head of the company was ignoring him. Then he learned they had shipped the device, late, but to customer satisfaction.

When he presented his bill for the hours he had spent on the project, the manager tore it up and tossed it in the nearest wastebasket. When John protested, saying that, although he had not completed the drawings on time, they had been able to use enough of them to ship the product.

"No," said the manager. "When you missed the deadline, we found someone who took it seriously, got an extension from the customer, and shipped them a quality product. We owe you nothing."

So, you see, all of these are examples of why trying to get out of a hard, dirty undesirable job does not work.

The number one rule in the military service has always been to not volunteer for anything. But this is definitely not true—there, or anywhere else.

Why not volunteer for—or at least accept—the outlandish jobs, and turn them in to rackets? Make sure there is something in them for you. It's easier than you might think!

CHAPTER 2

LITTLE KIDS WORKING

In our childhood, at some time or other we have all been asked (or told!) to do some type of work which we would just as soon not be doing— maybe not at that time, because something else seemed more important, nor in that place, or perhaps not even at all. We can remember ourselves dragging our feet towards it, or away from it, or just standing looking at it while wishing that it would go away. And it wouldn't.

But really there is probably no time in your life when you are better at turning an undesirable task into a racket than when you first find out that you have to do some work. The story of Tom Sawyer and his fence-painting project is a good example. Tom didn't try to convince Aunt Polly that it didn't need to be done, nor did he refuse to do it. He did not procrastinate or drag it out over time. He did not push it off on others either. He simply promoted himself to manager of the project, still taking responsibility for it—but tricking others into doing the actual work. It was still his dirty job, and he turned it into a racket by convincing the other boys to give him something in return for the privilege of doing his work for him. The ultimate racket from a outlandish job!

Now, unless you are a kid in grade school, it might be a little late to start learning how to utilize the jobs you or nobody else wants to do to your best advantage, but here are some case histories anyhow. Most jobs, requests or assignments that you get at the pre-teen age cannot be helped—someone simply forces them on you. But take a hard look, there is always something in it for you, if you work it right!

Coal and Kindling (Getting Somebody's Goat)

My first experience at turning an undesirable job into a racket was when my little brother got the easiest of chores at home and I got the hardest. He carried in the coal from the coal pile and I had to chop the kindling.

When I was eight years old and he was six our family moved out in the country from the coal camps. Our father, a miner, now had to travel further to work, so he assigned certain jobs to my brother and me.

Our house was heated in winter by a large cast iron cook stove in the kitchen, and a coal-burning fireplace in the living room. The cook stove, which also burned coal, was used to cook food and heat water for all purposes, all year round. My brother was given the job of always having a supply of coal handy for both coal burning units, while my job—since Dad had trained me in the use of an ax, a hatchet and buck saw a year earlier—was to have enough kindling available whenever a fire had to be started.

In summer, since the stove made the kitchen so warm, the fire in it might be started three times a day, but in winter a fire was built in both the stove and fireplace in the morning and kept going all day, then allowed to go out at night. My father got up first to build the fires—it was considered the job of the husband and father.

"He's so lazy his wife has to build the fires," was just about the most derogatory statement that could be made about a man.

But there was no way out of it. That kindling and that coal had to be there. If we didn't do it no one else would, and you know what kind of trouble that would put two small boys in immediately. We believed that refusal to do the jobs was tantamount to suicide!

The difference between my job and my brother's was that it seemed like I was working all the time, and he wasn't. I not only had to cut the kindling to a fire starting size, but I had to go to the woods, find it in the form of poles, drag them home, then saw them to pieces of the right length before splitting them. All he had to do was carry in five gallon buckets of lump coal and set them beside the stove and fire place and keep them full. I do have to admit that a five gallon container of coal could put quite a strain on the muscles of a six year old boy!

Then my little devious eight-year-old mind started working. First, there was no way out of the job, short of death—and I suspected that would occur at my father's own hand if I tried to shirk my duties. Second, I couldn't trade with my brother—even if I was able to convince him, or bribe him—because Dad wouldn't knowingly let him use an ax.

But wait, why would I want to trade? In looking at both jobs, I suddenly realized that since his coal was used continuously he could in no way stockpile it, he had to keep carrying it in whenever it was needed. But not the kindling! It was needed twice a day in winter, and maybe three times or less in summer. I could get ahead of the game.

Now for a container. Coal mining supplies, including dynamite, were delivered in tough wooden boxes of various sizes, and Dad often brought them home from the mines, so we had several around at all times. The cook stove sat across the corner of the room on an angle—"catty-cornered" if you will, or "whopper-jawed" to some. I found a box that just fit in this space, out of the way, and almost out of sight—and it would hold a week's supply of kindling!

My brother wasn't too happy when he saw me cut up a whole batch of kindling, then go on off and do whatever eight year old boys do for a week, while he kept lugging in the coal. Now he felt discriminated against, as I had before.

But it doesn't end there!

We were poor. (A friend of mine told me later that his family was so poor they thought "Day Old Bread" was a brand name. I told him that if he had store-bought bread he sure wasn't poor, he was rich!) As with most coal miners' kids, the only playthings we had were those made by our father—a see-saw, merry-go-round, (both made of planks), a tree swing and a wagon. To go with the wagon, Dad horse-traded (his term) for a large billy goat, for which he made a set of harness, and trained him to pull the wagon.

In the course of my exploring the woods in back of our place, I found an old rail fence, probably built over a hundred years before. Talk about seasoned wood! So, I would take old "Joe Bill" over there, hitch him to a couple of rails, and let him drag them home, where I would saw them to length and split them for kindling.

Then one day, just as I had Joe Bill hooked up, my brother, not knowing where either of us was, called the goat, who had learned to respond to that by coming to the caller. Joe Bill took off for home, towing my rails behind.

Big idea! My brother and I simultaneously! He unhitched Joe Bill from the rails at the chop block, then I called him. Here he came, back to where I was in the woods!

But it doesn't end there, either!

With the goat doing the traveling, we soon had a pile of poles 'til "who laid the rail", if you will pardon the expression. Borrowing Dad's crosscut saw, we started piling up kindling by the ton. So, we began tying it in bundles and selling it for a few cents to neighbors, mostly older ladies, who couldn't cut their own. I started helping carry in the coal, of course, to help out my partner.

What a racket! (Well, old Joe Bill might not have thought so.)

Cleaning Out the Stable (Shoveling What ?)

The Gentleman Farmer's hired man wouldn't give me a job, but the Farmer did. Boy, did he ever!

I was in sixth grade, fairly big for my age, and wanted, and needed, money. Some kids not much bigger than me were helping out on farms, especially in tobacco, which required a lot of manual labor. One farm in particular, which was so big they required a full time hired man, had quite a few younger workers.

When I learned they were working in the tobacco fields one day, I hiked off down there, walked up past the house and found where they were. When I told the grumpy old hired man what I wanted, he blew up. Told me I was too young, too little, too stupid, and lord knows what else, as I ran back down the hill to get out of earshot of his tirade.

It didn't help any to hear the laughter and catcalls of the dozen or so teenagers working in the field. I was to find out later that they were all his relatives and their friends, so he wouldn't have hired me, anyway.

As I walked past one of the barns close to the house, I saw some manure mixed with straw come flying through one of the window openings on the back side of the barn. I went in and found a red-faced, white-haired gentleman of advanced age forking manure out of one of a dozen horse stalls.

"Good morning, son," he said pleasantly, leaning on his manure fork. "You know, I'm getting too old for this."

"Why don't you have someone else do it then, sir?" I asked. "You seem to have lots of help."

"Because they are all busy in tobacco, today. They don't want to do it, anyway." he said. "Probably think it's beneath them."

"I'll do it," I said.

"You looking for a job?"

"Yes, sir. I'll do anything."

"And you want to do this?" he smiled. "By gosh, I think you do. It's hard work. We have to fork it twice, once out of the barn, then into the manure spreader."

So he put me to work, helping me himself that first day.

When the other kids came down off the hill I was still working, so they laughed at me again—making remarks about that being all I was good for, how I should feel right at home with that other stuff just like me—and worse.

My employer kept eight show horses in the barn, which had twelve stalls. I moved them from stall to stall in order to clean the one they were in. He was right, it was hard work. By the end of my third day the horses and I were old friends, but the other kids were still walking by and taunting me every afternoon.

On the afternoon of the third day, my employer brought the spreader around behind the barn with a team of workhorses, and helped me load all the manure into it. My sixth-grade head spun all night thinking about that.

The next day I went to his house and knocked on the back door. When he came out I asked him if we could park the manure spreader behind the barn under the windows and shovel directly into it from the stalls. It would reach across two stall windows at a time.

He looked at me so long I thought he was mad, then he started laughing.

"Why didn't I or somebody else think of that before? It's so simple. What made you think of it?"

"I don't know. I like to solve problems, or maybe I'm just lazy," I said.

"No, you're anything but lazy." he grinned. "Even now you will get less hours this way, so you'll make less money. Maybe I can find something else for you to do."

When he came out about mid-afternoon, I told him I thought one of the horses was off her feed, and she held her head low when I moved her to another stall.

He said, "I think she just needs exercise. Can you ride a horse?"

When I told him I could, he suggested we take her and one other out for a ride. He used a saddle, but wouldn't let me. "Horses can be bred, but saddles cost money."

Mounting up, we rode off in the direction of the field workers. He said he wanted to check on them.

It was just awful, me riding up on a high-stepping horse, alongside the boss-man, looking down on my taunters! I really felt bad. (And if you believe that, I've got some land down in Florida I'd like to talk to you about!)

When we arrived back at the barn, my boss said, "O.K., that's your new job. In addition to cleaning out the stalls, I want you to take one of the horses out whenever you can and exercise it. They all need it."

So, that's what I worked at all summer, then after school later. I don't mind telling you that the hired man tried hard to get me in the fields, and one of his sons in my job—but it didn't happen. I had done the job when it was hard, had improved on it to the satisfaction of the boss.

And you know, the only places I could ever find to exercise those horses was wherever those other kids happen to be at the time!

The School Spring (To Drink or not to Drink)

Sometimes dirty jobs and rackets can be found at other than work places or at home. At school, for example.

Our country grade school was located at the base of a mountain, at the upper end of a long valley, and consisted of six classrooms and an auditorium. In the hall was a single drinking fountain—from which no water came. All the students who wanted a drink during the school day had to bring their own water. This was most imperative during the hot September days just after school started, and in late spring before school closed for the summer.

Then, of course, there was no water for the summer playground activities, including the use of the baseball diamond by local and visiting teams.

One Saturday, after school started, my brother and I were on one of our exploring trips up in the hollows of the mountain when we came across a spring which we hadn't seen before. There were many springs in the mountains, but this one was hidden in a hollow, and the overflow ran down and joined water from others a short distance away.

We stopped to rest in the cooling shade among the ferns growing all over the rocks around it. When we bent over to get a drink we discovered a metal pipe leading out of it underground. It appeared to be about an inch in diameter, and had a screen over the end of it, which was completely covered with leaves and debris.

We looked at each other, and said, almost in unison, "The school fountain!"

The school was approximately fifty years old, and we presumed the pipe had been run the mile or so to it at that time, but there was probably no one left alive who knew where it came from, and would also know it wasn't working.

We cleaned it out as best we could with our bare hands, then went home—mentioning it to nobody. The next day we went back up there equipped with a hoe, a rake and a spade, with which to clean the spring out properly.

At the school on Monday, as we were turning on the fountain and letting years of waste get cleaned out of the pipes, the school principal came along, and after observing our activities for awhile, said, "I presume you boys had something to do with this."

We told him what we had done, and he seemed pleased.

Then a couple of months later, when the water slowed to a trickle, he called us into his room and asked us to go up to the spring again.

"I'm sending Benny and Tommy along with you boys, so they can help, and will know where the water source is for the future," he said, naming two older boys who did janitorial work at the school. In fact, they should have been in high school years before, but being poor students, remained in eighth grade, just to keep their part time jobs at the school.

My brother and I didn't really want them along, but the principal was tough, and not to be argued with.

As we left the school grounds, the other two let it slip out that the principal was going to pay them a dollar each whenever they cleaned out the spring. I looked at my brother and he looked at me, a wave of understanding running between us.

We led Benny and Tommy all around the mountain for the whole afternoon, about as far away from the spring as we could get, and never did find it!

The next day the principal cornered us, and he was not a happy man.

"You know I don't believe you couldn't find the spring," he growled. "I am fully aware of you boys' knowledge of these mountains."

We just stood and looked at him.

"Well, I could paddle both of you for this, couldn't I?"

We still just stood and looked at him.

"We need the water, and I don't like what you are doing, or what you hope to gain. Just what do you two think I ought to do to punish you?"

"Well, sir," I said, "why don't you try offering us a dollar apiece!"

His face turned red, I thought he was going to explode. Then he calmed down, and growled, "Fair enough."

Handing us each a dollar, he stalked away, hurling over his shoulder, "Do it today!"

And we did, and many other days, about every two months. For a dollar apiece. We later learned that the principal had told someone not to try to bargain with or threaten those brothers—it wouldn't work!

Several times we suspected that Benny and Tommy were following us, and when we did, we never went to the spring.

Of course, after we had discovered a family of spotted salamanders living in that spring on our first visit there, we never drank the water ourselves!

I wonder, just how clean is a spotted salamander?

The Play's the Thing (Me and Bodget)

Sometimes you can take on a school activity that isn't necessarily an outlandish job, or even a job, and turn it to your advantage. It might just be something nobody else wants to do.

Bodget, (her nickname), and I had been in quite a few school plays from third through sixth grades, and now we were in the seventh. One day we found out that the second grade teacher was putting on a stage play that involved almost all her kids, but needed an older boy and girl to play adults. All the seventh and eighth graders had run from the idea—but the teacher said it just wouldn't be the same with two second graders trying to look like adults.

"Let's do it," said Bodget.

"Why not," says I.

So we jumped right in, playing Mr. and Mrs. Vinegar in a funny play about an old couple who were granted three wishes.

One morning, while they were still deciding what to wish for, Mr. Vinegar (me) woke up hungry, and said, "I wish I had a whole pan full of sausages."

So, immediately, right in front of him (me) there appeared a pan of sausages!

Of course, at this, Mrs. Vinegar (Bodget) flew into a rage at him for wasting a wish, and shouted, "You and your sausages! I wish you had them hanging from your nose!"

And there the whole pan was, hanging from the nose of Mr. Vinegar (me). I won't tell you how we did that trick!

Then there was nothing the Vinegars could do but wish them off again—although Mrs. Vinegar (Bodget) had second thoughts about it! All the kids, in the cast and in the audience, roared with laughter, and Bodget and I were off and running. We were suddenly in great demand to play adults in many small children's plays for the next two years.

It got us out of a lot of extra schoolwork, as well as some other undesirable activities—and we still received good grades. We were both surprised, at the end of grade school's last year, when we each got an award for perfect attendance.

But for me the best award came when my teacher asked me if I knew where to get some ferns for use as stage decorations for one of the plays. When I told her yes, meaning the area around the school spring, she told me to go get some, and take Bodget along to help.

That's all I'm going to tell you, because the rest is another story, and has nothing whatsoever to do with undesirable activities!

CHAPTER 3

TEENAGERS WORK EXPERIENCES

Your first job as a teenager usually is whatever you can get—doing whatever is required by whomever will hire you. So, quite often you don't have the opportunity to pick and choose. You will be assigned tasks which you do not want to do, either as part of a job, or some other activity. Perhaps even the first job you get might be an undesirable one, but you could find no other. But even then, you still have the chance to do something for yourself, though the benefit might be outside the job itself.

Dish Washing at the Resort (Pearl Diving is Fun)

We learned of the resort, my brother and I—which employed many teenagers for the summer—several days after school was out, and feared that the jobs would all be taken. But we hitch-hiked the two hundred miles up there anyway.

It was a big, old-fashioned hotel complex built around some hot springs—which was what prompted the railroad to build it back around the turn of the century. But now it had a golf course, riding trails, tennis courts, steam rooms, exercise rooms, indoor and outdoor pools—and many other activity areas for the multitude of conventioneers and vacationers who came every week.

We could visualize ourselves working on the golf course, at the riding stables and other areas catering to the rich and famous. Imagine our chagrin, when the man in the personnel office said, "I'm sorry boys, but all I have left is washing dishes."

Noting our discouraged looks, he went on, "Hey that is not as bad as it sounds. I did it myself a long time ago. In the first place, we have automatic dishwashers now. Secondly, since our guests are all on the plan whereby their meals are included in their room rent, we serve meals only during certain hours, and if they aren't here they don't eat. Consequently, you have a lot of free time. You work only during mealtimes and for a short time afterwards, and your evenings are always free. To me, it's the best job here for someone your ages."

So we took the jobs, since we had no choice and needed work. We were pleased to find out that we could also use other facilities, such as the pools and tennis courts, when they weren't busy. After getting a chance to look around at some of the other jobs the kids were doing, and the hours they kept, and especially the way they had to kowtow to the guests, smiling at people they couldn't stand, I was glad to be hidden away in the scullery.

On my first day off, I wandered down to the riding stables, to discover a wrangler old enough to be my grandfather wrestling with a small gelding, trying to get him into a stall.

"They just brought him in from out west somewhere," he said to me. "I don't know what I'm going to do with him. He don't like nobody."

"Have you got a western saddle?" I asked.

"There is one around here somewhere," he said. "It isn't much, but it's all I got. These people all ride English style."

When he found the saddle, I led the gelding out into the paddock, walked him around a while, talking to him, then saddled him up.

"I'll be back in a couple of hours," I told the wrangler.

Heading up the mountain trail, I learned what I suspected about the little horse. We toured the trails, which crisscrossed the hills, and most of the time I didn't need to rein him at all. When I did it was neck reining only.

When I took him back to the stable, I told the wrangler he was a fine horse. Then a young lady, about my age, whom I had noticed as I rode up, walked over and asked, "How can you say that? I tried to ride him around the paddock yesterday and he gave me all kinds of trouble."

"That is the trouble," I said. "He is a range horse, used to being in the open. Don't ride him in an enclosed area. Take him into the mountains, he loves it there. And please don't try to keep him in a stall," I went on, to the wrangler. "Put him in the pasture, and I'll bet you dollars to dough-nuts that you can walk right up to him out there and put a bridle on him."

"Who is that guy, Grandpa?" I heard her ask the old man, as I walked away. "And how does he know so much about horses?"

That evening after it cooled off, I decided to walk into the little town nearby to see the sights, so I put on my best, and only, sport jacket and headed out. As I came downstairs from my room in the dormitory where we kids were housed—boys upstairs and girls down, (was that supposed to keep us apart?), she was waiting for me.

I had thought she looked charming that day, with her dark hair tied back, and wearing a white tee-shirt, jeans and boots. But now she was absolutely beautiful—hair down to her shoulders, pretty summer dress and white shoes.

"Hi, I'm Ebby," she said. "I won't tell you what it is short for. We are going to a movie."

As we stepped out into the cool night air, she smiled up at me and said, "Take off your jacket."

When I complied, she put it on herself, and said, "Now here, let me roll your sleeves up two turns."

After she did this, she locked her arm in mine and off we went for an enjoyable evening.

The next day I was met by the man from personnel.

"They want you to transfer to the stables," he said. "You can replace the manager's grand daughter when she isn't there."

"Nope," I said. "I'll stay where I am, thank you."

"Why would anybody that knows as much about horses as you do want to be a dishwasher?"

No way was I going to tell him I wouldn't take a job that had me working while Ebby was off, and vice versa! I was a most happy dishwasher the rest of that summer!

Drying Sand at the Mine (Does It Really Take Two?)

Coal mine jobs are all hard work, and extremely dirty, so it is most difficult to turn one into a racket—but Howard and Ed did!

They were my cousins, and our relatives didn't have enough influence with the mining company to get them one of the good jobs for high school students, such as working in the office, the company store, or driving delivery trucks. These were all allotted to the kids with important fathers. But Howard and Ed got jobs drying sand—hard, dirty work.

With mining equipment that hauled the coal out of the mine running on steel rails, like a down-sized railroad, the wheels of the electric locomotives which pulled the coal cars tended to spin on the rails sometimes—because of too long a string of cars, or inclines in the track in the mine. So the machines had sand boxes built into them from which, by pulling a lever, the operator could dispense sand to the rails when needed to give traction. The sand had to be dry in order to come out of the sand container properly.

This is where Howard and Ed came in.

Outside the entrance to the mine was a large oven used to dry the sand, from which it was put into a hopper from which the sand boxes on the locomotives could be filled.

The sand, always wet when received and from lying in a pile, had to be shoveled into the drier, then after quite some time of twiddling their thumbs, the shovelers had to direct the dry sand to the hopper, which might also require some shoveling.

One night Howard wanted me to go somewhere with him. I told him I thought he worked every night after school at the mine. So he asked me to accompany him to work. I watched as he and Ed did the backbreaking labor of shoveling the sand into the drying machine until it was full. Then Howard said goodbye to Ed and we left. He stopped at the company bath-house and showered. I did, too, although I hadn't planned to. I hadn't shoveled any sand. Then we went on to the party.

In answer to my inquisitive follow-up, he said it's only a two-man job up until the drier is full. After that, one man could handle it—and there was a lot of time to kill.

So, since they never saw any sign of their boss, and weren't really sure who he was, they had worked out a schedule of alternate nights—both of them working the first couple of hours, then one of them leaving. They were both still getting full pay, of course.

It was still outlandish work, but a racket nonetheless!

A Driving Job for No Pay (But Lots of Pleasure!)

Sometimes you can take on one of those undesirable jobs, which pays nothing, gives you lots of responsibility, can get you in trouble and takes you away from where you would like to be at that time. Sounds stupid, doesn't it?

Such was my position as a teacher chauffeur. I don't know how I ever got talked into it, but I'm sure glad I did!

Mr. Myers was a teacher in grade school next to the high school that I attended, and he seemed to be almost indispensable to all the extracurric-ular activities all of a sudden. Whatever was going on after school hours at the high school, he had to be there. It started with him selling tickets at basketball games, and went from there.

One evening he came to me and asked if I was busy. Even though I knew what he wanted, I couldn't think of any way out. He had asked a couple of friends of mine at another time to drive his car up to Dry Branch, a little community approximately five miles away, to pick up his wife, who taught school there, but didn't drive. They had done so, but after realizing the gravity of the situation, and that there was nothing in it for them, they had run from him ever since.

Besides, it took them away from whatever activity they would like to be attending at the high school that evening—the reason for Mr. Myers having to be there in the first place.

The man knew that my main activity was being editor of the school newspaper, and that made my time after school pretty flexible. So when he asked, I went. Mrs. Myers was a pleasant sort, but it still took me away from where I wanted to be for awhile.

I wound up picking her up three times that first week, but on the third trip, Betty showed up! Whoopee!

She was a year behind me in school, but I had long ago learned to appreciate her short dark hair, big blue eyes, open friendly face and a build like the proverbially brick outhouse! I had just never had any contact with her.

On my third trip to Dry Branch, she walked over to the car just as Mrs. Myers was starting to get in, and asked if she could ride back to the school with us—her question being directed more at my passenger than at me. When we both answered in the affirmative, she slid into the back seat.

I learned that she lived there at Dry Branch, right beside the school, had ridden home on the school bus, as she always did, but now wanted to go back to the basketball game. Fine with me. We sat together at the first game, played by the girls' teams, took a walk outside during the halftime break, then did all the same things during the second, the boys' game.

After the last game was over, Mr. Myers, discerning man that he was, came to me and said, "I'm going to be here for a while, yet. Maybe you ought to go ahead and take Betty home."

At that moment I would have washed his car, waxed it and thrown in a shoeshine for him!

The next time I was asked to go get Mrs. Myers, Betty was waiting for me at his parking place, (I don't know how she knew I was going), rode up to Dry Branch with me, ran into her house to do something, came back out ready to go.

Mrs. Myers, who was just as discerning as her husband, got in the back seat this time—with a wry, knowing smile on her lips and a twinkle in her eyes all the way back. Again, I took Betty home before the Myers couple was ready to leave.

This pattern continued for the rest of the school year, except there were many times when I would escort Mrs. Myers back to the high school, then Betty and I would take the car and find someplace else to go for awhile.

One of the boys who had made the first trip to pick up the lady told me I must be crazy to keep on doing that. I told him I sure was, but I didn't tell him who I was crazy about! What a racket!

Another Driving Job (For Pay and Pleasure!)

The second driving job story about teenagers, involves my own son. (He is as big a racketeer as his old man!) He didn't really ask for the job, either. It was sort of forced on him. But he was driving a new Cadillac!

I was editor of the top engineering magazine in a company that published eight such publications in a Chicago suburb. The maintenance manager and the mailroom manager tended to hire the sons and daughters of employees for part time work, whenever they were needed. I came back from a business trip once and found my son there—and I swear to you I didn't have anything to do with him being there!

A few days later I was telling him that he better do a good job, or I might lose mine. Just then the Old Man, the president of the company, walked up behind me and said, "I was just telling your son that if he can't straighten you out, I will have to fire him, too!"

With a loud guffaw he went into his office.

The following week I stopped at the service station across from the office to get gas for my car, and my son walked out. When I asked him what he was doing, he said he was having the Old Man's car serviced.

I warned him about how fussy the president was about his car, a new Cadillac Sedan DeVille, and that other part time employees had refused to drive it. I know I would not have.

My son said the Old Man told him he couldn't get anybody to take care of his car, because they were all afraid of him. But he couldn't take the time to get it serviced, or whatever else it needed.

I pointed out that it was still a big responsibility for a boy who had just gotten his driver's license.

"Well, all he can do is fire me," he replied, his usual realistic self. "And I was looking for a job when I got here."

So my sixteen-year-old son kept on having the responsibility for a car that cost more than my annual salary!

Sometime later I came home from the office to find a new black and white Cadillac in my garage—the Old Man's car! And there was my son cleaning it out. When I asked him about it, he said he had driven the Old Man to the airport, and was keeping the car overnight.

After supper he came downstairs all dressed up.

"Hey, it's Prom Night!" he answered in response to my obvious question.

"And you are driving —— ?"

"You bet," he said. "Wasn't it lucky the boss chose today to go away? Don't worry. I found a place to park it at the dance where no other car can get near it."

A few days later the company president came into my office just as my son was leaving.

With a mean smile on his face, he said to the boy, "Did that cute little blonde like traveling in style to the Prom?"

"She sure did," he replied, "but how did you know?"

"I'm the company president," he said. "It's my job to know—everything. And I do. Just tell me next time."

Looking around at me, he muttered, "What a couple of racketeers!"

Weighing Bananas (The Super Market Racket!)

Grocery stores probably hire as many teenagers as any business, or at least they did when I was growing up. And since there is such a wide variety of work to be done, it is hard to turn any of it into a racket. But I did!

Of course, some kids tried hiding in the back room and not doing anything, but they would soon get caught and relieved of their problems, and their pay.

No, the real racketeer in a job sees to it that he gets a lot done, but always to his advantage—one way or another.

In our store I preferred working in the produce department to anywhere, and that is where I was permanently assigned. Within that department, the worst job, agreed on by everyone, including the manager, was maintaining the banana tree.

We were selling bananas for three fourths of what they cost us. How could we make a profit, you ask? Real easy. By selling head lettuce for four times what it should cost! How did the two tie together? Here is how—a simple marketing strategy: the banana tree was located at the left end of the crisp vegetable case. On that part of the case was kept a mountain of beautiful head lettuce. The good buy on bananas was advertised greatly in newspapers and on radio. The head lettuce was not only omitted from the advertising, it didn't even have a price listed anywhere near it!

Oh, occasionally somebody might ask you the price, then you told them—but it hardly ever happened. Every customer who came into the store headed for the banana tree, and there was the head lettuce right next to it. If the bananas were so cheap, then the lettuce had to be, too!

And who could resist a great big crisp beautiful head of lettuce? The customers came back to the produce department to get a bunch of cheap bananas, and just automatically, without a second thought as to how much they were paying for it, grabbed a head of lettuce—or two!

Now here is where the undesirable job came in. Somebody had to break down the big bunches of bananas into groups of a half dozen or so, wrap them with tape, weigh them and write the price on the tape—then hang them on a framework we called the "tree". This same person had to keep the mountain of lettuce from becoming a prairie, or even a foothill. We all hated it! The customers constantly depleted both the banana tree as well as the lettuce supply. It was a hectic, frustrating job. Whoever was assigned to it, and it was rotated among all of us, complained constantly about having to do it.

After lying awake thinking about a better way to accomplish the job, as I was prone to do, and analyzing just what benefits I might derive from it, I went in one weekend and told the produce manager that I wanted to do that job whenever I worked.

He thought I was nuts, but he gave me the job.

I started by making more room to store the banana bunches prior to taking them apart, as well as more display space, by stacking up lettuce crates. Then I made more room for the lettuce the same way. Besides the more merchandise you have in one place, the more likely it is that people will think it is on sale. It worked for the un-advertised, high-priced head lettuce.

Now I didn't have to make so many trips to the stock room, and could stand there doing my thing while chatting with the customers, especially the young pretty female ones.

About the other benefits—what was really in it for me? Well, to begin with, I got to work as many hours as I wanted. No request for a raise was ever denied. And when I had time I might be out back washing my car with soap and water from the store.

Then, when I finally left the store, they tried to convince me to stay, with a produce manager's job in the offing.

A racket? Pretty darn close!

CHAPTER 4
RACKETS IN THE MILITARY

We have all been made aware of the Sergeant Bilko type of goof-off opportunist in the military. This is pure fantasy—it is utterly impossible to spend your entire career in one of the services milking everybody and not making a contribution to the country's defenses by performing your assigned duties. But there are many chances on a day-to-day basis to improve your lot while still doing what you are supposed to.

Running the Train is Hard Work (But Warm)

There weren't too many ways to find comfort or relieve tension in the Infantry in the First World War, but my father did—to some degree, at least.

The first time he was put on a troop train, not much better than cattle cars, it was in the dead of winter. Making his way up to the engine, he told the fireman and engineer, "I can fire this thing."

And he could. Growing up in the southern coalfields, he had hitched so many free rides on coal trains that the crews had started putting him to work, so one of them could take a nap. Then when he went in the Army, he did the same thing.

In France, his buddies made fun of him for always being dirtier than they were, until winter came.

"It's outlandish work," he would tell them, "but it's warm!"

Of course he didn't tell them that he also got warm on the inside, since every time they stopped to take on water or coal, they also took on a little of the French countryside's number one product—cognac!

Navy Boot Camp Rackets (But I really Like to Grind Onions!)

It's tough to turn any job into a racket during your first few weeks of training in the Navy. The best you can hope for is to use a little military psychology and get a more desirable one. That's why I volunteered to scrub pots and pans in the grease pit, much to the consternation of my shipmates.

During boot camp, the recruits were required to perform in two "service" weeks, three or four weeks apart, when the entire company spends the week doing the dirty work around the training center. Most of this work occurs in the chow hall—cleaning, washing trays and pots and pans, and helping the cooks.

After looking over the service week jobs done by other companies, and talking to their personnel, I learned that the worst job in the chow hall was grinding onions. And many onions were used in preparing Navy food. The job was so bad, they told me, that the people doing it had to be relieved often—sometimes several times during the preparation of a single meal.

Now, onions never bothered me much. I was the one member of my family that could cut them up for my mother without shedding a tear. But how to get the job?

When we were steered to the man who was to give us our chow hall assignments for the week, I stepped forward and asked that I be assigned to the grease pit, scrubbing pots and pans, which was about as far away from the onion grinder as possible. I told him onions were so offensive to me that they made me throw up, and I had to be far away from that operation.

My "Brer Rabbit" act must have been convincing, because, true to Navy fashion, laughing like a maniac, he took me over to the onion-grinding machine and put me to work.

(At the end of boot camp, when we were asked to put down our preference for type of ship—I had none, myself—one of my buddies, who knew about me and the onions, asked for a mine sweeper and was put on an aircraft carrier, which was what he wanted—or at least some large ship.)

I had to work only when the cooks needed onions, right before the noon and evening meals, so, since there was an ice cream making machine next to the onion operation, I took it over, too. I ate a lot of ice cream that week, but not too many onions!

Two weeks before our second service week, I was down at our outdoor theater waiting for the movie to start, and decided to visit the projection booth. The operators were complaining about their lack of help—they could hardly ever go on liberty. I told them I could run a movie projector.

They asked me if I would come down each night and help them—and I did. The other guys thought I was nuts, being tied up almost every night.

But it got me out of the Friday night scrub-up of our barracks, and I spent my next service week in a good, clean projection booth while one of the full time operators went on leave!

The boot camp rackets don't end there, however. One of my friends, Arnold, had been a star baseball player in high school and his one-year of college, so he went out for the base team. Again, the other guys thought he was crazy, tying up his Saturday afternoons and Sundays like that, when the rest of us had free time to roam the base or hang out at the library, reading or listening to records.

It wasn't long before Arnold had no duties, except his training classes, then when the baseball team was sent on a yearlong good will tour to play against military teams all over the world, he went with them. Don't know what ever happened to him—but if you don't plan to make a career out of the military, what a way to put in your time in the peace-time Navy!

Work Party Meal Chit (Hey, I Like to Eat Anytime!)

At the end of boot camp, and formal training for sea duty, and a short leave home, where each of us could be the "son in uniform", we came back to the Outgoing Unit, OGU in Navy terms, to be assigned to schools for further training or
to ships or shore bases.

Learning that the average stay in OGU was ten days, I began looking for a racket. Among other work party assignments was one to do maintenance and fix-up work on various buildings. I quickly got assigned to it, and took it over. We were taken around to several buildings and shown what had to be fixed, told where the tools were and shown where the materials were kept.

But, best of all—and this was what I was shooting for all along—I was given a chow chit!

This piece of paper, and mine was for up to sixteen men, gave us permission to go to the chow hall and eat at any time our work schedule allowed, and it was good for two weeks.

We got all our assigned tasks done, but on our own schedule. Whenever we were stopped for running all over the base and having a good time, I would just produce the chit and tell them we were on our way to the chow hall.

Our stay in OGU went pretty fast and pleasantly.

A small Navy racket, but a racket nonetheless!

Navy Truck Driver (The WAVES in the Port Director's Office!)

After having ridden out a hurricane in the Caribbean, getting my ship damaged in the Panama Canal, colliding with the pier at Alameda Naval Air Station and running aground off Okinawa, I was taken off and reassigned to a shore base in Manila Bay, driving a truck. I didn't mind. With the kind of luck my ship had, I was just glad the war was over!

The Chief Petty Officer in charge of the motor pool was a little wiry Texan with a spreading eagle tattooed in the red hairs of his chest, who loved to drink and fight —usually losing the latter.

I drove a ten-wheel truck, running whatever errands were assigned to me, along with a half dozen other drivers. When I first came there, along with another shipmate off the USS Accident-prone, as we called her, I told the Chief I had never driven a big truck, and would prefer a weapons carrier, which was about the size of a pickup truck. My companion used to drive a flatbed semi between New York and Bridgeport, hauling steel. Naturally he wanted the biggest truck he could get. True to its reputation, the Navy, in the form of the Chief, gave him a weapons carrier, and me a ten-wheeler!

They thought of it as crosstraining. We thought of it as a waste of talent and experience. Of course we had a few not-so-delicate Navy terms for it as well.

Then one night I was out in Cavite City just poking around when I found the Chief and some friends getting beaten up by some other sailors. I hung back until it was over, (I didn't get paid enough to get hurt), then I herded him and the others into his jeep and took them back across the causeway to the base.

The next day he looked me up at the motor pool and thanked me for my efforts. After he found out I didn't drink, he would never go out on the town without me. He would buy me a big tropical dinner, let me go where I wanted with his jeep—as long as I was there when it was time to go back.

As I got to know him a little better, I asked for the Manila run on a regular basis. Of course he couldn't believe his ears! Nobody liked the Manila run.

The setup was this: some truck from our motor pool had to go the twenty-eight miles to Manila every day, go to the office of the Port Director, who was a Navy officer, and run whatever errands they might have. The problem was, they never had any. So you sat on a bench outside an office full of WAVES, playing solitaire or reading a book all day.

All the drivers hated it, and would do any amount of horsetrading of jobs to get out of it.

Then one day I saw my opportunity.

I overheard one of the officers telling one of the girls to take some papers over to the Philippine Sea Frontier offices way out on Dewey Boulevard.

"Pardon me, sir," I said, "but should she be going out through the streets of this city alone? I'm not busy, sir, and I respectfully request permission to accompany her."

He knew me, of course, and she did, too, as did all the other girls in the office, since they liked to kid me, calling me the "Lone Ranger," because of my being the only one doing what I did. I told them I felt more like the "Lonesome Stranger," on this assignment.

He told me to go, and seemed to appreciate my concern.

Needless to say, it took us the rest of the day to deliver the material!

That's when I asked the Chief to assign me to the Manila run on a regular basis—so he gave it to me three days a week, and those were the only days I had to work. One or more of the young ladies found some reason to leave the office each time I was there.

So, I spent each Friday or Saturday night running all over Cavite City in the Chief's jeep, then three days each week tearing around Manila in a jeep, truck or staff car, seeing the sights, taking pictures and buying souvenirs, with one or more WAVES for company.

A racket? What do you think?

Working in the Chow Hall (Punishment or Privilege?)

Sometimes even a screw-up can be turned into an advantage, and it might not even be your fault.

The executive officer of the base kept an umbrella table and a couple of folding chairs on his sandy lawn in front of his living quarters, where he relaxed with his friends. Since he lived on a corner, they turned out to be a prime target for a careless driver.

My erstwhile friend, the New York to Bridgeport driver, and I came by there one day and, meeting the road-watering truck in the middle of the sandy street, swerved to miss it, drove across the exec's yard, completely destroying his furniture. We kept going, but somebody took the number of the truck and reported it. He was punished as the driver, and I for not reporting it.

I was given two weeks in the chow hall, doing the dirty work. (Even spent Christmas day there—my only Christmas in the Navy!) As my first day wore on, the cooks and mess cooks were complaining to me about the fact that they could not get the chow hall and galley cleaned up in time at night to see the first part of the movie. They knew that I was the part-time movie projector operator.

Since this was also a receiving station, where personnel come for reassignment, there were always many temporary people passing through.

That day, as the last of the eaters were finishing up, I jumped up on a table and, in no uncertain terms, described the dilemma of the cooks.

"If we all pitch in, we can have this place cleaned up in fifteen minutes, instead of the hour-plus it takes them to do it!" I shouted. "And anybody that doesn't help is chicken." (Or something like that!)

Most of them pitched right in, so the next day I did the same. Then the chief cook came to me and told me that if I did that every day for my two-weeks stay, I wouldn't have to do anything else. So I didn't. During the morning and early afternoon I hung out at the library, the welfare and rec department—even the motor pool—until I went back to my Manila run.

That racket reaches even further into the future!

By some coincidence, I came back through that receiving center later on my way home, and went directly to first the chow hall, then the movie projection booth. Some of my old friends were still there, and they made my short stay on the base very easy and enjoyable.

The Bread Man Cometh (How to Get Your Own Jeep!)

Got a cook that can't, and a hungry crew? Let them eat bread, and you can be a hero!

I was getting tired of baby-sitting the Chief on week-ends. I had heard a rumor that he was transferring, anyway. Also, there weren't too many

WAVES left in the Port Director's office, mostly officers and some civilian workers, and I was getting restless. Then a friend in personnel told me they were going to reduce the complement of men on our base—so I decided it was time to move on.

I had learned of a small ship plying the coastal waters of the islands that had some shortages in its crew because of discharges, so I had my friend in personnel make out a transfer form.

"The Chief will never let you go, until he does," he said. But I thought he would.

One morning after "the night before" I gathered up my courage, went to his quarters and shoved several papers under his nose for him to sign. Included in the bunch was my transfer. In his zombie-like state, he scribbled his name on all of them, then headed for the shower. Before he realized what he did, I was gone.

My new little ship had a crew of sixteen plus a skipper, and a cook who wasn't very good at his job, and couldn't bake at all. I guess if he could have he wouldn't have been on such a small ship. But it was a fun-loving crew to be with, even the young skipper was one of us.

One night the crew was going on a base liberty for the evening, leaving me and a kid named Hanson, on board to mind the ship. We decided to make a meat loaf, something neither of us had any experience at. By the time the other members of the crew left, we had all the ingredients in the recipe mixed up and were ready to dump them into an enormous baking pan.

Much to the chagrin and discouragement of the skipper, the cook and the rest of the crew, I opened a gallon can of salmon and prepared to mix it in, also. Smiling wry smiles, and telling me I was nuts—salmon didn't belong in meat loaf, they all left the ship.

After getting one big whiff of the fishy smell, I threw the opened can of salmon over the stern into the bay.

After midnight, when they all came back, the meat loaf started to disappear, and without exception every one of them complained about the fishy taste of the meat, with the cook starting it by saying, "This would be an excellent meat loaf if you hadn't put that damn fish in it!"

They couldn't understand why Hanson and I were in stitches!

Then the skipper said, "It would be a lot better if we had some bread to go with it." To which the cook scampered away to his bunk.

I did a little detective work the next day and learned that about six miles inland from one of our regular stops was a giant Marine base with an equally giant bakery. Getting the skipper's permission to check it out, and knowing that most cooks and bakers tend to be a little oversize, I spent a little time in the welfare and rec department on the base making a black tooled leather belt fifty inches long. Then, the next time we put in at that dock, I hiked up to the Marine base.

Finding the chief baker, I told him of my plight, and presented him with the belt—which really delighted him, with all its scrollwork of leaves, ocean waves and Marine Corps emblems. He said they were just in the process of removing a fresh run of bread from the ovens, which my sensitive nostrils had already discerned when I was less than halfway from the ship to the bakery.

From somewhere he produced a burlap bag, then another, then another—all filled with loaves of sweet smelling bread.

"Hold it, Chief," I said, "I'm only one man."

"Don't worry," he said, as he and his men tied twelve sacks of bread on a jeep, leaving a hole just big enough for the driver to see out.

"You can keep the jeep," he laughed. "We stole it, anyway. Come back when you need more bread!"

And away I went, back to the ship and a hero's welcome. Those guys ate bread like it was cake!

We repainted the jeep, put our ship's numbers on it, ran it up and down the beach a few times to give it that worn look, and kept it on board.

Several weeks later a Marine corporal with two privates in tow started to come on our ship. I stopped him at the ladder, asking if he had permission to come aboard.

He said it wasn't necessary, he was looking for a stolen jeep. The skipper came up, strapping on a side arm.

"I'm in command of this ship," he said, in no uncertain terms. "And I will shoot anyone who tries to board her without permission. That includes men pretending to be Marines."

The boarding party beat a hasty retreat—we all laughed—and we kept our means of furnishing the ship with bread, then cake, then pie, then — !

I sure made a lot of leather belts over the next few weeks!

Cleaning Up the Head (I Can't Stand to Live in Filth Either)

I wasn't trying to impress anybody in the things I started doing on my new ship, but I guess I did.

When I first came aboard I thought I had never seen such a rundown craft, for the US Navy. It needed everything, cleaning, scraping, painting, repairs. It had never been in dry dock, and there wasn't one around to put it in anyway. But the main reason for its condition, I suspected, was that none of the crew had been on it very long, even the captain. His predecessor had gotten yellow jaundice, had gone into the hospital, then been relieved of his duties and sent home.

The ship had remained at the dock for weeks as the crew had, one by one, became eligible for discharge and left. Now here we were with a practically new crew and a new skipper.

Even though I grew up poor, out in the country, with no plumbing, I still hated filth. My mother used to scrub the outhouse with her left-over wash water, with lye added. Our house, our clothes and we kids were always clean.

After taking one look at the head on the ship, which was shared by seventeen men, as soon as I could I attacked it with scrub brushes, cleaning fluid and scrapers. When it was finished drying, (I made the men do their business over the side while it did), I painted it, after repairing the drains and faucets where needed. When the skipper expressed his appreciation, in front of the other men, I told him that the first SOB that used it and left it dirty would be missing the next day—because he would be somewhere out on our sea lane trying to swim back. He said he would help me bring this about.

Within the next few days, the electrician's mate began cleaning up the fans, blowers, lights and other electrical devices. Then the motor mech and his helper started in on the engine room, and I helped them. Next came our one and only cook, asking for help to clean up the galley.

In two weeks, the little old bucket looked like new, inside—but outside she was still ugly. Then our captain had to go in the hospital for something, some kind of stomach disorder, and Jockers, the motor mech, was left in charge of the ship. We were told to just anchor her out in the bay and wait for orders, or the skipper to come back.

I got some paint and crawled up on the side of the conning tower and started to repaint our emblem, a green and red and yellow dragon discharging cargo from its mouth.

Jockers called everybody together, and said, "Let's make the skipper proud, and ourselves, too. Let's paint her while he's gone—from stem to stern, from the waterline up."

So we did, and a happier bunch of sailors you never saw. (Of course, later, when I showed a friend a picture of all of us on the dock by the ship, he wondered how we could ever win a war with such people!) There was a lot of tomfoolery, too. Since the Navy had only two colors of paint for ships, both gray—dark Ocean Gray for the bottom, and light Battleship Gray for everything above the main deck, that is what we used.

In fact, when one of the crew painted another's bare ankles, he used the dark gray, then when his shipmate retaliated by painting the first guy's neck, he used light gray. I, myself, was hanging over the side painting in a boatswain's chair when suddenly I went head over heels, paint and all, into the bay. Swimming around to the ladder and climbing back aboard, I was told that my line must have broken. But I told them I had never seen such a clean break, especially in a new line—looked more like it might have had a little help with a knife or hatchet! Naturally they stuck to their story.

When the captain was discharged from the hospital, I had the dubious privilege of running in to get him with a small boat. Jockers accompanied me.

As we cruised out into the bay, the skipper asked, "Where is old Plaster 33?" calling the ship by its code name.

"Right over there," answered Jockers, "with all the crew lined up to welcome you back."

Our passenger, who had been standing up in the stern, almost collapsed in his seat from surprise!

"You can blame this here guy," said Jockers, grinning. "He started it with his damn clean head!"

Harbor Patrol is Boring (But a way out of the Navy!)

The skipper came aboard from the shore base commander's office to tell us that our cargo hauling days were over. Half the ship's company would be transferred, and the rest would be doing harbor patrol duty in small boats—not assigned to the ship, just living on it. When he asked who would like to stay and who would like another ship, most of them wanted to go on another ship.

Hanson and I wanted to stay. I knew a little bit about small boats, and wanted to learn more. Some of our friends in the crew couldn't understand why we would want a job as mundane as checking ships going in and out of the harbor, when we could be out on the high seas having great adventures.

But I had a look at the so-called small boats we would use, and realized they were not so small. A forty-three foot boat with a diesel engine that will take it up to forty knots is not exactly a small boat!

My mate and I were hard on boats. We wore two out, sunk one, and had one burn—all without getting hurt ourselves. We worked twenty-four hours for three days, then were off six. We aquaplaned behind the boats.

(In shark-infested waters, no less! Stupid.) We drove them up a small fresh water river that flowed down out of the mountains, and where we could swim in some nice clear water. We toured the shorelines, the bays and the backwater.

What a racket!

And we almost hated to see it all end, except for one thing. We were going home!

The skipper informed me one day that my name was on the list for discharge, and I was to go ashore for orientation the very next day. I told him that couldn't be. They were discharging on the point system, and I knew I had nowhere near enough points to be let out.

"The point system was dropped yesterday," he said, "and all unassigned personnel are going home."

"But I thought I was assigned to this harbor patrol job," I said.

"Not really," he said. "We've been working at it, but not officially assigned to it. Don't fight it. I'm going, too."

"What about the other guys?"

"You mean the ones that sought other ships? They will be in at least another six months, unless their ships are decommissioned. Looks like you and I chose the right racket this time, doesn't it?"

I couldn't have agreed with him more!

CHAPTER 5

COLLEGE STUDENTS' OPPORTUNITIES

Most college students have some form of activity other than their studies. This might be athletics, social involvement or a job. Sometimes the job might be working for the school, or some arm of the school—or it might be outside the jurisdiction of the institution. There are also some "jobs" that have to be done in order to get what you came there for in the first place, which might not have any financial remuneration, but gain you some sort of advantage anyway. Still, all of these can be outlandish jobs. What you turn them into is up to you.

Sorority Opportunities (My, My—They All Need Help)

We think of a sorority house as some place where privileged girls live while attending an institute of higher learning, not as a place where some members can generate a racket—but it has been done by girls who didn't mind a outlandish job with a lot of responsibility.

Kandi had worked on the salad line in the cafeteria at the dorm where she lived her first year at a large mid-western university—her second year she had been made the supervisor. Then, at the beginning of her third year she had joined a sorority and moved into their house in town.

She felt pleased to be accepted, because the sorority was one devoted to her major subject—one which she expected to concentrate on for the rest of her life. But she suddenly realized that she was in with a group whose members, although they were serious about their studies and their future careers, had no interest in immediate responsibility. This was obvious when the sorority couldn't get anybody to accept an elected position to head up a committee to supervise the dining situation at the house.

Kandi knew it would be a time-consuming, thankless job, but somebody had to do it, so she volunteered. Soon she saw all kinds of opportunities.

After each evening meal, all the girls retired to the living room for relaxation, went to their rooms to study, or in some cases went out on dates—while two hired busboys, who were college freshmen, and the cook, cleaned up the dining room and kitchen. Kandi was shocked at how much they were paying the boys, which she thought was too much. But, since she controlled the budget, and with an ulterior motive in mind, she gave the two bus-persons a big raise anyway.

Getting together with her friend, Kathy, she proposed that the two of them replace the bus boys—and Kathy agreed. Then Kandi got together with the cook, who was also a good business-person, and proposed that she would establish a food purchasing budget. Then she and the cook would determine the menus on a weekly basis, and a part of whatever the cook could save by judiciously shopping would be a bonus to her, and Kandi would determine how to dispose of the rest of it later.

So, for the next two years, poor Kandi and Kathy labored in the dining room each evening, while the other girls, looking down their noses at them, went on with their own pursuits. Of course Kathy and the cook made more money in wages and perks than they could possibly have anywhere else on campus—and silly Kandi, all she was able to do was pay her tuition, room and board, sorority dues, and buy herself a good used car!

A racket? Or just good business sense, and an opportunity? You be the judge!

Straightening Out the Faculty (Hey, They Are Sometimes Wrong)

You don't argue too much with an ex-Marine pilot, no matter what your position on the school staff. It happened like this.

Fresh out of the Navy, going to school on the G.I. Bill, I had several classes, including math, on the fourth floor of a university building. The math was taught, or supposed to be, by a Mr. Gephart. But I was having a hard time. He spent our class period sitting in a window, which over-looked the football practice field watching the team activities. If he talked at all, it was about last Saturday's game—not about mathematics. But when he gave a test, it was on what you should have learned.

Now, my best subject had always been math—that was one of the things that led me into engineering in the first place—but no matter what anybody says, you cannot learn it at the college level from a book. Somebody has to talk to you, and you have to be able to ask questions.

Just about the time I became as close to frustration as a student could get, one of my classmates made a move. I had talked to him a couple of times, found out that he had been a motorcycle racer before military service, then a pilot in the Marine Corps. He was twenty-eight years old, had seen it all, and was now trying to establish a career.

As the class ended one day, and we all stood up to leave, he said, "Would you all wait a minute, please?"

His voice was so commanding that we just dropped back in our seats.

Approaching Mr. Gephart, the ex-pilot said, in a very firm but even tone, "Mr. Gephart, your job is to teach, and ours is to learn. Neither of us is doing his job. It's time that changed."

"Looks like you are looking for a failing grade," said the teacher.

"No," said the pilot. "You can't give me a failing grade on something you haven't taught. If you do, and if you don't start teaching, I am going to take my case to the administrators, and I am sure all these people will back me up."

"The administrators won't do anything," said Gephart. "I've been here longer than most of them. You'd better get on out of here."

"I will do that," said his opponent, "and when the university adminis-trators reject my complaint, if you are right, then I will go to the Veterans' Administration.

Currently over eighty percent of the students at this school are here on the G.I.Bill, and with people like you, the VA is not getting what it pays for. I'm giving you a week."

We could all see the color drain out of Gephart's face. Tenure or no tenure, if the VA cut the university off, it might be tough for a man his age, and with that kind of accusation against him, to find another job.

By the next class time, he was a different person—and I really think he and the ex-pilot became friends.

There is a little more to the story, though.

The only rest rooms on the fourth floor were marked "faculty." One day a woman in our class mentioned to me and the pilot that the first floor was a long way to go to the rest room. We suggested she just use the fac-ulty one, there were no women instructors on that floor anyway, and not too many men.

Later that week the pilot and I were standing outside the rest room doors when she came out, meeting Gephart going in the men's. He start-ed to say something to her, saw us and changed his mind. The pilot said, "Come on," to me, and he and I went in the men's rest room.

Within a few days all students with classes on the fourth floor were using the faculty rest rooms, and before long the signs just said "Men" and "Women".

Delivering Fried Chicken (Bell Hop Problems)

Long before anybody ever heard of Colonel Sanders, some of us college students had a fried chicken racket, except for one thing—a hotel bellhop.

One of the many things I worked at, and turned into a racket while in school, was delivering fried chicken. The business was called "Chicken

Delight," and they had no place to eat on premises. The customers had to take it away, or have it delivered. Most of it was delivered.

One of my friends had gotten me a job there, delivering chicken, and he said the tips were very good, especially if you were delivering to a party where everybody was too busy celebrating to notice what they were giving.

On the first night I worked, I was given a big order for a room in the only hotel in town. It must have been a party, so I anticipated a big tip. When my friend found out where I was going, he told me that was bad news. When I asked why, he said that the bell hop wouldn't let you deliver. He insisted on taking it up to the room, and he pocketed the tip.

By the time I reached the hotel lobby, I had worked up a pretty good head of steam. Sure enough, here came a bell hop, who asked me just where I thought I was going. I told him I had a delivery for Suite 402.

"I'll take it," he said.

"No you won't," I told him.

"That's the only way they'll get it," he said.

"Then give me forty-one dollars and twenty-three cents, plus a ten percent tip."

"No, I'll give it to you when I get back," he said.

I walked over to a house phone, called Suite 402, and told the man who answered that I had his chicken in the lobby, but hotel personnel wouldn't let me deliver it.

Soon a very irate red-faced man got out of the elevator and went up to the clerk and told him what he thought of him, the bell hop and the hotel.

"You close your damn dining room at nine o'clock," he screamed, "then try to hold up any food that we order. I'll be talking to your manager about this in the morning!"

He must have, because when I went back and told my boss that I wanted to make all hotel deliveries after that, much to the consternation of my fellow delivery men, the bell hop found some place else to be whenever I showed up.

Eventually it got to be that the hotel was the only place I went. Another bad job that worked out fine!

Getting the Lead Out (Dirty, Hot and Hard—But Profitable!)

Handling hundreds of pounds of molten lead a racket? Oh yes—at least it was for Charley.

Charley was a student who was lucky enough to get a job at the college's printing department. Since he was majoring in journalism, he thought the experience of learning how the written word is printed would help him in his career. The department was basically an offset operation, but still had some letterpress equipment left.

One day his boss pointed at an old lead melter, and said, "We have somebody who wants to buy that, and take it off our hands, but they don't want it with that lead in the bottom."

"Why don't we fire it up and pump it out?" asked Charley.

"We can't. The pump is broken. We could melt it and dip it out, but it isn't worth it. It hasn't got much in it."

After making a few quick calculations, Charley came back to his boss the next day and said, "I'll get that lead out if you will give it to me. You'll have to fire it up and loan me some molds."

Of course his boss was quite pleased, and the other employees felt sorry for Charley as he dipped and sweated, sweated and dipped—one whole day. But their expressions changed as his heavily gloved hand piled more and more pigs of lead on top of each other next to the machine. Eventually it was empty, and after Charley made a phone call, a couple of men with a truck came and hauled it away.

"That would make a lot of sinkers, Charley," said his boss. "It didn't look like much before. How much was in it, anyway?"

"Well, I got sixty-five molds at about a hundred pounds a mold," answered Charley. "The weight of that stuff fools you."

"It was nice of those guys to haul it away. Were they friends of yours? I hope they paid you a little something to make up for your labor."

"Yeah, a little something," said Charley. "They are buyers and sellers of low-grade lead. Paid me thirty-two cents a pound for it. I called them before I took on the job, after I calculated how much was in there."

"Why, that's over two thousand dollars!" exclaimed his boss.

"Not a bad days work, huh?" said Charley.

Working at the Front Desk (Hectic, But a Good Racket)

A receptionist's job can look like a good spot to be in, except for all the crap you have to put up with. The trick is to eliminate the crap.

Brenda had moved into the dorm on her first day of school, then made note of the turnover in girls serving as greeters and telephone operators at the front desk. At the end of her first semester she asked for the job, and the housing management staff was all too happy to give it to her.

Her friends and acquaintances, including the girls who had held the job, thought she was just asking for trouble.

The building consisted of twin dormitories connected by a single entry way where the receptionist's desk was located. The complement of the school was mostly girls, since it was primarily a nurse training institution. Several hundred of these girls lived in the two dorms.

The rules were simple: no visitors were to go up directly to the rooms, the occupant had to come down and register them at the desk; no male visitors were to be in the rooms at all, the girls could entertain them in the lobby or in an adjacent visiting area; and there was a curfew, but nobody paid any attention to it, and neither did the girl at the front desk. But these rules were not the problem—not what made the job so undesirable.

The frustrating part was the amount of complaints, and even worse, the types of complaints. The poor receptionist had to listen constantly to girls crying on her shoulder about the plumbing, the loud music next door, the girls who snubbed others, the cat fights between girls, even the way the rooms were decorated—and dozens of other complaints.

Brenda saw it as an opportunity—besides, she told herself, her mom didn't raise any dummies.

She simply made up a complaint form, had the college printing office print them in triplicate, and kept them at her desk.

The first time after that when some girls came to complain about some others, she handed them a form and told them to fill it out—listing all names involved, describe the incidents and sign and date at the bottom. When they asked what she intended to do with the forms, she told them one was for them to keep, one was for the dean of women and one went to whomever they were accusing.

There were not too many forms filled out! In fact, it got so that whenever any of the residents approached her desk, she just reached for a form and they would run. Within a few days, no one complained to her at all about trivial things, and Brenda just sat there doing her homework and getting paid for it!

She knew she had many detractors complaining about her to each other, but who cares—she had developed her own racket from a job nobody wanted.

Sometimes College is Hard (But You Could Become a President)

It is important to finish what you start, no matter how long it takes, but a lot can happen to you as you go along.

Take my college friend, Pratt. His folks were not too well off, and he had not been in the military, so getting the wherewithal to go to an institute of higher learning was a supreme challenge to him. He had gotten a job in a fast food hamburger and breakfast joint called the White Rock, and was able to juggle his hours to fit in with his school schedule.

He couldn't stand to see even one speck of dust where food was handled, so he cleaned constantly, whenever he had the time. He also organized the kitchen so that everything was at his fingertips.

The district manager of the eleven White Rocks in the area came in one morning before they were open for business and found Pratt scrubbing away, on his own time.

"Why are you doing this?" he asked.

"Because it needs doing," Pratt answered. "When I am the customer, I not only want food like it came from my mother's kitchen, but I want to eat it in a place as clean as my mother's kitchen."

"You'll do all right, Pratt," said the manager.

But he didn't. It wasn't long before his dream of finishing up getting a degree in Business Administration, and going into big business, was shattered by his father's death. Pratt had to find a lucrative full time position in order to take care of his mother.

"Come with us," said the White Rock district manager when he learned of Pratt's situation. "We have a manager's position open. You have really helped the one you work at to increase its business. I'm sure you can do better with one of your own. Besides, you can still take some business courses."

Although Pratt had never thought of going into the food service business as a career, he took the job. And he kept on going to school, part time.

In fact, he finally got the degree he had sought for so long. It took him eight years.

But by then it didn't matter—he was president of the company that owned the White Rock chain!

CHAPTER 6

EVENTS TURNED INTO RACKETS

There are many events in our daily personal or business lives that lie outside the normal call of duty, and we cannot avoid becoming involved in them. Most of us belong to, or are involved in some organization which holds regular activities. Also, we get involved in other types of functions, which require the services of a few just to get things done. Naturally we want the organization to serve its function, and we want the activities to go off successfully. But what's wrong with asking yourself what's in it for you whenever you have to do the jobs no one else will do?

The Flying Club Hog Roast (Or, My Family Gets the Best Cuts)

Everybody wanted to have a hog roast as part of the fly-in, but nobody wanted to work at it. We did, to our advantage!

My friend Moose and I belonged to a flying club based at a small grass field out in the country. Quite often they would hold a fly-in, inviting other flyers to visit from all over the area. It was always fun—the discussions, the flying, the visiting with other people and their families who had the same interests as you.

The first time this was done, the group decided to have a hog roast picnic in connection with it, where each participant could, for a nominal charge, have a pork picnic dinner. A man with a rotary hog roaster was hired to dress the hog, donated by a member of the club who raised livestock, and cook it whole.

He put it in the machine, started it up, and left—telling us when, at what time and temperature it would be ready. After that we were on our own.

Moose and I kept checking on the hog, then when we thought it was ready, we told the president of the flying club. He tried and tried, but just couldn't get anyone interested in that hog. All the other picnic materials were already on the table, when Moose sought me out.

"Ain't nobody gonna cut her up. I think they are going hungry first," he said.

"You think we ought to try it?" I asked. Neither of us had ever cut up and served a whole hog before, but we had seen it done.

"Well, it's one of those dirty jobs you are always talking about that nobody wants to do. I think there could be something in it for us," he said.

So Moose and I dragged the carcass out on a picnic table and carved and served away, much to the pleasure of those in attendance.

Then we retrieved the loins, our favorite cut of pork, from down under the table where we had hidden them wrapped in foil, warmed them up again on the cooker—and served them to our families!

And you know, in all the years we did that, not one person ever asked us why none of the hogs had loins!

Volunteers Get Rewarded (But You Have to Volunteer)

Not only can there be something in doing an undesirable job for yourself, but for your helpers as well.

I was employed at a small manufacturing plant, which was part of a large conglomerate, based in a Chicago suburb. But out in the boondocks, where we were, we didn't see too much of the headquarters personnel. Then suddenly that all changed.

A new plant manager was transferred to our unit from a larger facility, and he had a penchant for trying to make us one big happy family. This was to include those people with whom we had the most contact in Chicago. He wanted to have a company picnic and invite them out for it, families and all.

For some unknown reason, he tapped me to organize it—saying that if he did it himself, people would feel compelled to come, and he didn't want that. So after we discussed where we would have it, and what kind of food and activities we would need, I set about trying to get volunteers to help me with it.

The people I thought would be most cooperative laughed when I asked them, saying it might be fun, but why should they help—the company owed it to them. After I posted a notice on the bulletin board, six people came forward, four women and two men—three of whom were on my engineering staff.

During the week prior to the picnic I had occasion to visit the head-quarters building in Chicago, so I went to the public relations, sales promotion and advertising departments and asked for help. They rewarded me with company ball caps and jackets for each of my helpers, and myself—emblazoned with the corporate logo. They even put our names on them.

These were items normally reserved for customers, and it was next to impossible for an employee to get one. But we did!

When the seven of us wore them on the day of the picnic, and afterwards, the jealousy really showed in the eyes of other employees, especially those whose help I had sought and who had refused to join in.

Finally, one guy summed it up for all of them when he said, "Well, if we had known you were going to get jackets and caps for everybody, we would have helped, too."

"That's not the way it works," I told him. "First you take on the dirty job, then you look for its advantages. If you are rewarded right up front, then it's not an undesirable job anymore—everybody would want to do it. Sorry 'bout that."

But I wasn't, really!

Somebody Start to Eat (First in Line Gets to Choose)

The SME can be a land of opportunities, in many ways, some large from a professional standpoint, and some as small as getting to eat first.

For most of my working life I have been a member of the Society of Manufacturing Engineers, a worldwide organization with hundreds of local chapters. I have held many offices, as well as having been elected to their prestigious College of Fellows, and I have made technical speeches to many chapters and conventions. (It has been said that I will go anywhere that I can talk or eat, and if I can do both I will pay my own way!) But the most fun is at the local level.

The first chapter to which I belonged met once each month at a local hotel in one of its meeting rooms. The average attendance was eighty people. The hotel chef served a buffet dinner prior to each meeting. Then the business meeting was followed by a technical or educational presentation of some sort, usually by an "expert" in some chosen subject. That meant he had to be at least two hundred miles from home!

The chef would set up the buffet in typical fashion, with the salads and vegetables leading up to the meat at one end of the table, which he served himself—usually ham, roast beef, chicken, or all three. The problem was, nobody would start the chow line—nobody wanted to eat first. The poor chef would stand impatiently whetting his knife, but with no one to serve. After observing this at a couple of meetings, I decided I would start the line. (At six feet and two hundred pounds, I didn't get that big by being bashful!)

The first time I did it, I just grabbed a plate, called out, "Let's eat," and started filling it up.

This got to be a routine over the years that the members expected. I would always start the line. Of course I got razzed a lot about it. Then one night I was late getting to the meeting.

When I walked in, the line was already formed with my pal Wencil at the head of it, although the food wasn't out yet—and everybody looking at me with that "Ha, ha, we got you!" expression. They had known that I was coming in late.

I went into the hall, hung up my coat and went into the kitchen to find the chef.

"Hey, Thomas, let's reverse the line tonight," I said. "Put the meat at the other end."

Thomas was no dummy, and he loved a joke—besides, he had already looked out and seen what was happening. After I went back into the meeting room to very meekly fall in at the back of the line, he and his helpers came happily out carrying the food and lined it up backwards to what they usually did.

Now I was at the head of the line, and old buddy Wence was at the tail end!

"I don't believe it!" he shouted.

"Just doing my job!" I shouted back. "It's dirty, but somebody has to do it!"

My Life as a Bartender (Free Drinks for Everyone!)

This same organization made me a drink server, for just one night. They didn't want me to come back!

In the early years of that chapter of SME there was no liquor-by-the-drink allowed to be sold in that state. But, we learned, an organization such as ours could set up its own bar at meetings and serve drinks to members. So Wencil and I set it up.

We bought the liquor at the state owned stores, the hotel where we met was happy to provide the various mixes, and we found a couple of members who knew a lot about drinks and would volunteer to serve them. We called them the "Fellowship Committee," and reported their activities in the monthly chapter bulletin.

Wence and I calculated the costs of the various drinks, and set the prices accordingly. All we wanted was for the members to be able to get a drink, alcoholic or non-alcoholic, at a reasonable cost. We just wanted to break even.

Then as the years went on and he and I had less and less to do with it, the board of directors of the chapter started raising prices and listing a profit from "Fellowship" in the treasurer's report. We didn't think that was right.

But one night we made up for it!

Neither one of the fellowship chairmen showed up, so, winking at Wence, I volunteered us for the job. When the chapter chairman told us we could get some change from the hotel desk, I told him it wouldn't be needed.

After getting the bar all set up, with liquor and mix and ice all in place, I made a large cardboard sign that said "Drinks are Free Tonight, Compliments of the Chapter!"

Needless to say, the temporary fellowship chairmen were kept very busy for the next few hours.

The chapter chairman blew up—told us we couldn't do that to the chapter.

I said, "Wence and I took this on when it was a job nobody even knew could be done. It was supposed to be a non-profit operation, and by George, tonight it was!"

We were never allowed to tend bar again!

CHAPTER 7

WORKPLACE POSSIBILITIES

Traditionally there are only three criteria for taking or keeping a job: you have to like what you are doing and the people with whom you are doing it; the remuneration has to be adequate for the position and the area, compared to similar positions; and it has to look good on the next resume, if there ever is another resume. (And there always is!)

But I think there is a fourth reason: what else is there to be gained while doing the job? When you settle into the full time job of earning a living is when you want to take a look around at what is in it for you immediately—besides just a paycheck. There are lots of possibilities!

The Instability of Job Shops (But, Oh, the Opportunities!)

The business of some outfits is so spasmodic that it makes you wonder how you could ever survive, but I did!

Small contract manufacturing companies, especially those that produce tools and dies for manufacturing, are referred to as "Job Shops." Most of them maintain a small nucleus of professionals, then hire and fire as the workload requires, so the newcomer is usually subject to the whims of the marketplace. I was such a newcomer as a tool designer in a job shop while still in school. As low man on the totem pole, I would normally be the first to go when the workload dropped off.

Shortly after I took the job, the chief designer gave me a drawing to revise for a local office equipment manufacturing company. It was a tool to be updated, and the paper was yellow with age, which made it tough to make the required changes. But I struggled through it.

One of my cohorts told me that they all tried to avoid those jobs—some of those drawings were over a quarter of a century old—and nobody liked to work on them. My observations over the next few days revealed just how much of that type of repair work there was. Being more concerned with fulfilling my obligations at home and finishing school than finding easy, desirable work, I went to the chief and told him I would like to do all of those redesign jobs for that customer.

At first he seemed appalled at my request, then, being a smart opportunist himself, smiled knowingly—it was obvious to an old racketeer like him what I was doing. He started giving them to me. Sometimes they required longer hours because of their due dates, but I became the exclusive individual working on that type of job.

Over the next several months, until I finished school, the tool designers came and went from that job shop, sometimes getting down to as few as two people.

But there I was, fat, dumb and happy—doing the work no one else wanted to do. Talk about job security!

Undesirable Travel Destination (With an Opportunity Waiting)

Working as a civilian for the military can subject you to much difficulty in avoiding undesirable assignments—especially traveling to places you might not want to go—but maybe you shouldn't let it bother you. A friend of mine didn't mind at all!

Nobody wanted to go to the New York area on Air Force business any more than they could help it. I don't really know why, they just didn't.

I was working in tool and gage standards, and the group was buying airframes. All of us were required to travel more than we liked to venders we didn't like—all over the country.

Then Fred transferred from the group that procured engines into our group. He was immediately assigned to handle all contact with our east coast suppliers. Someone said he was dumb enough to ask for the assignment, which, of course, made everyone wonder about him. But he went along doing a very good job, getting compliments from our bosses, taking his work seriously and with no complaints. He was out on the east coast at least one week out of every two months, and sometimes for two weeks at a time.

Then the truth came out!

While walking through the New York airport to catch a plane home one night, who should I meet but old Fred. And with him was an attractive young woman. He introduced her as his wife. The next day at the office my suspicions were confirmed, but he asked for my secrecy in the matter.

The young lady, who obviously had an English accent, and Fred had been married when he was in her country in the military. He had volunteered for the undesirable east coast business so he could take her with him and she could go back to England to visit her folks quite often. I suspected our suppliers might even be furnishing her transportation.

Of course I kept his secret. I felt honored to have found a bigger racketeer than I was!

The Drill and Pin Jig Caper (Or, Writing for Magazines Pays)

Sometimes you can take one of those outlandish jobs and turn it into a racket so remote from what you are doing that it seems right off the wall to other people.

I was part of the tool design department in a large mid-western plant of an electronics company. I had been sent there on business, when I was in tool and gage standards at the Air Force base, and when the company offered me an engineering job sometime later, I took it.

I wasn't too impressed by the chief tool engineer, who had no formal training and very little experience, and I was even less impressed by the chief tool designer, who had been a bank messenger boy, just prior to being made chief.

The main problem was that these two would not let one of their staff people design anything they hadn't seen before, and they hadn't seen very darn much! So we wound up designing and building only the simplest of production tools, while they subcontracted everything else. In fact, I actually saw a note signed by one of them attached to a drawing, which said, "Too difficult to fabricate, farm out." Talk about shirking your duties!

But the one type of tool they couldn't "farm out" was a fixture for drilling and pinning assemblies together—drill and pin jigs. Nobody running a subcontract job shop would take them, except on a time and material basis, then my bosses would be criticized for their exorbitant costs. So, we designed and built them in house, by the dozens.

The function of the device was not complicated—it was its construction that made it complex. It simply had to hold several items, such as gears, couplers and cams in perfect alignment on a shaft, while a hole was drilled through each one. Easy enough. But then the drill guides had to be flipped out of the way, with the assembly still securely clamped, while a roll pin, tapered pin or dowel was pushed through each hole to permanently hold the items together in their clamped positions. Then of course, the clamping devices had to be swung away so that the whole completed assembly could be removed. Most of these things were less than twelve inches long, and might have as many as six separate items to be put together.

Whenever the chief designer issued one out to be designed and built, the recipient just cringed!

One day he gave me one, and I started thinking about what could be in it for me—so I went up to him and asked how many he had.

"Six", he said, warily. "Five more besides yours."

"Give me all of them," I said. "I'm going to find a way to standardize them."

He shook his head like he thought the guys in the white coats might be there to take me away any minute, but he gave them to me. And he never gave me any delivery date.

I played around with all six of them for several days, trying first one thing then another, using similar or identical components wherever possible, so that if they were all given to the same toolmaker or group of toolmakers to build, they could mass produce many of the components.

I had reproductions made of my drawings as I went, had pictures taken by our photography department as the jigs were completed and kept track of the hours required to make each component and assembly, and the costs of the purchased parts. By the time the six jigs were completed I probably knew more about drilling and pinning operations than anyone in the world.

At least it seemed that the world's leading magazine devoted to manufacturing thought so.

I put the whole package together in an article for them. They published it and paid me the equivalent of two weeks salary for it!

And that started my sideline of writing for engineering magazines. What a racket!

Nobody Wants a Boring Job (Unless You Do Nothing At All)

Sometimes you can get an assignment that looks dull, until you realize that you really don't have to do anything.

Most of us have to have some sense of accomplishment. That's why we can't adjust to living on a south sea island without doing anything. Even carving coconut heads is better than nothing. There are some people who work harder at not working than they would if they just worked, and I suppose even that can give them a sense of doing something.

But there is the breed of cat who can really enjoy just being at the workplace and accomplishing nothing at all. Like Rance. He found the ultimate racket, and it was handed to him, by his boss!

The company had grown so rapidly that all the early tooling and equipment acquisitions were not recorded. There were literally hundreds, if not thousands, of devices in house for which there were no specifications, no drawings, no information at all.

Then, inevitably, there was the day the boss called all of us in the manufacturing engineering department together to tell us about this. He asked for a volunteer or volunteers to go throughout the company, take measurements, develop capacities and capabilities, make sketches and list names and types of tools and equipment until it was all up to date—then put the whole kibosh in a book of standards.

Nobody stepped forward. It did not look like a highly technical job of accomplishment, like most of us wanted to work at.

He turned to Rance, whose normally hangdog expression became even more droopy, when the boss said, "You are in between assignments. You can do this. There is no pressure, unless the company goes up for sale, then it will have to be added to our list of assets. That is why management wants it in the first place."

We all felt sorry for Rance, but we didn't see a whole lot of him after that. He maintained a desk and a drawing board in our department, but didn't use them much. Whenever I would see him he always had a clip board or a manila envelope, or both, in his hands, and a tape measure hanging on his belt—and was somewhere in the factory among the machines. He spent a lot of time just talking to people—operators, supervisors, foremen, engineers, purchasing people, contract administrators, even me.

He spent much time in the cafeteria, just visiting, but he always had the tools of his trade with him. Then he started disappearing for days at a time—ostensibly he was at one of our other six buildings around town.

He lived in the country, kept and trained a few horses. I know for a fact that he built, himself, several new outbuildings during this period—and he wasn't doing it on weekends!

Occasionally some other supervisor would ask for Rance's services on some project or another. He was always too busy, right in the middle of something. He made reports at some staff meetings, which were called spasmodically, but all he ever gave was an estimated percentage of completion of his project. It didn't change much.

Since the company was not up for sale there was still no deadline for his project.

Twelve years after he was assigned the equipment specifications job, Rance retired. And the project was no further along than when he started!

Take the Outlandish Job With You (It's a Good Reference)

Sometimes, just as you finish a outlandish job, the wind shifts, and you are out on your ear. You can still use the job to your advantage. Nichols did!

Nichols was a draftsman, in a day when many of that type of skilled person were required—and he was good at what he did, and proud of it. His specialty was inked drawings, and he made few mistakes. He had been in that same department for several years, and consequently was the highest paid draftsman on the staff. He was the resident expert in making inked schematics—those drawings of information usually printed on instruction plates attached to a piece of equipment.

The ones for complicated electronics equipment could be complex and extensive, with great detail. Nichols was the only draftsman in the department entrusted to make the large ones, and he had just been given the task of producing the most complicated one of his career. Settling in to several weeks of inking a schematic on a sheet of special paper larger than his drawing board, Nichols didn't pay too much attention to what was going on around him.

He did know that the department soon obtained a new computer for the exclusive purpose of laying out schematics. Other people were being trained on it, but he thought his turn would come—probably when he finished his project. They were just doing the simple ones anyway to begin with. Besides, the computer couldn't ink drawings, so someone like him would still be needed. He concluded that the machine would eventually be his to operate as his own.

But as his project neared completion, he began to get suspicious. The day after he reported it completed to the chief draftsman, that individual called him up front and told him that his services were no longer needed. He was being given two weeks notice, with pay, but was not required to be there. It would be better if he left immediately.

So Nichols packed his briefcase with his drafting tools and personal things and went away, leaving the largest and most complex inked schematic in the company's history under the protective cover on his drawing board—or so everyone thought. But when he left, the drawing was gone!

I learned all this from Nichols several months later when I found out he lived in a west coast city I was visiting and looked him up to ask him about that last dirty job he did back in the mid-west.

"Dirty job, smirty job," he said. "That schematic made a wonderful reference in getting me a better job out here!"

Guiding Visitors—Thankless Job (Or Racket?)

When working in any given facility quite often you are asked to show outsiders around. Most of the time it is boring and a nuisance, since you are still expected to get your regular work done. But I liked making it a racket—sometimes just for fun.

One of my favorite classic lines about advancement was made by my friend Russ. When I asked him how he got promoted from the factory to the office, he said, "I was kissing everybody's fanny that wore good clothes. They promoted me because I was embarrassing the visitors."

I don't know if I embarrassed any visitors or not, but some of them sure provided me with a lot of laughs.

Take the group of nuns from a local school, who wanted to see how a factory worked. I kept asking, "Any questions, Sisters?" But nobody had any. Finally, out in the middle of the facility, one of them said she had a question. Great, now this can be a two-way conversation, because up to now I didn't know whether I was doing such a good job of explaining things that they had no questions, or if they were so completely confused that it didn't matter.

"Yes, Sister, what would you like to know?"

"Where is the closest ladies rest room?"

And I had no idea! I had to ask somebody myself!

Another time I was given the task of steering an inspector from some procurement branch of the government through the factory to check out our capabilities. He didn't talk. I finally got out of him what kind of work he had done before taking a government job and guided him into a similar area in our plant. I kept him buried there for two days. He went away happy, but knowing no more about us than when he arrived. He gave us a glowing report anyway.

Then the General came to visit. We did a lot of work for the Air Force, but this was the highest-ranking officer to visit, as far as I knew. I was shocked when the plant manager asked me to participate.

"He's flying here in a B-26 converted to a luxury craft," said the manager. "He'll have a pilot with him. Since you used to work for the Air Force, we want you to entertain the pilot while we take care of the General. They will be staying overnight."

So I showed the young airplane driver, who was about my age, around our facilities and the city, ending up at our extensive airport operations at the end of the day.

"Well, let's go have dinner," I said, looking forward to getting home to my family, "then I'll drop you at your hotel."

"Great," he said. "There's a place in St. Louis where I love to eat whenever I'm in the mid-west."

"That's fine," I said, "but it's three hundred miles to St. Louis. It will take us five hours to get there."

"Not in that!" he said, pointing at the B-26 parked on the apron.

"Can you fly it by yourself?"

"Yep, but you are a pilot. You can help me."

Off to St. Louis we went, don't know how much that dinner cost us taxpayers, but I never did mind showing him around on successive visits!

Then there were the bankers.

The company manufactured banking equipment—safe deposit boxes, vault doors and everything in between, and I was Manager of Manufacturing Engineering.

One day my boss told me the company president wanted to see me, he wanted me to guide a group of bankers, potential customers, through the factory.

"Why me?" I asked, "don't people from sales or customer relations usually do this?"

"These particular customers know something about manufacturing—they have been to all our competitors' plants, and the president says he can't take a chance on some sales department person telling them something they will know is not true."

Now, being a man who raises horses, and a sometime horse show judge, I have always dressed basically western. I'm not a K-mart cowboy. I wear good quality duds that are really conservative, and I wear boots—even to the office.

When I showed up at the president's office, he took one look at me and said, "Oh, god. Look at you! Don't you know bankers are conservative people?"

"How was I supposed to know I was going to be a banker guide today? Want me to run home and change?" Anything for the good of the business!

"There isn't time," he blurted. "They are on the way here from the airport right now. My secretary will call you when they arrive."

A little while later the secretary called me and I went up to the front entrance to find the company president standing there grinning like a jack-ass eating cactus, while greeting a group of bankers. They were from Texas.

And they were all dressed like me!

Concrete, a Really Outlandish Job (With Great Potential)

When a manufacturing company that basically produces electronics and mechanical items suddenly starts in the concrete business it looks like a lot of outlandish work. But my pal Vernon didn't see it that way.

That outfit that made banking equipment had decided to get into producing concrete products as well—vault doors, pre-cast vaults. I was told by my boss to find a liaison engineer, who was already in house, for the project, which I thought might be difficult.

I called in one of my department heads to discuss whom we might approach about it. Much to my surprise, he said he would like to do it. When I asked him why, he said that he felt confined in his present position. He thought this new job might get him out more. My other staff members and department heads looked at him kind of sideways.

So here was a guy who was used to being clean, wearing a suit and tie, while working in an air conditioned office—out at a cement plant wearing coveralls, a hard hat and hard-toed shoes, supervising pouring concrete into molds, vibrating them, and retrieving the product. Being out wasn't new to him. He came from a farm background, raised horses and hogs, and lived in the country.

His new job wasn't all pouring concrete. He also designed and procured equipment, created processes and calculated and controlled costs. When the company decided to establish a separate plant to produce concrete products, he and I started looking at buildings and property. Then one day he came to me with a set of figures he wanted to discuss.

"If we put a plant here, and haul the aggregate for the mix from where it is mined almost four hundred miles away, the cost will be tremendous," he said. "But if we build a plant at the source we will eliminate that cost.

And since we ship the product all over the country anyway, it can be shipped from anywhere."

He presented his plan to management and they bought it. Of course they sent him there to direct the establishment of the plant, then to manage it—with a big healthy raise in pay, plus a move bonus.

A year later they built a second plant there, for which he also had the responsibility. With the biggest employment in town, he became a pillar of the community.

Not bad for an old boy who just poured concrete, an outlandish job, at the beginning!

Don't Ever Take Part of a Dirty Job (Take It All!)

Every once in a while you will find one of your cohorts trying to push the hardest part of his job off on someone else, maybe you. Don't let him do it!

The company had set up a new production division, using a unique material in various quantities. The manager of the materials control department, which also included planning and scheduling of production runs, didn't like having to order the material for the new product—and seeing to it that it was available when needed. Since it was a time-usage oriented substance, it was a constant scramble to meet production demands.

He suggested—no, demanded—that the division manager be the one to order and expedite the material.

The manager said, "I'll be happy to, if I can also do all the planning, scheduling and purchasing for my division."

Although the materials manager, being somewhat of an empire builder, didn't think much of that suggestion, top management bought the idea. At first other managers thought the new division manager was out of his gourd to take on that much more responsibility, they soon realized that he also had the accompanying authority over his operation. This made it almost autonomous—except for sales.

There were five other division managers in the organization, and it wasn't long before they all requested that they, too, be given the same authority and responsibility.

So the poor materials manager, who had tried to unload the hard part of his job, wound up working for just one division, with an empire only one-sixth of what it could have been.

Be very careful when you try to get out of the outlandish part of your job—you might lose all of it!

CHAPTER 8

GETTING THE BOSS' ATTENTION

They say that trying to accomplish something without advertising is like winking at a member of the opposite sex in the dark—you might know what you are doing, but no one else does. You might be the best looking guy or gal at the party, but if you hide in a corner, you won't have much fun. I've heard it said about an engineer, "Bury him in a room somewhere, and he'll make you a million dollars." Note that it doesn't say he will make himself a million dollars. You have to advertise, let someone know you are there and that you are accomplishing great feats. And this person is usually your boss. Sometimes it means taking on some outlandish jobs.

Dave and the General (Or, I Can Fly as Well as You)
When I left my job with the Air Force, I was ranked as a G-4 civilian employee. My boss' boss was a G-11. Dave was one of my office mates with the same ranking as me.

Shortly before I left, a volunteer group of employees and servicemen started building a model airplane landing strip on the base. To most of us, with no interest in the sport, it looked like a lot of work for very little results. Dave joined in. He was out there every weekend helping out.

I kidded him about ruining his weekend with all that hard work, although I knew he had built some flying models.

Right before I left to return to private industry, he came to see me, saying, "I know you are wondering why I got in on that airstrip. It's like this, the commanding general flies models as a hobby. Let's see if he notices me."

A few months went by with no communication from Dave. Then I received my first letter.

"Remember I told you I was building a model flying wing?" he wrote. "Well, it caught the eye of the general. We have spent quite a bit of time out there flying it, just us two. By the way, my new rating is as a G-12!"

What a racket!

The Gardening Editor (I Didn't Really Think the Boss Cared)

I had made enough of an impression on enough editors of engineering magazines over the past few years with my articles that I had been offered a job as Engineering Editor by the number two publication in manufacturing.

Even though it had meant a thirty percent pay cut from my salary as a chief engineer, I still wanted to get in that field—so I joined the publishing company, which produced eight related magazines, in a Chicago suburb.

There were almost two hundred people working there, and I felt about one notch lower than the janitor. The building was a large one-story glass structure with a conference room jutting up as a small second story penthouse. I was shown a little office area surrounded by glass panels, which reached neither to the floor nor the ceiling. Reminded me of a horse stall—cleaner, maybe, but not as homey.

My magazine didn't have an editor at the time, he had been promoted to publisher, but it was being run by a managing editor. That worthy individual shut himself in his office and trusted no one—even did his own typing. I know he resented me. All I wanted to do was get along, and learn as much about the business as I could.

The building had been built around an atrium in its center, which had plantings of all kinds of trees, flowers, shrubs and evergreens—even contained a white birch clump much too big for the area. All four sides were of clear glass, which meant the occupants of the building should have a lovely view at all times. The plan had been that people working along the outside walls of the building could look out on the well-landscaped lawn, and those inside could look in on the atrium.

There was only one problem. The atrium looked like the kind of garden you see around an abandoned house, and the outside didn't look much better.

The second weekend I was there, after finding out that the key to the atrium door had long ago disappeared, I borrowed some gardening tools from my landlady, dragged a ladder across the roof and descended into the wilderness. By the time I finished, it looked like it should have. I even found a flagstone walk running through it, which no one could ever remember seeing. All the brush and dead trees went up and over the roof and into a pile out back to be hauled away.

On Monday afternoon, the president of the company, whom I had met only once, came into my cubbyhole.

"You did the garden?" he asked.

"Yep, it needed it."

"I looked at your resume," he said. "I believe you have a lot to offer this company."

"I hope so," I said.

"Do you have any problem with taking over supervision of the maintenance department, along with your other duties as Engineering Editor?"

"No, sir," I replied, "but my primary interest is in publishing."

"We'll start with a raise, if that will help."

I assured him it would, but I would have done it anyway.

Some of my cohorts, and especially the elusive managing editor, voiced their opinions that I had just committed publishing suicide—that the president would have me turned into a lackey. I would become his "boy." Well, I wasn't cut out to be anybody's boy.

But what it really did was get me the president's attention. Since I had to discuss property problems with him, it also gave me the opportunity to ask questions about publishing, learn from him, (he was fond of reminding me that he started in publishing the year I was born), and pass on a few of my own ideas and observations at the same time.

To make a long story short—within four months I was Chief Editor, in a year I was Publisher, and within three years I was Division Manager.

And all because of taking on the dirty gardening job!

What a racket!

Helping the Boss Whenever You Can (But Don't Become His Boy!)

Sometimes, all the boss wants is company, other times you can bail him out of some tough spots. Just be sure you benefit as well.

When I first joined the company, I overheard the president ask several people, one at a time, to accompany him to Boston to a convention. Each of them refused. When he got around to me, I figured what have I got to lose? So I went.

When we returned, several days later, one of the publishers cornered me and asked me how I ever let him sucker me into going. I told him I didn't understand.

He said, "I bet I can tell you just what happened. He kept you right with him all the time, and when the conversation with other people turned from world politics to technical stuff, he tossed the ball to you, because he is not a technical man. Right?"

I had to admit he was right, but what was wrong with that? After all I was an engineer turned editor, and I enjoyed technical discussions. Of course most of these other guys were journalists—maybe they were afraid of technical matters. But no, he told me, they just became bored with the president taking them away from work they would rather be doing, either at the office, or traveling to clients.

"He'll make you his 'boy'," one of them said. (That sounded familiar!) "You'd better start right now trying to avoid it."

But the president had introduced me to many people important to our business, and when I wrote to them thanking them for their input to editorial matters, without exception they all responded—so I felt like I made many new friends in the right places. And the word was fed back to the president by them, as well.

After my second trip with him to a meeting, at which most of the attendees were accompanied by their wives, I told him I felt like a fifth wheel because my wife was not with me.

"No reason why you can't take her to these things," he said. "We'll pay for it. I think she might be a big asset to you."

The very next convention was in the Bahamas—and she went. And she continued going, whenever she could. In fact, we had many great vacations, on business—and she made many friends among the wives of our clients.

Of course, when my cohorts in the company found out about it there was lots of weeping and wailing and gnashing of teeth, so to speak.

But she and I were having a good time. Such a racket!

Do Some Little Things for the Boss (Against His Own Rules)

Before I get away from this particular boss—the company president— I want to tell you about the coffee.

You see, he had a rule about no coffee makers in the building. Of course he went out a lot for coffee, which most of us didn't want to take time to do. There were coffee vending machines in the place, but I'm sure they were connected directly to the Mississippi River. All they did was heat it up. (You know the Missisloppy—too thick to swim in and too thin to plow!)

After he gave me the responsibility for the maintenance department, I rummaged around in the bone yard of unused office equipment in a storage room until I found a small cabinet with a shelf inside and a swinging door on the front. Cutting a hole in the appropriate place in the back of it, I placed it against one wall of my enclosed paneled office, right over an electrical outlet.

Then I bought a twenty-cup coffee maker and some supplies and put them in the cabinet. Hey, it looked just like any other office cabinet! I told my staff to bring their own mugs, and that I would buy the supplies, (out of my expense account), if one of them would make the coffee every morning. And we would all drink it.

Several months after I installed the coffee system, and we were all enjoying it immensely, I was bent over pouring myself a mug of coffee one morning when I heard my office door open. I looked around to be surprised at seeing the company president coming in. Wishing him a good morning, I just filled an extra mug and sat it on my desk in front of him.

He sat there, drinking the fresh coffee with relish, discussing everything but coffee, then sat his empty cup back on my desk and left.

Every morning, when I was in town, right up until I left the company years later, he would come in and drink his coffee. Not once did he ever thank me for it, or in any way acknowledge that it was there.

But he sure enjoyed it!

Big Jobs Get Attention, Too (They Just Require More Research)

Sometimes after everybody else gives up on a job as being impossible, a little more research—plus a good memory—can get it done.

As manager of manufacturing engineering, I was in on the planning of a facilities expansion. Fifty thousand square feet wasn't too big an addition, since we already had more than ten times that amount under roof. But the city engineers said no, when we applied for the building permit. There was something in the code that said we had already reached our maximum size of continuous building for our land area, but we could move out one hundred feet from the existing building and go bigger with a separate structure.

We were the largest employer for miles around, and the city tried to work with us—since we were also the oldest manufacturing company in the area—but there was that code. Our management backed off and began looking at alternate locations. We needed a continuous building to run the lines the way we wanted them.

The more I thought about it, the more I realized we were missing something. Then I remembered. My garage!

Ours was an older house at the intersection of two alleys. My old unattached garage had become difficult to maintain, and I wanted to replace it with a new one. The city said fine, but I couldn't build right on the lot line next to the alley, where the old one was. It had to be eight feet in, and I knew that would take up too much of my yard, since I planned to build a larger garage.

After looking at the code a little further, I applied for, and got, a permit to put an addition on the existing garage. After it was finished, I tore the old part off—and had exactly what I wanted in the first place.

Now about that factory addition—I visited with my friend the city clerk, we went over the code in detail, and soon I went back to management with a building permit. Two permits, really.

The clerk and I learned together that even though a new building on our property had to be a certain distance away from existing structures, any existing buildings could be connected.

So I got a permit to build a building a hundred feet away, then another permit to connect the two buildings. All nice and legal. Now the company had the space where it was needed, and the city didn't have to concern itself with its biggest employer moving out of town.

And the company president and some of the vice presidents were looking at me a little different. I wonder if they knew that move was really part of my racketeering!

Go for the Job Your Boss Should Be Doing (And Do It!)

No matter whom you work for, there are some parts of his job he doesn't like to do. Ease into them, take them over, learn from them while getting him forever in your debt.

I had a low opinion of the vice president of manufacturing, but then, I guess I'm a born boss hater. He didn't know enough about manufacturing to do his job the way I thought he should. (I wonder if people thought that about me when I became a vice president of manufacturing, then general manager, then president. Oh, well!)

But this guy hated the financial part of his job—didn't like budgeting for anything; manpower, tooling, equipment, facilities or purchased material. When I slowly slid into that part of his responsibility and authority, some of my friends, as usual, thought I was loco.

"That's the worst thing he has to do, and now you are doing it," they said. Didn't bother me though.

With the help of the data processing department I streamlined it, computerized it, made it easier to forecast financial needs and keep track of expenditures. But mainly, and this is where the development of a racket came in, I was able to get done some of my pet projects, or ones I considered important.

Besides, I knew that my next step was to a job like his—and this way I could train for it at his expense!

Little Things Can Lead to Bigger Ones (On the Next Resume)

If the boss wants you around for company, make it work for you.

"You got trapped last night, didn't you," said another manager to me one morning.

When I asked him what he meant, he told me that the vice president didn't like to go home on certain nights until dinner time, around seven o'clock. So along about five he would start up a conversation with someone, tour the plant, or find something else to do with them until about a quarter to seven, then jump up and run.

When I asked why he didn't want to go home, they said he had five daughters, a grand daughter and a mother-in-law that lived with him, and some nights there were so many feminine activities there that he delayed going home until he had to.

I was the new kid on the block, so now, instead of being flattered by his attention, I felt let down and used. Then I started thinking about what could be in it for me. I just told my wife to expect me home later on those nights, and I started milking him for all I could get in the way of information—while at the same time selling him some of my ideas.

Sometime later, the company, which was a division of a conglomerate, got on shaky ground—and found some excuse to let him go. I cleaned out his office of his personal things and took them over to his house. He was already on the phone
with a head-hunter.

To make a long story short, a couple of weeks later he called me. He was now president of our biggest competitor.

And me? I was soon his vice president of manufacturing!

CHAPTER 9

UNUSUAL FRINGE BENEFITS

My friend Harry makes hundreds of technical speeches all over the world. He starts each talk by saying that he has devoted his professional life to the type of industry he serves, and that he is going to tell his audience just what he has done, and how he has done it, for that industry.

One day, after hearing him speak for the tenth or twelfth time, I reminded him of how he starts out, then I said, "But Harry, all you talk about is what you do for yourself."

"Everything I do for my company and my industry I also do for myself," he said. "Haven't you ever heard of fringe benefits?"

Harry was right, there can be fringe benefits in almost everything you do, if you work it right—even the hardest, dirtiest jobs!

Roaming Around the Workplace (Necessary, But Can Be Fun)

There are inside fringe benefits, and there are outside benefits. Judge this one for yourself.

When I first moved to an industrial town, at age nineteen, I found employment as a tester in a plant where electric motors were manufactured. It was a multi-floored building, and we were on the fourth floor.

All of our products, after being tested, had to be placed on skids, whether acceptable or not. Our problem was that the motors arrived at our area by means of a conveyor, so there was no way that skids were delivered to us automatically. Other departments had the opposite problem—their motors, or parts, arrived on skids but left on conveyors, so they had to get rid of skids.

The undesirable job in my department was taking a manually operated lift truck and scouring the plant for skids to bring to our area. Of course this fell to the greenest employee in the department, which was me. I thought of myself as a big time motor tester, who shouldn't have to stoop to chasing skids. But my foreman thought differently.

On one of my almost daily search missions, I came to a place where there were more skids than I realized existed in that building, so I loaded up.

As I turned to leave, I heard someone say, "Hey, Handsome, skids are a dollar apiece in this department!"

A female voice, and I liked her already. Peeking out over a workbench was "Miss Cuteness," herself—all sandy red hair and freckles!

"Then you'll just have to arrest me," I said. "They don't pay me enough to buy skids."

"Too bad," she said, "I was looking for a rich man."

"Well, I'm rich enough for a couple of movie tickets, and maybe a bite to eat. How about Saturday night?"

"I'm game, if you are serious," she said.

I found out later that some of her co-workers told her she was crazy, she didn't know anything about this guy. She had told them she would, by next week. And she did!

I took on the skid search as a permanent job, went to that floor quite a bit—even took to eating lunch down there. Then when one of her girl friends told me she had gone back to Kentucky for the weekend and married some old boyfriend, I still kept going back to that floor. There were lots of other delightful, charming girls down there.

Sometime later my boss brought a new guy into our department and told me I was off skid duty. I told him no, I would still do it. What I didn't tell him was why.

The fringe benefits were too great!

Trailer park Maintenance (Someone Had To Do It, Why Not Me?)

If a outlandish job can be had right at home, and can be turned into a benefit, that makes it all the better.

I was still in school, working at a variety of jobs, when our first child was on the way. So we bought a mobile home. It was already on site in a trailer park, had been repossessed by a bank, and we just took over the payments.

We had to pay rent for the space, of course, and utility bills, but it gave us the privacy we wanted for a baby, which was difficult in an apartment, where other tenants objected to noise—even that which is made by a child.

The trailer park owner was a grump, but kept a clean, neat area. One day he was griping to me and some others about not being able to keep good part time help. I asked him what he wanted someone to do, and he said basic preventive maintenance and collecting garbage. The other men in the group began walking away, like the plague had just struck.

Then when he told me what the job paid, I could see why no one wanted to do it.

"I'll take the job," I said, "but I don't want to get paid."

"You mean you'll do it for nothing?" he asked.

"No," I replied. "I want my rent free, and my utilities paid for. No money is to change hands. I don't want to have to track it or pay taxes on it, and you won't have to carry me on your books as an employee."

"Sounds good to me," he said, smiling. "Can you start right away?"

"Of course," I said, "but there is one more thing. I'm doing the job, not working hours—so don't track my time. And I will do it whenever I can, fitting it in with my other activities."

It worked out well for both of us. He didn't have to manage somebody's time, and I didn't have to shell out money from my other hard-earned funds just to live there. In time I got the whole program down to about four or five hours each week, which cut into my study time hardly at all.

I continued doing that until I finished school and we could buy a house. The trailer park owner, who wasn't such a grump after all, said he really hated to see me go.

I almost did, too. I had developed this fringe benefit job into quite a racket, also!

Performing a Service (For Yourself, Too)

Sometimes, what you do for your employer can also be done for yourself, and at the same time.

During those school years one of my jobs was at a small cannery, employing twenty or so people. Their principle product was corn meal mush, which was either canned or rolled into round loaf-type packages sealed in wax paper.

On the mezzanine of the plant were three large vats, about twelve feet in diameter across the top and eight feet deep. The mush was mixed in these, then piped to the lower level where the canning and rolling machines were located. My job was to come in three nights each week, after they made mush during the day, and clean out the vats. I worked alone.

The vats were filled with water by the day shift and left to soak until I arrived. Then I drained the water out and scraped and hosed down the insides of the vats, without entering them, until they were clean for the next run. It was not easy work.

My first task was to disconnect the canning equipment from the bottom of the vats, while standing on a step ladder, then fasten an eight-inch drain pipe to each one, before draining the water out. One night I came to work and found the drain pipes already in place. Silently thanking whichever day shift employee did me this favor, I opened the drain valve on the first one. The pipe had not been fastened in place!

Immediately I had an eight-inch diameter flood of water hit me, knock me off my ladder, get me down on the floor and stomp me! Fortunately there was a large floor drain right under the vat drain. When I finally got upright again, while standing there cursing whoever put that pipe up there without attaching it, and myself for not checking it, I began to wonder about my condition.

I was soaking wet—outerwear, underwear, shoes, socks and me. It was the dead of winter, almost zero in Ohio, and I was a long way from home. Then I remembered the laundry.

Up next to the office in the cannery was a room with two washers and two dryers for processing the white aprons and jackets required to be worn by all food- handling employees. I slopped my way through the factory and into the laundry room. Since I was not only wet, but covered with the leavings of mush too, I took off all my clothes and ran them through one of the washers.

Thinking, "Oh, what the hell," I also gathered up all the dirty aprons and jackets and washed them, too. With two washers going, it was very warm in the room—so I found myself sitting there reading an old magazine stark naked. I was so mad at myself, and somebody else, I didn't know who, that I didn't care if someone did come in. But after awhile, as I put all the laundry in the two dryers, and sat my shoes on top of one to dry, my modest nature caught up with me, so I started looking around for something to cover myself with.

Just as I finished tying on two of the clean aprons off the shelf, one in front and one in back, I heard someone say, "Cute outfit! Shall we have all employees dress that way?"

I was mortified when I turned around and saw the boss lady, who, with her two sons, owned the place. Her house was right next door, but I had seen her only twice before.

"You don't have to tell me what happened," she said, laughing at my embarrassment. "It has happened before. But I must say your solution is a little more ingenious than anybody else's."

"I didn't really expect anybody to be here," I stammered. "Least of all, you!"

"Oh, I sneak around quite a bit," she said, "but tonight I came to do the laundry, which I have to do every few nights. Seems like nobody else wants to do it."

Thinking quickly, I said, "Why don't I do it? I'm here three nights a week, anyway. I could just stay a little longer and wash and dry the clothes."

She thought that was a very good idea, and so did my wife, when I told her we wouldn't be going to the Laundromat and feeding it quarters, anymore. I just simply took our clothes along with me to the cannery and tossed them in, then sat there and studied for school while the machines did all the work. What a fringe benefit!

Of course, I saw quite a bit of the boss lady, too. Sometimes she would bring her own laundry over to be done—and any number of nights she would have cookies or coffee, or both, for me. Maybe she was just lonesome—but she was very nice to me.

When our child was born, she gave me a very large cash bonus for a baby gift. Now that was a real fringe benefit!

Have to Work During Vacation? (Smile, Then Look for Benefits)

Occasionally what looks like a potential disaster can turn right around and become a pleasant event for you, with many fringe benefits.

When I first joined the electronics manufacturer after my government job, they shut down for vacation the last week of July and the first week of August every year. Those with vacation time coming had to take it then, whether they wanted to or not. Those that didn't have any time coming were just without a paycheck for two weeks. It took a year to earn one week, and two years to earn two weeks. I had just started to work there in May, so you can see where that left me for two weeks—broke!

Then right before shutdown the chief tool engineer came to me and asked if I could work during vacation, since there were a couple of projects to be completed. Of course I would—I needed it. He had also asked, or told, the night foreman in the tool-making department to work. The foreman didn't like the idea at all, having made plans for his family during those two weeks, but he acquiesced, and he and I worked in an empty plant.

Well, not really, we didn't exactly work, but we showed up—at least occasionally.

The unhappy foreman and I had finished all our assigned projects by Wednesday night of the first week, and had them in place. It is amazing how much you can get done in an industrial setting when there is no one around to interrupt or bother you.

"I don't know what we are going to do for the next week and a half," I told him, on Wednesday afternoon.

"We're going fishing," he said, "every day."

Now this guy was an avid fisherman, for all types of fish, and, being born and raised around that area, knew all the rivers, small streams and lakes like the back of his hand. Within two weeks I knew a lot of them myself!

The plant had a security officer on duty at all times. We would just tell him we were going to one of the other buildings, and head for some stretch of water. At first we would come in every morning to check things out, then come back that night to check for messages. There never were any. Who would they be from, anyway? The second week we didn't even do that—just fished every day, with one of us checking in occasionally.

We caught a lot of fish—catfish, crappie, trout.

The following year we volunteered to mind the store again, while everybody else was gone. It seemed like this happened every year, anyway—they always had hot jobs in our area to be completed at that time. The boss thought we were gluttons for punishment.

After a few years the company changed its vacation policy to one of staggered times, on a seniority basis. That move ruined a good thing for the tool room foreman and me.

But we sure enjoyed the fringe benefits of an undesirable job while it lasted!

Working at the Circus (The Worst Job Has the Most Benefits)

Part time jobs at entertainment events are hardly ever pleasant. The workers are neither spectators nor participants. But look around, the hardest job might be the best. Again, you have to look for possible fringe benefits.

I had joined an organization of special policemen, or "Saturday Night Cops," as we called ourselves, and was asked to work at the world's biggest circus when it came to town.

We were shown a layout of the circus grounds and asked where we wanted to work—parking lots, ticket booths, roaming the grounds to spot trouble and stop it before it happened. Being new to this circus job, I inquired about a spot that was shown inside the big top.

"You don't want that," whispered one of the others, "that's the worst place on the grounds."

But, just from looking at the layout, I didn't see it that way. The job was to guard a gate where the circus performers came in and out of the tent, and see that no one else did. It was hectic, but it was right in front of the best unreserved seats under the big top.

And who was sitting right in the front row of those seats, hobnobbing with all the performers? My wife and three small children, whom I had brought in free when I took up my post.

They thought it was a very important fringe benefit!

Step Down From Your Bridge (The Benefits Will Surprise You)

As you grow in your chosen profession, you might start to consider some activities beneath your dignity. Take a hard look, before you back off from them.

As a river boat captain, (yes, I hold a master's license), I have had occasion to observe just what other people in the crew do, and refrain from doing, on boats. And you know, no one wants to do the dock work!

But, whenever a boat, especially an excursion craft, comes in to port, someone must immediately pump out the sewage, pump in water and fill the tanks with fuel. Captains just don't do that, and other crew members run from it.

When I became auxiliary captain of a rather large side-wheeler excursion boat, filling in when someone was ill or on vacation, I noticed that the other captains hardly ever came down from the bridge, or pilothouse, except to eat or depart for home. Others were forced to take the responsibility for preparing the boat for its next cruise. Sometimes even one of the owners or a member of their families would be doing this. I couldn't see it that way.

If I had the authority over and responsibility for the boat, its crew and its passengers, I wanted it all. So when I was serving as captain, I would come down from the pilothouse, don my "pumpkin suit," as my family called my bright orange coveralls, and personally see to it that the boat was ready to go out again when needed. The other captains and some crew members would smile and shake their heads while seeing me doing these unseemly chores.

Then one day some members of my family from outside the area came for a visit. I called the owners to ask about special rates for them.

I was told, "You can have all the family and friends on the boat any time you wish. Let them enjoy everything to their heart's content. It won't cost them or you a dime! It's your fringe benefit!"

My family and close friends cruised with me quite a bit after that, and one of the other captains wondered aloud how we could afford it.

I told him we were rich. But I didn't tell him we were rich in fringe benefits from the job!

CHAPTER 10

OUTDOOR SPORTS RACKETS

Hunters and fishermen don't go hunting and fishing just to bring something home, any more than a sports fan goes to a football or baseball game just to see his team win. With the latter it is all the excitement of being there. It is the color, the noise, the bands, the young participants, the hot dogs and beer, the thermos of coffee, the pre-game festivities and, usually, the big party afterwards. And of course, there is the companionship.

But the fan doesn't have to justify being there.

The hunter and fisherman does, though. He feels guilty if he doesn't bring something home—and the bigger it is or the more quantity it is, the better he can justify going in the first place.

But that's not why he goes. He, too, goes for the color, the excitement, the thermos of coffee and the companionship. His problem is that he can't just go and enjoy the fun—he thinks that he has to come back and show what he got, or tell about what he almost got, or what he caught and released. Even the stuff the writers write has to contain the ultimate catch or kill of the object.

The fact is that the spring blossoms on the hillsides, the bright sun on blue water, and the color of the mountain hardwoods in the fall really serve as food for the soul—and the idiotic, as well as serious, things that can happen to a lover of outdoor sports and his friends can keep them in a constant enjoyable frame of mind, with an ever youthful attitude.

And for those of us who hunt or fish there are many opportunities to improve our situations as to availability of places to participate in our favorite activities, if we don't mind doing a little dirty work.

Helping the Traveler (He Might Be Your Best Contact)

Finding places to hunt on privately owned land is a big problem for today's outdoorsman. And doing so can come from some strange activities.

My young friend, Jim, was just being a Good Samaritan when he came upon an elderly gentleman with a flat tire on his car—Jim was like that. He was about twenty miles out in the country between his home and the next town, when he saw a man struggling with his spare tire, trying to get it out of the luggage compartment. Jim pulled up behind the other car and stopped to help.

Both he and the stranded motorist were very much chagrined to discover that the spare tire was also flat.

"Let's throw them both in my truck and we'll take them to town and get them fixed," said Jim.

So he and the appreciative man drove in to a service station where the tires were soon repaired, but the operator was alone and couldn't leave.

"He doesn't have to," Jim told the man, "I brought you here, I'll take you back."

So he drove out to the man's car, put the tire back on, and fastened the spare in the trunk. In the course of their conversation, the man learned that Jim worked in a sporting goods store.

"Then do you like to hunt and fish?" he asked. "Do you hunt turkeys and deer?"

When Jim informed him that he did, whenever he could find a place to pursue them, the man said, "I've got over nine hundred acres of woods down on the state border, where deer and turkeys are dying of old age. I don't hunt, and, since I run livestock, I don't let anybody else in there, either. It's yours to hunt in any time you want to. Just come by the house."

Jim and a few close friends have had their own private hunting domain ever since!

Everybody Requires Assistance (Some More Than Others)

There are five big lakes within an hour's drive of where I live, and I was trying to learn their best fishing spots, when I found help from a unique activity.

I was driving around in a small town near one of the lakes, when I saw the man taking a nap under a boat—at least that was what it looked like to me. I had come up an alley between some houses, and there lay a pair of feet and legs sticking out from under a boat, which was on a trailer. I stopped my pickup, got out and walked over.

I couldn't resist saying, "That's a heckuva place to take a nap!"

"Shut up and give me a hand!" snarled an almost human voice from under the boat. "Hold those bolts up there while I put the nuts on them down here."

I could see immediately what he was doing, trying to attach some new brackets to his boat trailer while the boat was on it, and it was definitely a two-man job. I've done the same thing myself, and lacking help, backed the boat in the lake off the trailer, then worked on the trailer in the parking lot—even painted a couple of trailers that way.

Finally a big redheaded guy crawled out from under the boat, and I could see he had an even bigger problem—his left arm was missing!

"The war," he said, when he saw me staring. "They gave me a new one, but I don't want to get it dirty, greasy or damaged working on the boat."

I wound up spending the rest of the afternoon helping my new found friend do a number of things to his boat, then came back the next day to help him get it ready for the lake.

"Ever fish this lake?" he asked on the second day.

I told him I hadn't, because I had no idea where to start, or for what type of fish.

"I'll give you navigation instructions," he replied. "I was born and raised here, and I know it like the back of my hand. I'll show you where to catch the biggest bass, crappie and catfish."

And he did, sometimes in his boat, sometimes in mine. We never became fishing partners in the true sense of the word, but during that spring and summer I became almost an authority on where to fish in that lake, and I still enjoy it immensely!

Always Help Other Boaters (They Might Help You in Some Way)

My friend Don and I had been cruising around the lake checking out our favorite fishing spots, when this activity led us up into a seldom frequented cove. Sitting in the cove was a pontoon "party boat" with several people on it, mostly middle aged men and women. They began waving to us, motioning us towards them.

Cruising up alongside the boat, I guessed it at about thirty-two feet—not a bad size for that type of boat, small enough to be trailered, but big enough to carry a dozen or so passengers. They informed us that their motor wouldn't run.

"Well, we're not mechanics," I told them, "but what can we do to help?"

"I am," said one of the men, "but when I went to fix it, I dropped my only spare part in the water. Can you tow us?"

"Not very far," I told him, "my boat isn't big enough. Where did you launch?"

When he told me, I realized it was a good ten miles to that ramp, and my little boat would be under a strain to get that big pontoon there.

"There's a ramp just about a mile away," I said. "Why don't I pull you there, then I'll run you down the lake to the other ramp, you can get your vehicle and drive around on land to your boat."

It took us an hour to get them to the closest launching area, then we ran him to his car.

When he expressed his regret at taking us away from our fishing, and offered to pay me for my trouble, which of course I refused, we told him we were about ready to give up and go trout fishing, instead.

"I have a stream full of native trout running right through my place," he said. "Why don't you fish there? I don't fish."

Boy, did I ever take him up on that! Trout fishing the back-country streams has always been my favorite, anyway. It is much more fun than sitting in a boat. I haven't kept any fish for many, many years—preferring to release all of them so they can grow bigger. And it is especially satisfying to release them in a small stream. Of course, I've been told that since I don't keep any, I can stretch the truth a little about what I catch. I don't subscribe to that statement that says, "I fish, therefore I lie," anyway, no matter what my friends might tell you.

But now I have a great place to fish, on private property, and it's all mine!

Mending Fence is Hard Work (But Profitable)

What has repairing a fence to do with outdoor sports, you ask? Everything, if it crosses a trout stream.

I had spent the morning, with great satisfaction, on my favorite trout stream, and started home. I decided to go out the other way from which I had come in through the mountains, when I came to a place where the stream flowed right across the road. After surveying the situation and checking it for depth, I put my truck in four-wheel drive and drove through it. Standing on the other side was a bearded young man, in his forties, I guessed, looking intently at the water.

I stopped.

"You look perplexed," I ventured, in my usual shy manner.

"That big rain last week took out my fence," he said, "and my horses need the pasture. I was just dreading getting in that cold water to replace it."

Looking up and down the fence row from the creek, I could see about a hundred yards of barbed wire fence on the ground, some of it in the creek itself.

Looking at his work shoes, then at my chest high waders, I said, "You don't have to. I'll do the wading."

"You mean you'll help me? Why?"

"Because I'll enjoy it, that's why. I've done a lot of this in my time, and I sort of miss it," I replied. "Let's get at it."

So there we were, crawling around among the cottonmouth moccasins and poison ivy, driving fence posts and stringing barbed wire. (Poison ivy has never bothered me, and apparently it didn't bother him either. And as for the cottonmouths, do you know how to tell them from other water snakes? No? Well, the cottonmouths are the ones that run towards you!)

After a while, he said to me, "I don't see how you can say you actually are enjoying this!"

"It's easy to explain," I told him. "I don't have to do it. You do. You need the additional pasture. But I can walk away—I can quit and go home!"

"What are you doing here anyway?" he asked.

"I fish downstream where the creek cuts through the ridge," I said. "I know the man that owns the land there. I decided to go home the back way, when I saw you."

"Well, now you know the man that owns this land, too. So consider it your fishing spot. And I bet you do better here than down there."

And he was right!

Hey, I'll Take the West Coast Trip, Boss (And Go Fishing!)

Sometimes you are forced to go somewhere you don't want to go, especially if it is a repetitive situation. Just analyze it—there has to be something in it for you.

Someone from my organization had to go to the west coast four times each year for a week. All of us got tired of it, including me. And then I met Rod!

He was the father-in-law of my wife's brother, who had asked me to look him up sometime. Said he was that rarest of individuals, a native of that area. So on my next trip, I called him. Before I even finished identifying myself on the phone, he said, "I know who you are, you old S.O.B., we're going fishing tomorrow."

I tried to tell him I had things to do related to business, but he ignored me. Said he would pick me up in front of my hotel. And he did. Such a delightful old guy, and

such a pleasant day out on a commercial fishing boat. We caught rock cod, striped bass, red snapper and barracuda. I couldn't wait for my next trip!

Of course I had to be very cagey in telling the company president that I wouldn't mind taking all the west coast trips, since I had found a shirt-tail relative out there to visit with. I was willing to make the big sacrifice, just for the good of the company, and to relieve the pressure on the other executives. This way I could plan my four trips in advance, in order to get the most good out of them.

But you can bet I didn't tell him that one day on the ocean was included in those plans, or he might have suspected just who was getting the most good out of these trips!

Driving a Sand Point is Hard and Dirty (But hunting is Not!)

This is another of those "help the landowner and gain privileges" stories, and it completely surprised my hunting buddy and me.

Moose, my life long hunting, fishing, golfing and flying partner, and I were driving down a back country road to visit a friend who owned some land on which we hunted, when we came across an older man sitting on the ground in a little valley by a dried up creek bed. He had a post driver and some pipe lying next to him. Suspecting what he was up to, I stopped my pickup, and we walked over.

"Looks like you have taken on a tough job, Mister," said Moose. "I don't want you to feel insulted, but driving one of those things is for younger men."

"I'm too tired to be insulted," he laughed. "I wouldn't have to do this, but the creek went dry this year, and I thought that by driving a sand point near the creek bed and putting a small pump on it I could get enough water for my livestock."

"We'll drive it," I said. And we did.

When he asked us what we were doing there, and we told him we were on our way to visit a friend on whose farm we hunted, he said, "You can hunt here, if you would like to."

He told us his wife had passed away, and his only son had gone into the Army, so he had put most of his land in a set-aside program, except for the pasture. Most of it was meadow and slough grass, surrounded by his neighbors' cornfields—an ideal habitat for pheasants and quail.

He posted "No Hunting" signs all around, so that Moose and I with a few friends were the exclusive hunters of that vast area.

Another outlandish job turned in to a racket!

Always Help the Old Guys (You Might Be One, Too, Some Day)

Sometimes, in the outdoor world, you just do things that need to be done, as they occur. Sometimes they come back to haunt you, but good deeds bring on other good deeds. Or so it was at the lake.

Due to the nature of our professions, for a time Moose and I could take off on Thursdays in the spring and go fishing. We preferred launching our big tri-hull fishing boat at a small boat ramp on a steep slope back of the ranger's station at our favorite lake, because it was not used very much by other fishermen.

Early one morning we found the ramp blocked by two older men, octogenarians at least, who were trying to pull a flat back canoe out of an old pickup. I stopped the boat trailer and we proceeded to get the canoe in the water for them and mount their little motor on the stern.

As we pushed them off, Moose said, "I hope they don't venture far from shore in that thing. It will capsize for sure. Maybe we should keep an eye on them."

And we did—not letting them out of our sight all morning.

This became a regular Thursday morning routine—they blocked our way, we launched their craft, and, if the lake was at all rough, we stayed within yelling distance of them. No words were ever exchanged between us.

Later, when we complained to my old uncle about it, he said, "Don't be too hard on them, boys. Some day you will be too old to do what you do now, too."

Then one day their motor didn't start.

Moose said, "Why don't you guys just go with us."

They seemed most happy to do so, and thanked us profusely.

After that, they didn't even bring their canoe on Thursdays—just waited for us.

As we became better friends, they asked us one day if we ever fished small streams. We told them that was our favorite type of fishing, that we had several good places to fish for trout, and did so all winter.

"Would you like to fish for bass in a small stream?" one of them asked, and we told him we sure would.

It turns out that they owned adjoining farms, and the state's best kept secret ran right through them—a cold, rock-bottomed creek full of small mouth and rock bass, with no one fishing for them. They said that used to be their favorite fishing, until they got too old to wade. That's when they obtained the canoe.

Long after our two friends had passed on to a better fishing stream, the Moose and I were sitting on the tail gate of my truck, after fishing their favorite stream for about the ten-thousandth time, struggling to remove our waders. Amid all the grunting and groaning, I looked over at him and we both died laughing.

"Are you thinking what I'm thinking?" I asked.

"Yep, our two old friends and their flat back canoe!"

"My uncle was right," I said. "We've come full circle. Let's just hope there are some younger guys out there somewhere who will take time to perform a outlandish task when we require it!"

CHAPTER 11

ENTERTAINMENT ON THE JOB

We have all heard the story about the guy whose job in the circus was to go along and shovel behind the elephants and clean up after them in their railroad cars. When he complained constantly to the other circus employees about what he did, they asked him why he didn't just quit and find another type of work.

"What! And give up show business?" he replied.

Well, he was in show business, but he was not the one being entertained. You can sometimes do him one better in your own position.

Within the confines of most jobs are some opportunities to be entertained, and this goes for the outlandish ones, too. In fact, I have known of a few cases where the main reason the employee kept the job was for the entertainment value of it!

The Roughest Job in the Store (And the Most Entertaining)

Why did Georgie prefer working in the basement, we wondered. We all knew he was a sixteen year old girl-crazy teenager, and there were certainly no girls down there, although there were plenty of them passing through the store.

The oldest grocery store in town was in a long narrow typical storefront building on the main street. Its single cash register on a checkout stand was at the front of the store, right in front of the big plate glass window. We teenage boys who worked there enjoyed watching the girls in their thin summer dresses pass between us and the bright sunlight shining through that south-facing window.

What we didn't like was hauling grocery stock out of the dark, dingy basement up to the main floor where we could put it on the shelves. But Georgie did.

Since the building hung on the side of a hill that dropped away to the back, the lower level opened out on a dock to which the supply trucks could back up and unload. Someone had to help remove all the grocery cartons and put them away in the basement—and all of us part timers helped with that. Then every day, somebody had to pull out the appropriate boxes, put them in a dumb waiter and send them to the main floor to be put on the shelves. Georgie loved that job, much to the consternation of everybody.

I almost felt sorry for him, down there in the dark among the cobwebs. Then one day I went down in the basement for something, and didn't see him anywhere. I finally found him up under the front part of the store, right about under the checkout. He had his head tilted back and seemed to be looking up. Seeing me, he wasn't even startled.

Putting his finger to his lips to signal me to be quiet, he pointed upward. In the old wooden floor, right where everybody had to walk to get past the cash register, was an old screened heat register, long unused, about two feet square.

Motioning for me to follow him away from the area, Georgie whispered, "You'd be surprised how many girls don't wear any underwear in the summer time!"

A teenager with a dirty mind? Some sort of young pervert? Naw, just a red-blooded American boy taking advantage of the entertainment opportunities of his job!

Observations of a Lineman (More Visual Entertainment)

We have all heard the stories that ice men told, back in the days of door-to-door delivery of that commodity, about the various stages of undress, deliberate or not, in which some of their lady customers greeted them. But a utility lineman? Why would one keep doing an unpleasant task?

One of the tallest utility poles went almost to the third floor of the hotel, and right up against the wall. And something on that pole required service quite often, but the linemen disliked doing it. Then one day after my friend Hubert spent most of the afternoon on the pole, taking twice as much time for the job as normally required, he told his boss he would volunteer to climb that particular pole whenever it was required.

"Well," he said, when I asked him if he wasn't becoming a glutton for punishment, "I keep hoping the entertainment will be as good as it was that first afternoon. Right inside that window, not ten feet away, was a beautiful young lady

taking a nap. She had on no nightclothes, or day clothes, or evening clothes. In fact, all she seemed to have on was the radio!"

A peeping Tom? Watching a brazen hussy? Nope, just a utility lineman and a tired young lady, doing what they should have been!

Another Pole Climber (Do They All See Things Like This?)

When you are not even supposed to be climbing a pole, but you get entertained anyway, just relax and enjoy it.

While managing a concession stand at a drive-in theater when in school, I heard the wife of the owner-manager complaining about a problem, which he would normally fix, but he wasn't there. Although I didn't work for them directly—the concession stand was operated by a separate company—I asked her if I could be of service.

"Two of the moonlights are out," she said, "and the bulbs need to be replaced."

Clear past the back row of the theater was a steel pole about seventy feet high, with a service platform on top and, above that, a bank of green and orange lights—two of each. They were put there to provide enough light in the area for people to see to drive in or out with their automobile lights off, or to walk to the refreshment stand—but were not strong enough to have an effect on the movie screen. Hence the designation, "moonlights."

Now, I've never had any problems with heights, so I volunteered to replace the lights. The steel pole was equipped with climbing spikes, so it was an easy climb.

After replacing the bulbs and climbing down to approximately twenty feet from the ground, I was aware of a dark colored convertible backing quietly right in under the pole. Before I could descend any further, the young couple in the car climbed quickly into the back seat, both of them slid out of the lower part of their clothing and started a wrestling match just below me. I hung on to the spikes on the pole and didn't move, not wishing to embarrass them with my presence.

Soon they separated, so I thought they might drive away, but just the opposite happened. They started up their activity again, except this time they removed all their clothes! After it was all over, they separated again, but made no effort to leave, or even put their clothes back on. By now I was getting tired of hanging on to the spikes in the pole, so I climbed on down.

As I dropped off the last spike, right beside their car, I said, "Good evening, folks."

There was an immediate starting of motor and spinning of wheels as they left the drive-in—still undressed!

There is an aftermath to this incident, though. When I told the theater owner about it, he had an idea for a joke. The following Saturday night, he got on the public address system and announced that there was a very irate husband up at the ticket office, claiming that his wife was there with some other man.

"We don't want any trouble," said the manager, "so if the couple in question will just drive out quietly, we would appreciate it."

The end of the joke was that he had arranged for a couple of friends to drive out, pretending to be the wayward ones—and the audience would laugh.

All of us in on the joke laughed even harder when three cars left!

CHAPTER 12

SHAPING YOUR FUTURE

How many people do you know who are doing exactly what they set out to do professionally? Not many, I'll bet. Oh, maybe a few doctors and lawyers, and not even very many of them. My dentist said he was forced into it by family pressures. My pharmacist is a computer whiz, and would rather be in that field. Another friend is personnel manager in a large manufacturing company, but studied art. One of the best engineers I know has a degree in drama. No, he never acted. But he designed lighting systems, computerized them and operated them.

Even myself—I was meant to be the world's greatest baseball coach, while teaching high school math, or so I thought. I never intended to wind up as an engineer, riverboat captain and publisher.

But all too often some simple thing we do at some point in our youth, or in our work, deliberately or inadvertently, can point us in some direction from which we do not wish to retreat. Or maybe we can learn about what we do not want to do. And some of these career changes can be outlandish jobs.

Bottom Job in Publishing (Can Lead to the Top)

It is possible, no, probable, that your very first job can determine your future.

My friend, Lewis, in high school, felt lucky to get any job at all after school and on Saturdays. He had wanted to get into retail sales, and shoot for either a lucrative commission position or a managerial spot—whichever he might prove to be best at doing. But part-time jobs in that field in his town were as scarce as chicken teeth.

Then the local newspaper, which also did a limited amount of book and magazine publishing, needed someone temporarily to pack up some files and move them to their archives. Lewis found out about it from another student who had taken the job, but got called away to do more chores at home. Lewis suspected that the guy just considered it an undesirable job, and found a way out. The job was expected to last all day Saturday, and evenings the following week.

When Lewis showed up for work on Saturday morning, the lady in charge of the files told him what to do, then he overheard her talking to another employee about being gone on vacation that afternoon, and would be away all the following week.

Lewis set up a system whereby the storage boxes he was to use were on an angle for ease of filling, as the file always slid to the front. The file drawers were set on a table above the storage boxes, so he could reach into them quite easily. Two stacks of four-drawer files had already been emptied, and there were twenty-four to go.

Shortly before noon Lewis went to the boss lady and asked her what he should do after he finished with these files, since he was told to plan on working all day, then after school all next week. She told him to just finish up the file project and he would be done.

"I'll be done shortly after noon," he said.

The boss couldn't believe it. She told him his predecessor had done only two of the twenty-six files all week after school.

Lewis finished up and went home, once again jobless—until she came back from vacation and hired him on a permanent part-time basis.

About his retail career? Never got to it. Of course the fact that he is now president of one of the largest publishing houses in that part of the country just might have something to do with it!

Take the Job, Anyway (You Might Learn Something Negative)

Most of us develop ideas about our future based on what we see around us, and the people we respect—thinking we would like to be like them. A little experience at what they do can sometimes change that thinking.

Since I was a fairly good student, and had a respectful attitude towards most of my teachers, I decided early on that I would like to emulate some of them. I hadn't really thought much about what they actually did all day—just what kind of people they were. Then I was more or less forced to learn more. I became a teacher!

During my senior year in high school, the man who taught freshman mathematics along with some other courses had to be away for an extended period due to a family emergency. There were no substitutes to be found, but the school administrators were able to shuffle other teachers into most of his classes, but a first year math class had no teacher. I just happened to have a study period that coincided with it, and they asked me to teach, or at least to baby-sit the class. Many of my friends were horrified that I would even consider such a thing. But I thought of it as preparation for my future as a teacher. No pay, but a lot of experience.

On my very first day, two smart-aleck boys decided to try me, so I sent them to visit the principal—who had promised he would back me up when he talked me into taking the job. Then two little over-developed girls in the front began crossing and uncrossing their legs. The mother of one of them was a teacher, and the other one was my neighbor. At the end of the period I stopped them as they left the room.

"I have a note here for the mother of each of you," I said, "but I think I will wait until tomorrow to give them to them."

From then on they were perfect ladies, and I never did give my non-existent notes to their mothers.

I walked into the noisy classroom on the second day, and after I finally got everybody's attention, I said, as forcefully as I could, "Now here is the deal, students. After yesterday I don't like this any better than you do. We have two choices, and neither one of them will hurt me—but one of them will really have a negative effect on you, all of you. No one knows how long your teacher will be gone, and I'm giving up a study period to do this. We can all settle down, respect each other, and try to have some kind of a math class to keep up until he gets back. I can help you all. All of your teacher's other classes are covered by real teachers, but there is no one for this one. The only other choice, if I walk away, is for the administration to suspend this class. Since it is required, you'll just have to take it some other time in the ensuing years, after a teacher becomes available. I wouldn't want to do that, if I were you."

By the time the teacher returned three weeks later, I had seen all of teaching I wanted to, from his side of the desk. Since then I have taught industrial courses in plants, and even some engineering classes—but I completely forgot my original plans to teach high school.

It takes a special breed of cat to do that—and two of my kids do it—but my outlandish job left me with some memories I would just as soon not have. We've heard of teacher "burn out".

I was burned out in less than a month!

Working Your Way Up (All It Takes is an Opportunity)

If you can't get into the type of work you want, maybe you should take something close to it, then sort of sneak in. That's what Jack did.

The personnel manager told me he thought the job applicant was not qualified to do production work, and he seemed a little too "slow on the up take" to put him in shipping, where the guy wanted to work. Still, the manager knew him to be a good solid honest man, who had a mentally handicapped daughter—but had not been able to find a job other than part time janitorial work at the local super market.

"I wish we had something for him, though," he said.

Now, factory cleanup was done by the production workers, who were required to keep their areas clean, but we used a janitorial service to do the offices—and they were not very good. I suggested we hire the applicant as a part-time custodian for the offices, and see how he worked out.

So Jack ordered all the supplies he needed, and proceeded to do a remarkable job for us. With the shipping offices also in his bailiwick, he spent quite a bit of time

back there. Then, since our shipping chores were heavier at times, that department started using him during those busy times. He was overjoyed when we put him on full time, at the request of the department manager, with full benefits. He continued his janitorial duties.

Turned out he was not "slow on the up take," as we had thought. Jack was just thorough. He was very accurate in what he did, which was a desirable trait in the shipping area.

To make a long story short, when the shipping department manager left us for family reasons three years later, we gave the job to Jack!

Even a Golf Outing Can Be Good for Business (And You!)

You are more likely to get fired over screwing up one of those "Swiss Navy" jobs than for making a mistake in your regular work. Those extracurricular activities you are requested to do can cost you your job, or enhance your future.

The head of the publishing company got it in his head to hold a golf outing for fifty or sixty select advertisers. After mentioning several times at his staff meetings that he would like for someone to get involved, I jumped right in. Again, my editor and publisher friends in the organization told me I was nuts. One mistake, one customer with a bad taste in his mouth, and I would be history. I kept going.

Now the Old Man was a very good golfer, but he only wanted to play—not get involved in the outing itself. So I approached Moose. I had been instrumental in establishing an annual tournament for the chapter of the Society of Manufacturing Engineering of which I was founding chairman, but, even though I play golf, I didn't know anything about the details of running a golf contest. Moose did.

He was a member of my editorial staff, and was, without a doubt, the best golfer in the company. He played in tournaments all over the world—sometimes with me in tow. I was to manage the overall event—and he was to manage, and participate in, the tournament. I asked for, and got, a budgetary figure for the outing. The Old Man took care of the invitations.

When Moose asked me what if we screw up and get fired, I told him we ought to meet enough important people at the event to find another job with one of them—especially since both of us were engineers-turned-editors, and these were all executives of manufacturing companies. We held our noses, so to speak, and jumped in.

We bought a bunch of golf shirts, identical except for sizes and colors, from the club where the event was held, put them out on a table and insisted that each participant take off whatever shirt he or she was wearing, and put one on. Now we were all readily identifiable. One executive, or other person who had customer contact, from the publishing company was in each of thirty foursomes. With the Old Man's help we juggled foursomes for compatibility. At the dinner the evening after the tournament, we saw to it that everyone there got some sort of prize. We even had a category called the "I didn't get any other prize" award!

We held the golf outing every year for many years, until the club established a policy of no more than ten foursomes in a tournament at once.

The future for Moose and me?

I became a division manager, while he was director of sales. Eventually the two of us owned our own publishing company with nine publications.

Many of the friends we made at the golf outings were instrumental in bringing this about!

Getting All the Employees Involved (And Yourself)

The union complained that they had no input into manufacturing management's affairs, so we offered a way.

Perhaps the union officials expected top management to step aside and let them take over. Of course that didn't happen. But we did devise a way to let them participate in day-to-day activities—and they rejected it.

My proposal was for an employee participation program, whereby all ideas for technical improvements would be heard by a review committee made up of manufacturing engineers and production personnel. The ideas did not have to be reviewed by the presenter's boss. The system was designed to bypass him until a decision was made on its value.

The union rejected it when they were told that none of this—the factory representatives, whether or not an idea would become fact, or what type of rewards might occur—was not to be negotiable. I proposed we do it anyway, and we did.

There was almost one hundred percent participation on the part of the workers, much to the union officials' chagrin. (Of course, some of those officials were not officials after the next election.)

No monetary rewards were offered, but we did generate our own newspaper. Unfortunately, within a few years, the company was sold, the employee participation program was eliminated at the insistence of the union and things started to go down hill. By the time the plant was closed I was long gone. (I wonder where those hardheaded union officials are today?)

Many of my friends asked me why I was hanging my career out to dry with a project like that—especially since, as Manager of Manufacturing Engineering, I had no bargaining unit production employees reporting to me. I told them it was for the future—and it was.

First I wrote a series of articles and made many speeches on the workings and success of the program, then, as a consultant, instituted an employee participation program in other plants!

Branch Plant, a Pin in the Map (But It Could Be Your Pin)

I've heard that getting involved in your company's first attempt at diversification into off-premise facilities can be tantamount to professional suicide. If all goes well, somebody else gets the credit, and if everything goes wrong, they look for a scapegoat. Your plant is just a pin on a map, and it is easy for them to pull the pin out and throw it away, or to remove the green pin and replace it with a red pin. But it can also be a racket for you.

My organization's initial stab at relocating part of its facilities was a move for the electronics department. I'm the guy who proposed it, and, over the protests of others, carried it out.

I've always been convinced that there are only four reasons for branching out.

1. Your customers are somewhere else.

I once worked with an outfit in the mid-west that manufactured tool boxes. They did a lot of business on the west coast. When you ship a box, you ship mostly air. With their shipping costs high, and many customers there, they just naturally built a plant on the west coast.

2. Your raw material is someplace else.

There is a good example of this in the WORKPLACE POSSIBILI-TIES section of this text—the concrete products plant.

3. You run out of space, with no room to expand.

There is a case of this almost happening in the GETTING THE BOSS' ATTENTION section, where an addition was made to the plant by juggling the rules.

4. You run out of people.

This happens to most of us who are in an area of low unemployment.

You will notice that nowhere have I mentioned lower labor costs. That's because no matter how hard you try, wages always catch up with you.

The reason I proposed a move for our electronics division was the fourth one above—we ran out of people. Not only did we use up all the available personnel where we were, but another company closed their electronics plant a short distance away in another town so that all the people they laid off were available, and the plant was also available. I went after it.

Our own top management liked the proposal so well that they went for it, much to the chagrin of many of my cohorts who were opposed to it. Within a few months it was up and running—quite successfully, I might add.

Soon the proposals were flying left and right for us to move other departments, as people tried to get on the successful bandwagon of the corporate moves. I looked at them all very carefully, but at the chance of being declared a negative thinker, I couldn't agree with any of them.

Then one day the executive vice president called me into his office to tell me that the vice president of manufacturing, with the help of the production manager, had leased a production facility a hundred miles away, with the idea of moving one of their departments there. He wanted me to go and take a look, without disclosing what I was doing, and report back to him.

I detested an assignment like that—preferring to keep everything open and above board. I disliked even more what I had to come back and tell him.

"They didn't look up," I said.

"What do you mean?"

"The highest ceiling in that building is sixteen feet," I said. "The shortest machine in that department they plan to move is twenty-two feet high!"

I left him on the phone, not too happy.

Meanwhile, my electronics division was humming along nicely.

A branch plant can save you or kill you—you just have to look at all sides, and know what you are doing.

Expecting Failure is Realistic, If You Learn from It (I did)

I know it seems ridiculous to go into something knowing it will fail, but if it gives one experience to use on the next job, it is worth it.

The company was looking for a plant manager, and I was interested. What got my attention was the fact that there was no plant, just a foundation—and a lot of plans. But I never go into anything blind, and I had heard much about the area in which it was located.

The town was controlled by a unique educational institution, and most of the residents, especially the business people, were connected in some way to the school.

As soon as I met the founder and principle officer of the company, I knew it couldn't last. I gave him a year, unless he made some great personal changes.

But I took the job anyway. For two reasons. One, I liked the product, and thought it had a great future—I still think it has, although it hasn't been produced for many years. Two, I wanted to start a manufacturing plant from the ground up—with total responsibility and authority.

I had been instrumental in new plant start-up for many facilities, all over the world, but had never had it all. I figured a year on this one would give me the experience I wanted, to do this as a full time job. When I voiced my opinion to my friends about the expected failure of the company, they would shake their heads and look at me kind of sideways—especially after I had the facility up and running and was elected president.

Then what I expected to happen, did. The owner jumped in with both feet and started screwing everything up—sales priorities, production schedules, quality control, and even the sales themselves. Things started to slide downhill—orders cancelled, backers getting cold feet, disgruntled employees—but he wouldn't listen.

One day I asked him a question for which I already knew the answer. "Why do so many businesses, started by people from your school and which show great promise, simply go broke?"

"It's because they are wonderful entrepreneurs, they have great ideas for businesses, but once they are up and running, don't know how to handle the day-to-day operations," he said. Then, with a little hesitation, followed up with, "I guess I'm describing myself."

"You said it," I said, laughing as friendly as I could.

But nothing changed. Then when he started to insist that I buy stock in the company, and go out and hustle the backers for money, which he paid to himself as bonuses, I bailed out.

Thirteen months had passed, but I felt like I had the experience I wanted! He hired a friend from the institution to replace me, but within just a few short weeks the company closed its doors.

Don't Take On a Branch Plant (Without an Ulterior Motive)

There are many reasons why an individual would want to take on the creation and management of a branch plant for a company. Make sure yours is a good one. Mine was.

Although I had been instrumental in starting over twenty off-premise facilities for a variety of companies, I had never actually managed one. Somebody else, much more qualified than I, always did that—taking over after it was up and running. Then I had the opportunity to do so right in my secondary hometown, where I had a home near a lake.

My friends, whom I contacted, knowing they had managed branch plants, told me I was crazy. First, they said, this company is over a hundred years old, and has never done anything like this before. Second, trying to start a plant in the small town where you live, even part of the time, will get you in trouble with the local populace.

But I did it anyway. I had an ulterior motive.

Although the parent company made me Vice President and General Manager and a member of the board of directors, there were still people from the home plant trying to shoot me down—jealousy, I suppose. Some of them, who were proposed to me as the ones who could help me the most, were just the opposite. They had a habit of coming for a visit, then going back to report on the problems we were having—which we didn't have until they came.

Still, I had the plant up and running, making production schedules, within a year. The company gave me a big fat bonus, plus a raise in pay.

We had developed some great employees from inexperienced people. But we also had a few of the other kind.

One waitress wouldn't serve me in a restaurant because we didn't hire her husband. Two cops picked me up on ridiculous charges. I learned my production manager had fired the daughter of one of them. She had worked forty days in a one hundred and twenty day work period.

I let the husband of the county clerk go for incompetence, and was called for jury duty the following week.

Between these incidents, and hundreds more like them, plus the management changes at the home office—all my old bosses were gone—I bailed out after three years.

Why did I take the job, and hang on for so long?

My ulterior motive!

I wrote a book on the pros and cons of branch plants!

HAPPY READING!

CONCLUSION

Do the Outlandish Jobs First, Do them Well (And Make them Work for You!)

We have all learned that the best way to take a timed test, whether it be in school or to obtain a license or certificate of some kind, is to breeze through it as quickly as we can, answering all the easy questions or solving all the simple problems first. Then we can tackle the next toughest, then the next, and so on. That way we don't get bogged down on the first difficult problem or question that we come to and get fewer answers than we could. Usually we aren't expected to answer them all, anyway, so why not leave the toughest ones unanswered?

Just the opposite is true with outlandish jobs. We know they have to be done, so why not jump right in and get them done first? It gives us a chance right up front to see what is in it for us, as well as the opportunity to improve on it for the next time.

Let me say, right here, though, that if your boss tends to follow up on each outlandish job that you complete with another of a similar nature, just because he knows you will do it, when you look around to see what is in it for you, you might decide that the most you can get out of it should be yourself. Then do it! Go somewhere else to work. An opportunist is one thing—a sucker is something else!

But most of the time there will be something in it for you, either now or in the future. Your boss will be impressed enough to make things better for you, and sometimes, without suspecting it, help you turn it into a racket. And that is the whole point in this book!

Don't try to convince anyone that a outlandish job does not need to be done. Usually this has already been decided.

Don't refuse to do it, unless you have subscribed positively to the First Law of Wing Walking, which says, "Don't Let Go of What You've Got Until You Grab on to Something Else!"

Don't try to pass it off on to someone else. They might be a bigger racketeer than you, and you can only lose.

Don't procrastinate on starting it. It will catch up to you sooner or later.

Don't drag it out once you do start it. Just get it done, and look for other opportunities.

And don't try to hide, hoping it will go away. You might be asked to before it does.

ABOVE ALL, FIND WAYS TO TURN THE OUTLANDISH JOBS INTO RACKETS. IT'S EASIER THAN YOU THINK!

PART TWO

OUTDOOR COMRADES—Me And Jake

These are hunting and fishing stories that I shouldn't tell anybody, because they are all true!

There's a song that goes:

"I won't go huntin' with you, Jake, but I'll go chasin' women."

Well, me and Jake are both too old and fat to go chasing women—besides we wouldn't know what to do with one if we caught it, probably wouldn't even know how to clean it—but we have spent over two-thirds of our lives hunting and fishing together. And we haven't shot each other yet, although we both admit we have thought about it from time to time.

Jake "Moose" Vavra is a six-foot-five, 265 pound Engineer, Farmer, Business Man and Publisher. (He used to just weigh 250 pounds, until I found out his scale only went that far!) And what hasn't happened to us in many years of hunting and fishing together just isn't worth mentioning.

Hunters and fishermen don't go hunting or fishing just to bring something home, anymore than a sports fan goes to a football or baseball game just to see his team win. With the latter it is all the excitement of being there. It is the color, the noise, the bands, the pretty girls, the hot dogs and beer, the thermos of coffee, the pre-game festivities and, usually, the big party afterwards. And of course, there is the companionship.

But the fan doesn't have to justify being there.

The hunter and fisherman does, though. He feels guilty if he doesn't bring something home—and the bigger it is or the more quantity it is, the better he can justify his going in the first place.

But that's not why he goes. He, too, goes for the color, the excitement, the companionship and the thermos of coffee. (Although there are damn few pretty girls!) His problem is that he can't just go and enjoy the fun— he thinks he has to come back and show what he got, or tell about what he almost got. Even the stuff the writers write has to contain the ultimate catch or kill of the object.

The fact is that the color of the mountain hardwoods in fall, or bright sun on blue water, really serve as food for the soul, and the idiotic things that happen to him and his friends keep the hunter or fisherman in a constant enjoyable frame of mind, with an ever-youthful attitude.

In a brief anecdote form, I have herein set down some of the most ridiculous happenings that have come my way so that you can see why hunting and fishing isn't all that serious a business. And I haven't even changed any names to protect the innocent!

THE BURYING AGREEMENT

Me and Jake long ago adopted the "golf adage" which says, "Anyone who mentions his job or business on the golf course has to buy a round of drinks when we get back to the clubhouse."

We had also adapted this slogan to other sports, including hunting and fishing. Who wants to be with someone who either gripes continuously about his job or tells all the juicy gossip at the plant or office—or perhaps is trying to sell you something—when you are out enjoying nature?

Then, as time went by, we invented another rule: "Whoever dies on a trout stream or in a duck blind or corn field will be buried where he falls."

The survivor is not going to suffer a heart attack or double hernia dragging the other big carcass out!

Then when I fell in a hole full of water on a duck hunting trip I had to hurry up and tell him he could not leave me there, because the agreement did not include burial at sea!

Later on a brilliant fall day, with the leaf color at its best in Fayette County, we were descending the bluffs to Bear Creek when the Moose stumbled and fell.

I turned to inquire if he was alright and he said, "I wouldn't tell you if I wasn't, because I'm sure you'd implement the burying agreement even if I was just crippled!"

He's right, I would!

DUCK HUNTING COWBOYS

Me and Jake turned out to be duck hunting cowboys. We drove into the farmyard on a cool spring day to be greeted with a scene normally reserved for a sale—cars, trucks and people all over the place. I inquired as to where the owner could be located, and someone pointed out a big burly man in coveralls.

This had all started when we decided that the river bottoms between Anamosa and Olin might be a good place to hunt ducks. We had discovered Muskrat Slough, a large shallow lake about a mile in diameter that made up a public shooting ground. (They even blew a bugle to signal shooting time!)

All the idiots and skybusters were there, so we didn't like to hunt there. But, since the Slough was only a few miles from the Wapsipinicon River, it stood to reason that when the "army" opened up on Muskrat, that the ducks would head for the river.

So, in taking a canoe down that twenty-mile stretch of river, on one of the trips we shared with our wives in summer, we found the ideal spot for a duck blind—an island in a place where the river was wide, and so was the surrounding open country. There were even a few potholes back in what timber there was.

Apparently the land on both sides of the river belonged to the same owner, so we set about finding him. Hence the Saturday morning trip to the farm about four miles away, to meet the owner.

Approaching him, and introducing me and Jake to him, I asked him for permission to hunt ducks on his stretch of the river.

Instead of answering that question, he said, "Can you boys handle a horse?"

We told him yes, we had both grown up with horses.

"What about cattle?"

We told him we had also grown up with cattle.

He said, "Good, we're about to drive over two-hundred head over to that place you are talking about, and we need all the help we can find to get them over there."

He told us to get ourselves some saddles out of the shed, and catch a couple of horses out in the barn lot. We found two old beat-up saddles, and threw them on a couple of harmless looking old stump suckers, still rough with their winter hair, adjusted the stirrups to our long legs, and climbed on board.

There were about a dozen of us, and some had to continually ride ahead to block off roads and lanes as we drove the herd along the back country gravel roads to the river. It was kind of fun playing cowboy, and it took us all morning to move the cattle the four miles.

When we had finished putting them through the gate into the river pasture, several women drove up in pickups and set out hot coffee, beer, pop and sandwiches—a welcome sight indeed!

We then rode our horses back to the farmhouse, unsaddled them, rubbed them down with a burlap sack, cleaned and oiled the saddles (something that hadn't been done in years, if ever) and again approached the boss farmer.

I said, "Well, what about it, can we hunt over there?"

He said, "I can't give you permission to hunt over there, because if I do, I'll have to let everybody hunt."

"We only hunt ducks," I told him, "and we are very careful of livestock and property."

"I'm sorry," he replied, "but I cannot give anyone permission to hunt in there!"

But he had a grin on his face and a gleam in his eye!

Taking the cue, I asked, "Will you run us out if you catch us in there?"

Again, "I said I can't give you permission."

This time without laughing.

Me and Jake built a blind on that island and hunted there off and on for seventeen years, and, since we missed his spring and fall cattle drives, never saw him again.

But you bet he knew when we were in there!

SKY SHOOTERS

I am sure you have seen and heard of many lucky, or just plain good, shots. There are several that I remember well.

One day we were standing there back to back in that island blind when suddenly Jake's gun went off in my ear. I wheeled around to see a lone mallard drake dropping from the sky.

I said, "Why didn't you say something?"

To which he replied, "There was only one!"

This was carried even further one year when Ray and Bob were hunting the river bottom ponds with us. (I'll tell you about Ray later!) A pair of woodies came whistling in on our end of the pond while I was pouring a cup of coffee.

Jake fired one shot and, since the ducks were side by side, both fell. Frankly, in all my years of hunting, that is the only double I have ever seen taken.

Bob and Ray yelled their congratulations from the other blind and I told them I didn't shoot because there were only two ducks, and since they came in on the Moose's end of the blind, and we always get doubles, I let him have them.

And those two nuts believed me!

Later that same day a lone Canadian honker came over, and since Ray didn't know what it was, he pointed up and shouted, Yo!"

The Moose said, "Yo, hell!" and bagged the goose.

Then "Yo" became a standard call with us.

The next morning two birds of undetermined species zipped in over Jake and me, so to have some fun, we shouted "Yo," and, with two shots from the other blind, two poor old pigeons fell dead on the water in front of us!

"What kind of ducks are those?" Ray asked.

We couldn't answer for laughing!

Once, on Lake Odessa, we were surrounded by sky shooters. A flock headed our way was flying high over the next blind boat when a single shot rang out.

"You can't hit anything that high, you stupid son of a ———" shouted Jake. And then, "Nice shooting, fella!" as one duck came tumbling down.

CRAZY DUCK HUNTERS

You don't have to be crazy to hunt ducks, but it helps!

The first time I ever hunted ducks in the Lake Odessa region was late in the season, after the flight was really on. Me and Jake had planned to hunt our usual spot on the Wapsipinicon that weekend, but decided on Odessa instead. The idea was to go down the river in our boat and go in over the dike to the marshland after shooting time. No one was allowed in the hunting area before that.

So we put the boat in at Grandview at about one o'clock in the morning, and since it didn't take as long to get to the spot we had all staked out, we wound up with a long wait on a sandbar on the river side of the dike.

Moose said, "Let's build a fire and take a nap."

So, there we were, two idiot duck hunters trying to keep warm around an open fire on an icy twenty-degree winter night. I dozed off once, and while I was asleep he had worked his way around between me and the fire. I woke up with my legs so cold I could actually hit myself on the thigh and couldn't feel a thing!

Hours later, in a blind on a little pond, we really lambasted the ducks. Then, with me in the blind, and the Moose out in the brush hunting downed ducks, the conservation officer came up. After checking me, he asked if the guy out in the brush was with me. He also asked if we were the ones who had spent the night on the sandbar. When I answered yes to both questions, he just walked away. But not before giving me one of those looks that said, "Anybody as crazy as you guys has got to be legal. I won't even check that guy out in the brush!"

NEW SHOTGUN

The duck season had just opened in mid-October when me and Jake and our basketball coaching friend were entering a floating duck blind from a john boat. We didn't like taking visitors with us on hunting trips, but this guy had prevailed—wanting to learn the ropes. Instead of handing his new Browning automatic to one of us, Coach chose to crawl into the blind, gun in hand. When the boat moved a few inches away, as boats tend to do, he sought to balance himself by grabbing onto the blind. Down went the Browning into the Mississloppy!

I was hunting with an old Remington pump, and Jake with his father's ancient double—not much money between us for hunting equipment, so we envied Coach his new automatic.

After the early morning shooting died down, we began to feel sorry for Coach, who had sat there not participating. I told him we could go back home and get a grappling hook and try to retrieve his gun, but he said no, that he was all done with this sport forever—didn't ever want to see that Browning, or any other shotgun, again!

He asked if I would crank up the boat and take him over to the home of a friend on shore where he could call his wife to come and get him— he didn't want to ruin our hunt. After taking him all the way home, because there was no one at the friend's house, I rejoined Jake in the blind, and we finished out the day.

Several days later Old Moose and I were back in the same blind and he pulled a new Browning out of his gun case.

When I congratulated him on his acquisition, he just said, "Well, the price was right—too good to pass up."

"Yeah," I said, "just fifteen feet of cold water and some clean-up effort. Right?"

Old Jake just grinned!

CONSERVATION OFFICER

I know I said everything happens to me and Jake, but this isn't necessarily always true—sometimes it just happens to one of us. So I might as well tell you what happened to me one opening day of duck season, a Saturday when I had an appointment at the office.

I took my favorite Black Labrador, Dixie, and went to the river bottoms real early with the idea of getting some shooting from the railroad tracks. Legal shooting time was a few minutes after six.

At about five-forty another hunter came along and sat down by me, petting Dixie and engaging me in pleasant conversation. At five-forty-five a flock of ducks flew over us.

I said, "It's tempting, but it's too early."

Other hunters in a blind further down the slough really cut loose on the flock.

This happened several times, and each time I remarked that the game warden must be around here somewhere, and he should get after those guys.

Eventually shooting time came, and my newfound friend and I got some ducks, which Dixie retrieved.

Then my friend said, "Can I see your license and duck stamp, please?" And he flashed a badge!

That son-of-a-gun went on down below, and he was still writing tickets when I left for my appointment, a half hour later!

FIRST DOG

Old Jake had just gotten a new dog. She was a bit small for a Black Labrador Retriever, but at nine months of age she was partially trained by her former owner, a service station operator who decided to go back to college. At least the price was right—he gave her to Moose free.

Duck season, back then, used to open on Wednesday in Iowa (so all the doctors and lawyers could get first crack at them, I guess), but we used to take off work and go anyway. (I remember telling the boss that I would work sixteen hours a day for him all year, but opening day of duck season I would take off, even if he fired me. He never did.)

So, we took the dog, Ebby was her name, and headed for the Iowa River bottoms between Tama and Chelsea, as we still do on opening day. We were sitting back in the timber on a backwater when a whole flock of "malyards", as an old Mississippi river island buddy of ours from "Quinsey" calls them, came wheeling in over the trees. A beautiful sight, all brown and blue and white and green against the yellow leaves of the river bottom maples! After the initial opening day fever left us, there were four dead mallards on the water. Ebby, good dog, went off the bank in a streak of black, and all ducks were retrieved. It looked like a good day.

But later, as the shooting slowed, we hiked back to the car, about a mile, and started driving down the dirt road for another pond. About a half mile down the road we met Moose's brother-in-law, Bill, who had come to join us. Bill suggested another area back the other way, so we turned around and went back.

There, sitting along the roadside, where our car had been parked, was old Ebby. Moose had completely forgotten that he had a dog!

We hunted with that old dog for nine years, and she never forgot that day. Every time a car door was opened, Ebby would knock us down being the first one in!

THE DOG, THE COW, THE HAT

Another day in the life of Jake's dog was the time the cow ate his hat. It was late in the season of the first year he had Ebby, his first Black Lab. We were still hunting, although most of the ponds were frozen and the river had ice floes in it.

There was a timber pond across the river on the cattleman's place, which was really good for late season mallards if you took the time to break some of the ice on it. Since it was only about knee deep, this was easy enough to do. The problem was that it was on the wrong side of the Wapsipinicon River, and the river had to be waded to get to it. Fortunately there was a cattle crossing not too far away where the river could be waded with hip boots.

We came to the river and the Moose said, "Here, carry my gun."

I said, "What for?"

"I'm going to carry Ebby. I don't want her out in all that ice."

"You're kidding!"

So I carried the gun and he carried the dog.

When we got to the pond and started breaking the ice, here come old Ebby, jumping around and helping us!

Later, back at the river crossing on the way home, I didn't say anything—just reached for Moose's gun.

"Go to hell!" was all I could get out of him.

Oh yes, about the cow eating his hat. As we had approached the pond earlier, there was a flock of mallards working, so we crawled into a thicket for cover. In the act of getting in the bushes, Moose knocked his hat off, and didn't get back for it until the ducks were gone.

So was the hat. We couldn't find it anywhere. But there was an old red cow standing by the thicket placidly chewing her cud.

Even though no one believes it, especially me, the old Moose swears the cow was chewing on his hat!

RETRIEVERS

And now, Jake the retriever versus Ebby the retriever.

I'll never forget one day at Lake Odessa. We had built the ultimate in duck blind boats. It had everything but hot and cold running water—and on this particular day it had cold running water. There had been a storm the night before and it was full. Moose and I bailed it out in the dark with a garbage can and we shoved off.

Moose expertly guided the big boat (it was eight feet wide and eighteen feet long) through the channels and cutoffs toward the open water and found a nice spot to drop anchor.

The shooting was good, and soon we had dead ducks on the water. Jake, who wore chest waders, bailed out of the boat after the first volley, racing "Ebby" for the ducks.

Exasperated, he turned around and shouted, "I forgot about that damned dog!"

I said, "Come on back, Jake, she'll get the ducks!"

But next time we shot ducks, over the side he went again!

On the third time around, I swear to you, Ebby looked around at Jake to see what he was going to do!

DUCK HUNTERS' BREAKFAST

The Moose grew up around the Tama Indian settlement, and started hunting and fishing as soon as he was old enough to walk. He calls himself "The Old Indian Guide," and it used to upset him when I would tell people that he was half Indian.

Especially when I would say, "That's the front half. It isn't something that he inherited—it's just something that rubbed off."

Two brothers, Walt and Bill, are married to Jake's two sisters—and how those guys love the outdoors!

One of the first times they hunted ducks with us, or us with them, we were invited up to the home of one of them, I don't remember which one, for a late breakfast. We were tired, hungry and dirty from hunting—and sitting by each plate was a glass of brew that looked just like we did. I took a premature sip of mine very gingerly—and oh, brother, home-brew for breakfast!

Amid the smiles of the others, our hostess said, "You don't have to drink that stuff. How about some orange juice?"

Having learned a long time ago that making an ass of yourself is no way to prove your manhood, I said, quietly, "Anything at all, Ma'am, even water."

Soon the Moose and I started on our fifty mile journey home in his Buick Roadmaster. About five miles down the road he suddenly shuddered and gave out with an "Aaarrrgh!"

I said, "Want me to drive?"

"No, I feel alright. It's just the taste backing up on me."

After another five miles or so, he turned a very green face toward me and said, "Still want to drive?"

COLD AND WET

It's the natural state of the duck hunter, right?

Me and Jake hit Muskrat Slough one cold November day when the Northern Flight was on, and the ducks were really moving. There were times when just about all you had to do was stick your gun barrel up in the air and pull the trigger to get a duck.

There was only one other pair of hunters on the slough that day, and he and I had put up a temporary blind out in the water a ways, where it was about a foot deep. We were both wearing hip boots, and we had dragged a good sized log out in the water to sit on.

After the early morning shooting had died down, we were sitting back relaxed, enjoying our pipes and a couple of cups of coffee.

The Moose said, "You know, I never get cold around the butt, normally, but it's so cold today that even that is chilled."

"By George," I said, "mine too. It's as cold as a well digger's in January."

With that we both stood up. Our log seat had slowly and imperceptibly sunk into the mud so that we had both been sitting in about three inches of water! But the weather had been so cold that we had not noticed.

All we needed was a hungry gut, right?

COLD AND WET, AGAIN!

The island in the Wapsipinicon had been a favorite duck hunting spot of ours for years. Most of the time you could walk up to the back side of it in low rubber boots, the water was so shallow, while on the river side it was over your head. There were real neat places for decoys above and below the blind, and the island was situated in a bend in the river so that everything that flew that way passed right over it.

One day we went over there and the river was up, so that there was a lot of water behind the island. I had torn my hip boots and had left them home, expecting to walk out to the blind easily.

Jake said, "Come on, I'll carry you."

I said, "You're kidding."

"No, you carry both guns, and I'll just wade out to the island with you over my shoulder."

So he did—we both only weighed about two-hundred pounds back then.

When we came to the island, he proceeded to deposit me on a steep edge, and my feet proceeded to slip out from under me, and I proceeded to slide down the mud bank of the island to end up sitting in about eighteen inches of cold water!

My turn came about three years later, same place, same way—but I swear to you it was an accident!

Moose had lost a hip boot, and since he had acquired another retriever, just didn't bother to buy a new pair.

Again, the river came up. This time I volunteered to carry him. As we approached the island my feet got stuck in the mud and I couldn't move. As I thrashed around trying to get loose, his dog came over to see what we were doing. Just as I extracted one boot from the mud, she ran under it and in trying to regain my balance, I dropped Moose.

As I said, it was strictly accidental—but you can't get him to believe that!

AND AGAIN!

Me and Jake were hunting the river bottoms between Tama and Chelsea on cold November day when we both took a dip. First it was me. We were on our way out to go uptown and eat lunch when it happened. The bottoms were flooded from some late fall rains, so we had to wade in and out, for what seemed like miles. I simply stepped in a hole and went in over my boots.

In trying to extract one foot from the mud, I lost my balance and went in even further—clear to my waist!

Moose laughed, threatened to bury me there, then thought better of it and helped me out of the hole. Back in town I changed clothes. I had learned a long time ago to carry extras when hunting or fishing. But I had no other waders, just a pair of knee boots—and it would be a long time before my hip boots would be dry enough to put back on. And I did want to get in some evening shooting.

While having lunch with Jake's dad, the old man suggested we take his little john boat back with us. We could float down the river and get some shooting.

Jake said he had a better idea. Since he still had dry boots, he would walk through the marsh and pull the boat with me in it, until we reached one of our best spots.

This worked just fine, until we started home in the dark. Moose was tired and hungry, so he decided to take a shortcut across the marsh, instead of going back the way we had come.

I was sitting in the boat enjoying the ride, as he pulled me through the shallow water, when suddenly he disappeared from my line of sight. I jumped up on the front seat of the boat, to find him lying on his back in the cold water! The boat had caught on a grassy hummock and stopped its forward motion, jerking him backwards by the rope, which he had over his shoulder.

"Are we still burying at sea?" I inquired.

"Shut up and help me out," he growled. "I should have known better. Everything that happens to you eventually happens to me."

DECOY RETRIEVERS

At one time me and Jake had identical black Labrador retriever pups, seven months old, from the same litter. Oh, his was bigger than mine, but they still had the same lines and seemed to have the same intelligence. Both were females.

Since I lived near a lake, I had worked with mine all summer around the water. He had no such convenience. So, when we took them to the river bottoms on opening day of duck season, his was still a little inexperienced in water, although both were retrieving the scented dummies well.

We had two blinds on a large pond, and our intent was to put out decoys in front of each blind. Moose stopped off at the first blind with his dog, Belle, and a sack of decoys, while I continued on to the second with my dog, Dixie.

Of the first eight decoys I threw out, my dog brought back five—before she really believed I was mad! You should have heard the razzing from the other blind about my well-trained decoy retriever. Until I walked over and found that Moose had tied Belle to a tree!

Later on, when we had dead ducks on the water, I threw a mud clod out by one and yelled "Fetch!"

Both dogs swam out to the duck, sniffed it a couple of times, then each brought in a decoy!

Then, we finally had a duck fall on land. Moose threw it out a ways on the ground, and Belle would retrieve it every time. Dixie just sniffed it and walked away.

Then I threw it in the water and Dixie got the idea—and brought it in every time. But Belle wouldn't enter the water.

So, we decided we had one good dog between us!

By the end of the day, though, they were both working well.

HUNTING WITH RAY

We had a hell of a time with Ray. He was from Long Guyland (as he pronounced it), and liked a shot of Vodker, (as he called it), once in awhile—but he had never hunted ducks.

I brought him into Iowa the day before opening day, where we met the Moose.

Now Ray was fat—not exactly obese, mind you—but good solid fat, probably about three hundred pounds.

He had no hunting gear, so before accepting our invitation to go, he went out and bought a new automatic shotgun, insulated hip boots, hunting pants, coat and hat. I think he invested more that one day in gear than the two of us had in our entire lives! He was ready, and it was really too bad what happened to him.

The early morning shooting was really good in Otter Creek Marsh in those days, before they civilized it, and we wouldn't miss it on opening day for the world. But Ray did.

We got a little worried when Ray climbed over the first farm gate. Now Jake and I are big, but we don't have trouble with farm gates. Or slogging through a foot of water and mud. But Ray did.

About a hundred yards into the marsh I heard a shout. Turning around, I could see only Ray's head and shoulders. He had stepped into a hole up to his armpits—all cold water!

And he had no other dry hunting clothes to put on.

I'll say one thing for him though. He insisted on sitting in the car alone while we got in on the early shooting. I offered to take him back to town but he wouldn't hear of it—wouldn't ruin it for us.

He got the last laugh that day, though. Two of them in fact!

After we got him uptown and dried off, and ran his clothes through a laundromat, we were back in the marsh in a makeshift temporary blind.

A Canadian honker came along straight overhead and Jake said, "Shoot him, Ray. You need a little target practice."

I still don't know if he deliberately planned it that way, but when that goose fell, it came directly at the Moose! As he dodged around trying to avoid it, his feet stuck in the mud and he lost his balance. As he went down he grabbed at something to sustain himself, and that something was me! As we both lay there, spread-eagled in about a foot of mud and water, Ray couldn't keep his laughter in—but then neither could we!

SWEETEST DAY AND RAY

The second year Ray went with us his wife was madder than hell! It never occurred to her that his duck hunting was not a one shot deal. Besides that, the day after he left was his son's birthday.

But, after all, he had invested in all that equipment the year before— and, since he had gotten ducks, he was now an enthusiastic duck hunter, and would be for the rest of his life.

As we drove out of town the day before the season opened, we passed a florist.

I said, "If my wife wasn't speaking to me, I'd go in there and send her a dozen roses."

Ray said, "I will! Turn around."

Once inside, we saw a sign which said, "Tomorrow is Sweetest Day. Say it with flowers."

Now, we had never heard of Sweetest Day, but it comes the third Saturday in October. It could be just another trick to sell gifts and flowers, but then again it might have been invented just to ease the consciences of duck hunters.

Anyway, it sounded like a good idea—so I, too, sent home a dozen roses, with an appropriate card.

The Moose, saving his money for more shells, I guess, decided that half a dozen was enough. But we found out later that the florist goofed up and put in seven by mistake.

Upon our arrival back home after a successful weekend of hunting, we dropped the Moose off first. As he was unloading his gear, his wife came out and expressed her appreciation for the "Sweetest Day" flowers.

"But why seven?" she asked.

"Er, ah," stammered Jake, "one for each day of the week!"

He was always fast on his feet for a big man!

HUNTING WITH LARRY

Me and Jake have hunted together, usually just as a two-person team, most of our hunting lives, but we seem to draw all kinds of characters along with us sometimes. One of these was Larry. Now, you know you have to either be half nuts or have a ridiculous sense of humor to hunt ducks in the first place. And it helps if you have both attributes. Larry was just such a person.

When some guy invites himself along, it seems like the hunting is excellent his first time out, and he becomes a duck hunting nut. That's the way it was with me.

But, if you spend a lot of time trying to convince some friend of yours to try this great sport of shooting ducks, you can almost bet that neither of you will see a feather—let alone fire a shot.

On Larry's first time out it was the former.

He was a cowboy, steer wrestler, rodeo performer and judge—and an auctioneer. Showed up in a cowboy hat and carrying the world's rustiest shotgun. (Said he stored it under the couch in the basement.)

He really got the ducks on his first time out. So, his second time out was when his sense of humor had to be tested. That's an unwritten rule among duck hunters.

Like most second timers, he was all eyes and ears in the blind—ready for any sight of a duck. After the early morning shooting had died down, Larry sneaked back in the trees behind the blind about twenty feet to pour himself a cup of coffee. (I don't know why he left his thermos so far away.)

On a signal from me, Jake and I grabbed our guns and made like a flock of "malyards" was directly out in front.

Larry poured his coffee all over the ground!

(We have done that to guys who were eating a sandwich, lighting a pipe, taking a crap, picking up decoys or retrieving ducks. Of course it's been done to me, too.)

Then while we laughed (and he cussed us), a lone mallard dropped right over the blind. Larry was the only one with a gun in his hand so he threw it to his shoulder, and it clicked—no shell in the chamber!

SAVE YOUR SHELLS

Sometimes you don't even need to shoot, like the one time Jake got a goose at our Mississippi island blind. It was apparently shot on the Illinois side of the river about two miles away, and chose to fly over and drop among our decoys.

"It was a nice Canadian honker," said Moose, "but I wonder who shot it."

He kept it anyway.

The same thing happened to him again pheasant hunting, only it was a double. Four of us had just entered a field of standing corn to walk the rows, when a lone cock came down the row right at Jake. Just as he raised his gun it fell dead in front of him. When he went to pick it up there was another nearby—both still warm!

Back to the Big River blind again. We were standing watching thousands of ducks fly over and by—all out of range.

"Here ducky, ducky, ducky, ducky," I called. "C'mon down here and I'll shoot you in the fanny!"

"Still shootin' behind them, huh, Bear?" said Jake, in his most pitying voice.

THE BARE NAKED DUCK

Everything kept happening to me and Jake!

I had seen an ad in the newspaper about an old upright piano for sale, so we drove down to the farmhouse on the Iowa River to take a look at it. I thought it might go in my basement rec room for my kids to beat on. We figured that if I bought it, we could round up enough guys to move it later.

The old farmer, who had recently become a widower, was more than generous with a new bottle of Jack Daniels we had spotted on a kitchen shelf. By the time me and Jake were ready to leave, we could have rolled that piano end for end—so the three of us loaded it into my pickup and away we went.

As we drove out of the farmyard, I said, "Did you see that pond in back of his place?"

Looked more like a small lake, to me," said Jake. "You thinking what I'm thinking?"

"Yep," I said. "Let's go back before opening day."

So, with a bottle of Old Jack as a bribe, we got exclusive permission to hunt ducks on the best pond anywhere near that stretch of the Iowa River.

Opening day was excellent, as we lambasted the ducks from our hastily constructed blind, and so were many days following. But as the season wore on, and the shooting tapered off, we started jump shooting other small ponds and potholes on the place.

One day, while Moose was out checking potholes with the dog, a couple of mallards came over and I shot one, retrieved it and hung it up in the blind. Sitting there alone, smoking my pipe and sipping coffee out of my thermos, I absent mindedly started to dry pick the feathers out of the duck. I had most of the feathers removed from its body—you don't pick the head and wings, anyway—when another big flock flew in over the decoys. I jumped up and blasted away.

When the excitement was over, my picked duck was gone! I had thought it was dead, but apparently it was just stunned. I spotted it running down the sandbar along the edge of the pond and took off after it. You can imagine Jake's consternation, surprise and reaction when he came back to the bank overlooking the blind at this moment.

There I was, running down the sandbar, chasing a bare-naked duck, which couldn't fly (no tail feathers), and which would jump in the pond then jump out, shivering, and run some more.

"I would have given anything for a movie camera," the Moose said later.

THE TRUCK, THE POND

With apologies to a favorite country singer, I love pickup trucks! I don't know anybody that doesn't. I don't even want to know anybody that doesn't!

I remember reading once that the raw material in a car is worth only about twenty-one dollars before it is processed—untouched by human hands or machines. Some of my pickups were only worth that much, and I was driving them around!

As a kid, you always knew that if you stuck your thumb out in front of a pickup, you would get a ride. I have owned small ones, large ones, supercabs (my wife doesn't like those, too long), automatics, stick shifts, sun roofs, camper tops, flat beds, racks, four-wheel drives.

I have hauled grain, seed, lime, gravel, feed, fertilizer, furniture, stone, cross ties, fence posts, firewood, sawdust, manure, hay, corn, calves, colts, peaches, watermelons. I have towed stock trailers, camping trailers, boats and farm wagons.

I couldn't imagine myself without one.

I have buried them in mud, sawdust, manure, over a bluff. No one ever got hurt.

And then, me and Jake put one in a pond—it wasn't planned, it just happened.

Like I said earlier, what hasn't happened to us isn't worth mentioning, but maybe some of the things that did happen shouldn't be mentioned either!

Take that Thursday, for instance. We had downed three pheasants in a cornfield between New Sharon and Tama, when we decided to drive out along the Iowa River marshland between Tama and Chelsea to check out our old duck hunting spots. (All the ponds were frozen.) Jake was driving my pickup—claimed he knew the territory better than I did, having been born and raised there. All day long he had kept saying he wanted to buy the truck.

"I'll write you a check right now," he kept saying.

(The truck was worth at least twice what he offered, at that time, being new, and with a topper on it and all.)

We had just passed an intersection on a mud road, where I had tried to convince him to turn around—but he refused, saying he knew that country well. Soon we came to a familiar spot where the road was touched on either side by a frozen pond. They were small lakes, really. Next thing I knew we were sliding sideways—then right onto the ice on the left side of the road.

As the truck broke through the ice and slowly settled into about two feet of cold water, Jake looked over at me and said, "You want to drive!"

I said, "Write me that check first!"

WINTERTIME ON THE MISSISSIPPI

Recently, during an early winter cold snap followed by a blizzard here in the mid-west, I received a letter from a southern California friend. Included in the envelope was a full color picture of said friend standing in his green grassy yard, with blooming flowers in the background. A caption on the back of the photo said, "Sorry to hear about your weather."

I immediately had a color photo taken of myself sitting in front of one of the three fireplaces at the Bentonsport house, my shoes off, a drink in one hand and the other resting on the head of my dog, Dixie—a picture of pure contentment! The caption on this picture, which went with a Christmas card to the Californian, said, "Is that a lawnmower in the corner of the photo you sent me?"

Winter does come early sometimes—and the snowmobilers love it! Look at all the tracks in the roadside ditches, and the gatherings on Sunday afternoons. It's really a great sport for the snow addicts. Don't you feel sorry for those poor southern Californians?

Of course the boating enthusiasts and duck hunters hate to give up early, as they had to this year. In fact, Jake and I had planned a final hunting trip to Lake Odessa, near Wapello, for November 30, but everything was frozen up there—so we didn't go.

Much different from another year, when we went all the way to Keokuk on the river on December 16.

We kept a real nice floating blind straight out from the mouth of Devil's Creek near Ft. Madison. One Sunday towards the end of duck hunting season we went down there to find it gone—floated away. We searched for it but couldn't find it.

A couple of weeks later we were discussing where that blind could be when the Moose said, "Let's take my big boat and go look for it—I would like to take the boat out one more time, anyway."

So, on the blue cold day of December 16 we launched at Don's Riverview Marina and shoved off. We went all the way down the Iowa shore, searching with binoculars, to the dam at Keokuk, then we crossed over to the Illinois side and searched it on the way back. Still no blind.

How could a floating duck blind, about ten by twenty feet, of welded construction, just disappear?

Several hours later, cold and tired, we went into Don's to get warm. (Jake hardly ever puts the top up on his boat—and today was no exception.)

Don said, "What in the world are you guys doing on the river on a day like this?"

"Hunting a duck blind," we chattered.

"I wondered whose that was," said Don. "It floated upstream to the lower edge of Riverview Park, and I tied it up. You can see it from here."

That darn blind had really been blown upstream, and we had passed within one-hundred yards of it on the way down to Devil's Creek to start looking!

BOAT RETRIEVER

Jake had no business going up to our river blind by himself that Sunday morning, but he did anyway. We had planned to meet later that afternoon to put out the rest of our decoys—but, since he wasn't tied up, as I was, he went on up without me.

When I arrived, he said, "I don't have to tell you what happened to me this morning, but I will."

And here it is, in his own words.

"I came up too early because I got fouled up on the daylight savings time. But since I thought some other hunters might be up at the correct time, I decided to put in at my cousin's cabin and wait. It was still dark, so I had driven the boat up the river under a spotlight. I noticed that part of the dock was missing, so I ran the boat up on shore.

"Instead of running her further up on the bank, I had eased her up into the mud, grabbed a line and jumped out over the bow.

"As I jumped, I kicked the boat backwards away from shore and the wet line slipped out of my hand. So there I was, watching that big john boat drifting downstream about fifty feet out from shore. My gun and all my equipment were still in it—and so was my Labrador Retriever, sitting on the bow barking her head off.

"All I could think of was the ribbing I had to take that summer I lost my boat by getting it swamped in a storm—so, after about two minutes hesitation, I stripped to my shorts, plunged in the cold water and swam out to the boat.

"After bringing it back to shore, I went in the cabin, built a big wood fire in the stove, dried out my shorts, made a pot of coffee—got dressed and went on hunting. Got two big mallard drakes, too!"

He looked at me in consternation when my only comment was, "At five o'clock in the morning, in the dark, on an isolated chute in the river, why did you keep your shorts on?"

SNOWSTORM ON THE MISSISSIPPI

I had let the Moose talk me into getting an Illinois hunting license that year so we could hunt on the other side of the channel. We had put a blind in the stump field below Oquawka and the hunting had been excellent, although it was really tough picking your way through the stumps in a john boat.

We usually put in on the chute below our island, ran up the three miles to the island, then cut across the channel to the stump field, then went back in it another three miles. Also, to make the trip even more interesting, that was one of the widest channel crossings on the river.

On a warm summer day there is no more beautiful place on the river—lots of blue water and various shades of green foliage. It is also nice in the fall, with multi-hued yellows, reds and browns all up and down the water's edge, and in and out among the islands. But on a cold, gray winter's morning it can be very unappealing, and under certain circumstances, downright frightening.

All that fall we had made that run up and back two or three times each week, and had good hunting each time. Then, around December first,

NO RUTS FOR ME!

with the season almost over, we ignored the forecast of "a little snow" and went up there again. About mid-morning a few white flakes began to fall, which I pointed out to Jake.

"Must be some ducks overhead," he laughed, "and they are shedding their feathers."

Pretty soon it looked like all the ducks on the Mississloppy were shedding their feathers, and even Jake agreed that we had better make like two old hockey players and get the puck out of there.

Bucking an icy wind, we picked our way through the stump field very slowly, him handling the motor and me in the bow peering downward into the cold gray water and ahead into the impenetrable snow and waving directions back to him. I could hardly see him in the stern of the eighteen foot boat. Both our Black Labs were huddle in the bottom of the boat, keeping each other warm.

When we cleared the stumps I shouted back to the Moose to open her up, because all we needed was a set of barges as we crossed the channel. So, twisting the throttle wide open, he took aim by the seat of his pants and blasted full bore through the snow.

At about what I deemed to be three-fourths of the way between channel markers, my heart almost quit pumping as I heard a tow-boat horn— and close! Looking back, I saw the first barge, and then another, as their long, vertical rusty sides slid past Jake's end of the boat, just a few yards behind him. We were buried in the snowstorm's lack of visibility too much to see the others as we sprinted for the chute.

Later, Jake said he heard the horn but was afraid to look around. If we had been running just a few seconds later, we and our boat—and the dogs—would have been history!

And, you know, the Moose has never even mentioned getting an Illinois license since!

OVER THE DAM

Me and Jake have seen a lot of water go over the dam—and one day we went over it too!

It was a big Fourth of July celebration in Bonaparte—food, carnival rides, contests and a canoe race down from Bentonsport on the Des Moines River, where I owned a home, and our favorite of the old river towns.

We were fishing upstream several miles, in the backwaters, and since the river was extremely high, we decided to run down and check out the festivities. I was driving a little red and white fifteen foot runabout, which would really scoot along the smooth surface of the high water.

When we arrived on the river opposite the town, Jake asked, "Can you run the dam?"

I assured him we could on the south side of the river where the dam had washed out—especially with the water so high. As we went past the dam and slowed down below it, a young couple we knew waved to us, so we went over and invited them to join us for a boatride—which they were all too happy to do. After we made the pass up and down the river several times someone got the idea of putting in at the creek above the dam and going up to town and getting some lunch. This meant going back up through the washed out portion of the dam, then running across the river above it to enter the creek, where we could tie up and go eat.

About half way across the river, the gas tank on which we were running went empty. I looked around to the back seat and told the couple to switch tanks.

"What?" one of them, the man, asked.

I told him to just pull the one gas line loose from the motor and snap the other one on it.

"I don't know what you are talking about," he said, as the fast water took us backwards towards the dam.

"I'll go back and do it," said Moose.

"Better hang on, instead!" I shouted, and soon we were looking up at the dam from down below, in the tailwater. Fortunately, we did not capsize—but it was a lesson in boating. Make sure the occupants of your boat know a little something about what to do in an emergency.

Later, one of my neighbors said he and a friend were standing on the bridge, when the friend said, "Look at those idiots in that red boat going over the dam!"

My neighbor told me he said, "I hate to admit it, but I know those idiots!"

DOC'S BOAT

Me and Jake have long been aware of the humor involved in the medical profession. Maybe it has something to do with the types of personalities that are drawn to that kind of work, or perhaps after seeing people in all kinds of dire physical straits all day you have to develop a sense of humor to keep from going nuts.

And there is no one in the world with a drier sense of humor that Doc. And that brings us around to Doc's boat.

Rosemary and I had bought a large pleasure boat. We had spent quite a bit of time on tri-hulls belonging to friends, so we wouldn't settle for anything less. We hadn't much more than got it home when Doc and his wife came over to see it. Doc went down to Don's marina the next day, the way I heard it, and told Don he wanted one just like it. So Doc bought a nice shiny green two-tone tri-hull with a hundred horse motor.

Paul got to looking at it and so he traded his boat in on one just like it. Sonny traded his boat in on Paul's, then Rick bought Sonny's. If I had known Paul was going to trade, I would have preferred his boat in the first place, but if I hadn't bought mine, Doc might not have—then Paul might—oh, well, you get the picture.

Doc said that when he went down to resister his boat the girl at the courthouse asked him, "Do you have a toilet on your boat?"

Doc says, "I told her we carry a three pound coffee can—and she just went right on typing, didn't even look up!"

Now, Doc is an avid fisherman, and he is always out in those stump fields in the Missisloppy where angels fear to tread—but he does catch a lot of fish. (Of course his first prop only lasted a week!)

The following Sunday Rosemary and I were cruising up the river with Jake and Bettie when we spotted Doc's boat way over in a stump field on the Illinois side. Doc and his wife were both standing up waving their arms.

Jake said, "I'll bet old Doc's busted a prop, or knocked a hole in his boat, and is stranded."

So I gingerly edged our brand new boat and motor through the stump field, where we had been almost afraid to take a small flat bottomed john boat before, and pulled up alongside Doc's boat. Whereupon Doc said, "Hey, your boat is just like ours!"

And that was all he wanted!

FAST WATER AND COTTONMOUTHS

Me and Jake have always liked canoeing—especially when it was connected to fishing. We thought we were pretty good at it, and were never really afraid on the streams or lakes.

Neither of us were afraid of snakes, but we still gave them a wide berth—especially in cottonmouth moccasin country. Somebody once asked me how you can tell a cottonmouth from any other type of moccasin. I told them that the cottonmouths are the ones that run 'towards' you!

We canoe and fish several backwaters in which many logs and stumps are half submerged—and they are usually infested with moccasins, but no cottonmouths. Too far north and too cold for them. But we do fish southern streams where they are prevalent.

Recently we were on the Eleven Point river in Missouri fishing for trout in a big nineteen foot cargo canoe, when we ran some fast water which brought us close to a cliff. Jake had to really lay into his paddle against the rocks to keep us from being bashed against them. This brought my end of the canoe even closer to the cliff. What I saw made me almost turn the craft end for end!

"What's the matter?" shouted Moose, above the roar of the current, and I had to swallow my heart again before I could tell him.

As I had leaned my paddle against the cliff to push the canoe away, I found myself staring into the eyes and open mouth of the biggest cotton-mouth I had ever seen—all coiled up on a ledge, about six inches from my face, and ready to strike!

'COON HUNTERS

Me and Jake had our 'coon hunting careers cut short by a hair-raising experience. Although both of our fathers were 'coon hunters, they had both gotten too old to climb the hills by the time we were big enough to be interested, so they had quit. But Jake's dad still had Old Joe around, and he liked to run—so one brilliant autumn moonlit night we decided to give it a try.

We didn't get any 'coons, but the old dog did tree once.

We could hear him barking down the slope a ways, so we started towards him. Soon we came to what seemed like a small cliff or outcropping of rock below us. After walking each way for a hundred feet or so, we decided that it must run the entire length of the slope. We could see the tops of some saplings five or six feet out from the edge of the cliff, so Moose suggested we jump into them and climb down. So, as he held the light for me, I dove headlong from the rock into a tree, grabbing on to a branch. Then I turned and held the light while he did the same.

Down we climbed—and down, and down. Soon we ran out of limbs, and the trunk was almost too big to reach around.

By the time we reached the ground, we had decided that our grove of "saplings" was a full grown tree reaching to the top of a seventy foot cliff!

Old Joe had lost his treed 'coon by then—so, two shaky amateur 'coon hunters went on home empty handed.

OLD JOE

Jake's dad has a collection of dogs as only he could have. When you drive up to his place you are liable to be greeted by two pekingese/terrier crossbreeds, a white hound with hemorrhoids, a nondescript long-haired Heinz-fifty-seven mixed female, and "Old Joe."

Old Joe is the star of the show. He is a little rickety when he walks, can't hear himself bark, and is a little absent minded, forgetting to come to eat sometimes. But you would too, if you were ninety-eight years old—because at fourteen, Joe is the equivalent of almost a hundred human years.

The old dog is a Blue Tick coonhound, which his owner raised from a pup, and who was his constant companion for many years. He came into this world with several strikes against him, being the only male in a litter of seven. Moose said it was a cold day when he was born, and Joe was so cold and stiff that they didn't think he was going to make it. So they took the pup in the house and gave him a shot of whiskey. That started him on a long and fruitful life.

Jake's dad said that once when he was in the hospital, the old dog missed him so much that he couldn't get along with anybody. Then the summer when he was twelve and the coon dog swimming races were held locally—and someone had the gall to suggest putting a life jacket on him—not only did Old Joe swim the pond three times, but he took second place in the contest!

Joe travels the surrounding country at will, and he knows where he can hop through or crawl under the fences, since he can't jump over them anymore.

But his real crowning glory came at the age of fourteen, when he became a father again—and of six pups, no less! Who knows, maybe Old Joe is just getting his second wind, and will be around for another fourteen years.

TROPHY PHEASANT

I never took my hunting and fishing seriously. It was something to do for fun, and, of course, I do like fish and most game to eat—especially if I cook it outdoors, even at home on the patio. But neither was I ever interested in trophies. But, however, I do have a good friend who has learned to stuff things, and occasionally he has wanted to do one for me at no cost.

After a day of pheasant hunting once, in which he participated, he insisted on mounting a rather large rooster, which I had bagged—so I let him.

Since he did have reasons to visit my office sometimes, I hung the bird on a paneled wall behind my desk. There it was, for all to see, in its ring-necked, wingspread beauty—in full flight, hanging from a wooden ring.

During the night someone took a piece of white paper about three feet square and ran over it with a car, so that a big black tire mark traversed the sheet from side to side. When we all came in the next day the paper was attached to the wall and the pheasant was hung over it. There, in all its glory, was a pheasant hit by a car!

Not knowing whether to laugh or cry, I just left it there—until my friend the taxidermist came in.

Talk about fire in a man's eye! If he could have found the culprit, I'm positive his hide would have decorated that paneled wall! Then he started to see the humor in it.

From then on I noticed the whimsy he was adding to his mountings—and he seemed to be enjoying his hobby more.

PREACHER'S PHEASANT

We were pheasant hunting with two of Moose's neighbors. The father of one of them owned a farm about thirty miles away, and we had been invited up for an exclusive hunt one day.

When we got there, the local preacher was visiting, and the old man suggested that he go with us. So they dug up an old rusty single barrel twelve for him, and away we went.

Now it was cold. We were wading slough grass and icy bogs all afternoon. The preacher was well dressed for it—in a ball cap and canvas shoes! I think his jacket was made of chicken skin, or something just as translucent. He didn't complain, though. He didn't shoot anything either—in fact, he didn't even take his gun off his shoulder—but he didn't complain.

At the end of the afternoon we had eleven pheasants—and Jake and I had seven of them. We had shot three apiece, and we had shared one. Oh, had we ever shared one! (I'll bet that if you laid it on a screen, it would have gone right through!)

Anyway, when we got back to the farmhouse, the old man suggested that since there were five families represented we take two birds apiece—and that he would take one.

As Moose and I were taking the birds out of the trunk of the car, he muttered, "I sure hate to give that preacher any of my birds. That S.O.B. didn't contribute anything to this hunting trip."

"Aw, quit complaining," I said. "Just be glad we didn't tell him about the 'no talking business' rule. The way you have been cussing him, he might say you were bringing up his business, and make you buy drinks. As for the birds, you can't keep them all—and besides, I know one bird we will definitely give him!"

"You mean the one that would go through a sieve?"

"That's the one, pal. Here, you hold this newspaper while I scoop the bird onto it."

So, we went home happy, and the preacher was happy that he had gotten two pheasants. At least until he got home and tried to clean them!

CLEAN BIRD

While we are on the subject of pheasants, you will find this story hard to believe, or maybe not.

A new young couple moved in right across the road from the Moose. City slickers, I guess, if there is any such thing anymore. Anyway, she found out Jake hunted pheasants, and kept telling him how badly she wanted to fix one.

So one Sunday afternoon Jake returned from hunting and presented her with a nice plump bird.

A few days later he asked her how they enjoyed their first pheasant.

"You didn't tell me they stink," said she.

"Stink?" asked Jake.

"Yes, stink," she said. "I tried roasting it in the oven, and when I took it out, it smelled so bad we couldn't eat it. I threw it out with the garbage."

Jake said, "You did get it good and clean, didn't you?"

"Oh, yes, we picked it real clean, just like my mother used to do a chicken."

"What about its insides?" asked the Moose.

"Insides? What insides?"

WHOSE SON ARE YOU?

It was the best hundred and twenty acres of pheasant hunting any-where—slough grass along a stream down the middle, with corn on both sides—and it belonged to Jake's uncle.

That opening day, Moose's cousin was home on leave from the Army and decided to join us.

As we approached the far fence in our first pass across the field—bag-ging a few birds—some hunters came out of the road and started yelling at me, since I was closest to them.

"Get out of here," one screamed, "I don't allow anyone to hunt in here!"

"Just who are you?" I asked.

To which he replied, "This is my property, so get off!"

I called to Jake's cousin, who was farthest away, to come over.

"I just wanted you to meet your new father," I said. And turning to the slob hunter, "His father owns this property, so he must be your son."

"Well, I tried," said the idiot, sheepishly, as he and his buddies headed for their car.

GETTING PERMISSION

Me and Jake had flown over the place, up above walker, several times, and thought it looked like an upland game hunter's paradise. A couple hundred acres at least, and all obviously in a government set-aside program—what some laughing called "Jackie's Acres" during the Kennedy administration, or named them after whoever happened to be the President's wife since then.

We decided to find the owner. Luckily he lived on the place—in a big old two-story run-down farmhouse reminiscent of the "Peter Tumbledown" cartoons we had seen in our newspapers when we were young.

When we drove into his farmyard, he was sitting on the dilapidated steps of the front porch petting a large dog. Several other dogs were lying or standing around the place.

"I think it's your turn," I said to Moose.

We had long ago adopted the policy of taking turns in asking for permission to hunt or fish on private property.

Jake got about twenty feet from my truck and the old man said, "Sic 'em," to the dogs.

The whole mob came tearing at my partner, barking and growling their displeasure at his presence. I pushed the door open on his side and he dove headlong into the seat. I started the motor.

"Wait a minute, boys," called the old man.

Then he chased the dogs away and walked over to the truck.

"I was just having fun," he said. "You boys want to hunt here?"

"Well, yeah," I said. "We had planned to ask for permission, but we don't want to get eat up."

"You got it," he said, "and don't worry about the dogs. They're a bunch of pussy cats. I just use them to scare off people who invade my place without asking. In fact, you two are the first ones this year to ask. Come on in and have a cold drink, and hunt anytime. If you drive a different car sometime, just let me know—so I won't sic the dogs on you again."

We hunted there for years, and became very good friends with the old man—and the dogs!

JAKE'S HOLDING PEN

Me and Jake pretended to be farmers for awhile. I raised horses. But not him—he raised hogs! I used to tell him anything but hogs. Horse manure doesn't smell all that bad—good fertilizer for the garden. Cow manure I can tolerate. But hog manure, with that acidic smell, is repulsive. Of course he just said it smelled like money to him!

Because we hunted so much on other people's land, with permission, of course, we would let anybody hunt on ours—if they asked for permission. If they don't —.

One day I stopped to see him about some business, and he was studying his property some distance away with binoculars.

"What's up?" I asked.

"Some guys are hunting across the road without permission," he answered. "Come on."

I got in his truck with him and he drove to one of his hog holding pens. Taking a shovel out of the truck bed, he proceeded to scoop up a pile of wet, juicy, smelly manure and set the shovel gingerly back in the truck bed.

We drove to the interloper's car, Jake opened the door and tossed his load into the front seat.

Laughing, I asked, "What if the door had been locked?"

"I'd have broken a window."

Some unhappy landowners put sand in the radiator or gas tank, but he's too nice to do permanent damage.

I said, "What are the chances of those guys coming back and doing something destructive?"

"Oh, they'll be back," said Moose. "But after they tell what happened in town, somebody will tell them what the rules are, and they will ask permission next time."

RABBIT CHASERS

In Iowa, during a recent twelve-year period, 1.9 million hunters have killed 21.6 million rabbits, according to the Iowa Conservationist magazine.

Since me and Jake were out on a day on which three cottontails were bagged, we are well on the way to the next twelve years, with only 21, 599, 997 rabbits to go. And I got all three!

But I must admit, though, that I gave Jake his chance. He and I were walking down one side of a brushy draw, when we came to a secondary draw, which ran for about a hundred yards at right angles to the one we were following. I told the Moose that I was going to do him a favor and cut across to the head of the short draw and herd the game down towards him.

It didn't work. I kicked up one measly cottontail and, let me tell you, I shot behind that rabbit three times in order to chase it down to Jake, and he still didn't get it!

CHICAGO RABBIT HUNTERS

Remember what I said about giving permission to hunt on my place to anybody that asked?

The sound of barking dogs drew me away from the warm fire at the Bentonsport place and out into the yard. There in the driveway in the closing dusk sat a nondescript green beat-up old Ford station wagon, with a large wooden box tied on the top rack.

Getting out of the front seat was a skinny little dark skinned man, grinning from ear to ear. He asked if I was the new owner, and upon being told that I was, asked if they could hunt rabbits there. He then told me that there were six of them, from the south side of Chicago, and, with my predecessor's permission, they came there every year for two days of hunting—nothing but rabbits. They stayed at the hotel in Keosauqua.

When I asked about the contents of the box, he said, "Beagles, eight of them."

Early the next morning I heard them banging around up in the hills, while the dogs would occasionally howl as only a Beagle can. When the shooting stopped, and I presumed they had come down to their car to eat their lunches, I rode my horse up there. I was looking at the skinniest bunch of dogs I had ever seen—all their ribs were easily discernible, right through their skin!

I asked them how the hunting was, and they said they had gotten only half as many rabbits that morning as they had the first morning last year.

"And how many is that?" I asked.

"Just thirty-six," I was told.

"You mean you got seventy-two rabbits in just one morning? What do you do with them all?"

"Oh, it's a regular thing every year. We take them home, have a big feast, then share them with our friends and relatives. We only hunt these two days, and with no limit in this state, usually get over two-hundred rabbits."

They came back every year, for many years, and it was always the same—skinny guys, bony Beagles, old Ford wagon, box on top, and dozens of rabbits.

Talk about meat hunters!

BRUTUS AND THE QUAIL

There are quail, rabbits, turkeys and deer on the backside of our Bentonsport place, where the big spring and all the ravines are located—and I think most of them die of old age, since nobody hunts them. Remember, I am basically a duck hunter.

Just when I thought I was all through raising horse because all three kids had grown up and moved away, my oldest daughter sent me four quarter horses down from Wyoming to keep "temporarily." One of them was a big sorrel gelding which no one could do anything with, but I was determined he would earn his keep—so by hook or crook, and with a lucky break or two and some help from Jake, we became friends, and I rode him at will.

Moose would come down and we would trail ride up in the ravine country just for kicks, and the old gelding seemed to enjoy it just as much as we did. He had an Indian name that meant "The Wind," but I called him Brutus.

The turkeys came down and ate horse feed, and the deer were always licking the salt blocks, so the horses got used to them.

Then one sunny Saturday in the fall I was riding Brutus and Jake was riding Buck, a big buckskin more to his size, when we decided to make a pass high up through the hills just to look at the view. As we separated the two horses to ride around a stand of colorful oaks and hickories, I walked Brutus right into the middle of a large covey of quail! They went up on all sides, and he went straight up in the middle. Caught off guard, I kept going. There is no worse feeling than being fifteen feet in the air, all spread-eagled, with no horse under you. Fortunately, the ground was soft and grassy, rather than hard and rocky.

Old Brutus ran off a little way and waited for me, and Jake said the horse was looking back as if to say, "What are you wallering around down there on the ground for?"

FIVE-BELOW-ZERO BUCK

Although basically me and Jake are duck hunters, we will try something else once in a while. Like deer. I have never hunted deer. I don't know why, I just never had any interest. But Jake did, at least once. He even tried bear hunting once, joining an expedition to Canada. I needled him about that—he didn't get a bear, but he got a picture of a guy that got one!

But back to his deer hunt.

It was five below zero that morning, and the Moose was in a tree in the Iowa River bottoms right over an active deer trail in the snow. A few minutes after climbing the tree, he had a nice seven-point buck dead on the ground. After field dressing the deer, he attached it to a harness he had brought along, and started dragging it towards his pickup, about a half-mile away.

Now, the river is so crooked in that area that it is easy for a native to get lost—much less a stranger. And Jake was no stranger. So, Jake dragged his deer. And he dragged it. And he continued to drag it. He had parked his truck right in the edge of the woods, so it should be easy to find. Besides, who needs a compass in Iowa?

Several hours later, he broke out into an open field and looked around for his truck. He spotted it about two miles back! He had been dragging the deer parallel to the edge of the woods, and had passed within a hundred yards of his truck, and kept on going!

JAKE'S TURKEY

Jim, Jake's youngest son, has an excellent place to hunt turkeys down in Van Buren County on a friend's place. He met the guy a long way from home when the guy had car trouble and Jim helped him out—so they became fast friends.

Jim and some others talked the old Moose into going with them one fall. I don't know what it is about your kids, but as soon as they get past twenty they think you are senile, no matter what your age and condition. And that is the approach Jim was taking on Jake that day—they were really worried about something happening to him.

So they took him out in the turkey woods and sat him under a tree, with instructions not to move—the turkeys would be along near him later.

Let Jake tell it in his own words.

"I sat there for what seemed like hours, and, even though I could hear the boys calling turkeys further away, I was bored stiff.

"After awhile I got thirsty, and seeing no activity, and knowing the car wasn't far away, I decided to walk back to it and get a cold drink of water or pop.

"I came out to the road about fifty yards from the car, and, as I laid down on my stomach to slide under the fence, pushing my gun ahead of me, here come a big tom turkey trotting down the ditch. Immediately he belonged to me.

"Shortly thereafter, while I was congratulating myself, Jim and the others, having heard the shot, came up at a pretty fast clip and started chewing me out for moving. They had worked back around to my tree, and not finding me there, had feared the worst and started looking for me.

"I said, 'Hey, look at my turkey!' They didn't even look. Just kept telling me how I could have a heart attack, could have broken a leg or could have shot myself. I tried to tell them they knew I had done this all my life, and how about my turkey?

"And you know, those worrisome boys weren't the least bit interested in my successful hunt—just my health.

"I told them there was no sense in all of us worrying about my health—so while they stood there and worried, if that was what they wanted to do, I was going back in the woods for another turkey!"

SEA SICKNESS, OR NOT

We met in downtown Los Angeles for a big breakfast of potatoes, eggs, sausage and toast at four in the morning, boarded a friend's boat at San Pedro harbor at six, had corned beef and bloody marys at ten, and by noon I was sick to death!

I have never been seasick in my life. In fact, any kind of motion sickness is foreign to my system. I was in the Navy—rode out two hurricanes at sea. I have owned and driven every kind of boat imaginable. I am a licensed marine pilot and marine engineer, and hold a Master's License for inland lakes and rivers. I have flown airplanes upside down, and will ride any ride at the carnival or amusement park.

But that day I was sick. Of course, those Californians put more tabasco sauce in their bloody marys than you can imagine, and I do really like corned beef, so I tend to over indulge in it. It must have been that!

The captain/owner of the boat kept asking if I wanted to go back in, and I kept telling him that I would die out there first!

We did catch fish, but the climax came when Jake hooked something with dorsal fins, which the captain said was a sand shark. Harmless, he said.

Moose finally got it up alongside, and the captain expressed his disappointment when the twelve-foot monster got off the hook.

"I don't know," said Jake. "I wasn't too crazy about being in a boat with anything like that. And I wouldn't get out, because I don't know what else might be lurking in there waiting for a big overweight fisherman!"

BIG FISH

Personally I have never caught a really big fish. But I have been with them that have.

Back when my business used to take me to southern California several times a year I would always take an afternoon off and go out on a sport fishing boat in the blue pacific. In fact, for years I kept a fishing outfit hidden at a friend's place in the wilds of Burbank awaiting my repeated returns.

We always made up a pool on the boat for the biggest fish caught. I never won it. But others thought I did—at least once.

The first time the Moose accompanied me out there on a business trip he won it. But nobody knew but us.

The skipper of the boat told us to rig for bonito, because they were running. The very first strike on the boat was on Jake's line. Now, a large bonito is something like having a tiger by the tail. Their bones must be coil springs. That fish dragged Moose down the starboard side, across the stern, and halfway up the port side before he got control of it.

Later, as we were enjoying a sandwich on the way back in to the harbor, I said, "Moose, they are weighing in the fish, back on the fantail, and yours should win the pot."

He said he didn't think so, whereupon I took the big bonito out of the sack, took it back and had it weighed, collected the money, accepted everyone's congratulations as if I had caught it, tipped the boat boy out of the prize money, and didn't turn the rest over to the Moose until we were in our rental car and far from the wharf!

"You were being a little generous with my money, weren't you?" he asked.

"Since when did you get so bashful," I said. "I think I should have taken the cost of my fishing trip out of it, too."

The next time I left for the west coast, he said, "Who are you taking to catch the big ones for you this time?"

I don't get no respect!

FIRST ON THE LAKE

"Well, you're first," said the bait shop owner as we walked in. It was a cold March 9 afternoon, and he had just opened—just got his first load of minnows in, he told us.

Jake and I both had a bad case of cabin fever, so I had brought my boat and he brought his foldout camping trailer to Lake Rathbun to fish for early crappies.

We spotted the trailer in the unopened state park, launched the boat and proceeded to fish for the rest of the afternoon. Aside from catching only two little measly crappies, the day was uneventful until we found ourselves hung up on a log when we decided to give it up. It was well after dark by the time we bounced the boat around to clear the obstruction.

"How about some hamburgers and hot coffee?" said Jake, as we arrived back at the trailer—alone on the whole lake.

The gas stove wouldn't light! So, with a lantern, we went out in the cold and checked the bottled gas tank—plenty of gas. So we crawled under the trailer on the cold ground and started tracing the gas line—it was O.K. up to where it entered the trailer. Raising up the stove and sink unit, we found a flexible gas line wedged shut underneath—when the unit was folded over for use, it had flattened the soft line.

The hot coffee warmed us up, and the hamburgers filled us up. By now it was quite cold. The old Moose assured me that with a portable gas heater he had borrowed from his dad we would sleep warm. So, we lit the heater and climbed into the two outboard bunks, sleeping bags, insulated coveralls, thermo underwear, insulated socks and all.

In the wee small hours of the morning I woke freezing to death.

I kept thinking, "Why are we sleeping out here in these two bunks suspended in air, with only canvas over us, like it was summer, when we could be sleeping down by that heater on the couch and breakfast nook which made beds?

I heard Jake move, so asked if he was awake.

"You know we could be sleeping down by that heater," I said.

"I thought of that," he said, "But it's out of gas! Let's light the stove and cook breakfast. That'll warm us up."

"Let me know when it's ready," I said.

Daylight found us breaking skim ice off Honey Creek inlet in order to eventually catch some more little measly crappies.

When we finally got hungry enough for lunch, I nosed the boat up on shore and against my warning, the old Moose grabbed a line and jumped to shore. His feet slipped and he immediately fell backwards into the lake. The boat started to drift away, with me still in it. I nosed it up on shore again, and, wearing hip boots for just such an occasion, I stepped out. The wind swung the boat broadside to me, and in attempting to recover it, it pulled me in over my boots.

Looking over at the Moose, sitting disgustedly in the weeds, I said, "Anytime you want to go home!"

"Right now," he said.

BEFORE THE WIND

Thursday was a good day at Lake Rathbun—for us crappie fishermen, that is.

Moose's brother-in-law used to be the sheriff in Little Rock, and he had a home on Nimrod Lake, about fifty miles from there. A few years ago we joined him on a fishing expedition there for several days while the lake was up about ten or twelve feet. We were catching crappies so big that the Arkies choose to call them "saddle blankets" or "slabs."

So when we heard that Rathbun was up a similar amount, we knew it was going to be a good day.

Jake had a fourteen-foot deep vee fishing boat and a five-horse motor, such as it was, so we took that, knowing that my big boat would never take us where we wanted to go. The object, under all these circumstances, is to ease back up in the inlets among the trees and bushes, preferably over a creek bed. That's where the crappies are when the water is high.

We put in at the state park ramp and motored straight across that area of the lake to a small inlet, actually passing over a submerged pasture field fence. There we tied into what turned out to be a whole herd of slab crappies. I cleaned and brought home fourteen, but we must have thrown back three time that many.

After we got tired of catching them, we decided to go exploring, so we ran in and out of inlets until, guess what, we ran out of gas!

So the two old Indian guides took a sight on the spur at the state park, checked out the wind down the lake, and decided that with a little luck we would drift right to the boat ramp. It worked, too. We only had to row about fifty feet!

And we caught several more crappies and a couple of walleyes as we drifted.

CRAPPIETHON

They started holding a Crappiethon at the lake every year, and me and Jake would enter. We never won, but once we were still in the running until very late in the day. It's tough to compete against hundreds of teams, even on your own lake.

The first time we competed, we caught only sixteen fish, and none of them were very big. The contest paid twenty places, for the heaviest twenty fish. That first time we were really disgusted with ourselves, especially when we went back two days later and caught forty-one crappies, any twenty of which would have won!

LADIES' DAY

Me and Jake had taken our families to Lake Rathbun for swimming and skiing that first summer when it opened up, but had not been fishing with them. In September we went fishing there for the first time with our wives. Rosemary and I met Jake and Bettie one Thursday after the kids were back in school. It was too cold to swim, so we picked up minnows at the marina on the north side of the lake and went crappie fishing.

We went way back up in an inlet and tied up to some buck brush that was sticking out of the water about two or three feet. The water was six to eight feet deep. Being nice guys (?) we baited our fly rods with those "slippery slimy" minnows for the gals to use, and before we could get our own poles rigged there was a "whoops" from the bow of the boat, Rosemary, and another "whoops" from the stern, Bettie, as they each hooked a crappie simultaneously.

"Whoops" became the cry of the day, as they proceeded to catch one crappie after another. About the time it warmed up enough to go skiing, and the ladies were tired of catching fish anyway, a conservation officer pulled up alongside our boat.

"I'll bet you came to tell us where the people are catching all the fish, didn't you?" Moose asked.

"Well, I am making a survey of who is fishing and what they are catching," he answered.

In answer to his questions, we told him that we had been there about two hours and had caught over sixty crappies—mostly caught by the girls—and that we had also caught and released two walleyes and a large-mouth bass.

He asked if we fished there often, and we told him yes, that on the last trip the two of us had taken home twenty crappies for a fish fry, but had released about three times that many. Three or four twenty to twenty-four inch walleyes were not uncommon to us.

So he said, "And you want me to tell you where the fish are?"

EVERBODY HAS TROUBLE ON THE LAKE

The next time our wives went with us turned out to be "one of those days."

Rathbun is a great sailing lake, and there are some great sailors on it—and some who are not so great. Me and Jake went down early to fish in the morning. Along about ten o'clock we headed for our favorite crappie cove, after fishing several inlets.

Strung across the cove were about a dozen large sailboats. We saw them all the time, especially on weekends. Sailors who never saw their sails, and probably didn't know what to do with them, anyway. They went down to the marina, boarded their boats, fired up their kicker motor, pushed the boat across the lake into a cove or inlet, partied all weekend, fired up the motor, and "sailed" back to the marina to their berth. No sails were ever raised.

As we cruised under the line which tied the string of boats to a tree, some guy came out of a cabin and started yelling to us to stay out, that was their cove. We gave him a "Hawaiian Salute" and went on back in the cove. When we came out later, there were a series of lines strung between the end boats on either side and trees on shore. We presumed to keep people like us out.

"You still got that hatchet in your toolbox?" asked Jake.

"In the bow, under the middle seat."

I eased the boat up to the lines on one side, and the old Moose had a good time cutting them with the hatchet, while all kinds of threats were called to us from the decks of several boats.

"Should we report it to the Corps of Engineers?" I asked.

"Hell, no!" said Moose. "Just keep that hatchet handy."

Me and Jake were sitting on a picnic table at the marina later, waiting for Rosemary and Bettie to join us, since they didn't want to fish all day, and we had already been out for several hours. The typical middle-aged couple came down to launch their boat, in a typical middle age fashion— she was backing the trailer in the water, while he sat in the boat ready to start the motor and back the boat off the trailer.

If I talked to Rosemary the way he talked to her I would probably be on the wrong side of the grass by now. He kept calling her "Dummy" and "Stupid," telling her she couldn't do anything right. We thought she was doing pretty well. Soon he backed the boat into the lake and she drove their car up on the hill to park. The lot was full, so she had to go quite a distance to do so.

Jake said, "Look at that S.O.B. I think he is in trouble."

The man was running the boat around in circles at a high rate of speed and was waving his arms and shouting to get his wife's attention. She was casually strolling down the driveway looking at the scenery and other boats.

As she neared our perch, I said, "Ma'am, I think your husband forgot to put the plug in the boat, and he wants you to go get the trailer, so he can put the boat back on it. That's why he is running around in circles, to keep the water from coming in. If he stops, the boat will sink."

And you know, that woman stood there for what seemed like several minutes deciding whether or not to go get the trailer!

That was the day we decided to keep a bunch of fish, so we could have a big crappie feast for our friends. My tri-hull, which we had opted to use in deference to the ladies, did not have a live well, so we kept our catch in a wire basket hanging over the side when we were not moving.

About three dozen crappies later, we headed for the marina. While I went to get the trailer, Moose prepared the boat for retrieval. He had set the fish basket in the shallow water beside the boat ramp. When I picked it up later, to go over to the fish cleaning station, it contained only five fish!

He had put the basket down over a rock, and since the bottom door in it had not been fastened, the rock pushed it open, and the fish swam away! So much for the fish fry!

But the day wasn't over yet. As we drove home late in the evening, we came across a car stopped by the side of the road, and a wrecked john boat in the ditch back a little way from it. It was the couple with the plug problem.

She was sitting quietly on the back bumper of the car, while he ranted and raved about her not noticing that he had not clamped the trailer tongue down on the ball of the hitch. The boat had simply come loose from the car.

"Looks like she forgot to tell you to hook the safety chains, too," said Moose, winking at the woman—as we dragged the boat up the embankment and attached everything as it should have been.

"I'll bet that ends their fishing together," I said.

"If it was me, it would probably end us ever doing anything together," said Moose, while Bettie smiled in agreement.

YOUR BOAT, OUR BOAT

Me and Jake had a little old Cessna airplane, which was supposed to be a four-place, but with him and me at over five hundred pounds, it was a two-place—especially with all our fishing gear in it, too.

One nice spring day we flew it to Minnesota to go walleye fishing below lock and dam number three on the Mississippi. There is a gravel road that runs all the way from our home airstrip to Redwing. We always followed this road. "IFR" means "I Fly Roads," not "Instrument Flight Rules," as some people suspect! Two of our friends were going to drive up a day early and meet us there.

They picked us up at the little airport and we stopped for groceries on the way to the cabin on the river. It was dark when we got there, but no one mentioned supper—they just flopped down in front of the TV set and started drinking beer instead.

I went out in the kitchen, peeled some potatoes, fried them, plus a bunch of pork chops, made a salad and coffee, opened and heated a can of corn, and yelled, "Come and get it!"

They all ate like pigs, got their coffee and headed back to the television. I started clearing the table and washing dishes and Jake came to help.

Four a.m. found me up and in the kitchen again, and with the old Moose's help, making up a bunch of "fisherman's special," toast and coffee. Again, after everyone ate like there was no tomorrow, me and Jake did the dishes, leaving the kitchen spotless.

When we walked out on the sandbar in front of the cabin later, I observed two john boats pulled up on shore—one about sixteen feet long with a twenty-five horse motor, and the other a twenty footer with a sixty-five horse. The big one had fishing tackle in it.

I called to Jake, and we started taking the tackle out and putting it in the smaller boat, then putting our tackle in the big one.

The other guys came running out, coffee cups in hand, yelling, "Hey, that's our boat!"

"That was your boat," I said, laughing. "It's ours now, and will be as long as we're cooking!"

Needless to say, it was our boat all weekend.

ALPINE INN

The Alpine Inn in Elkader was a stagecoach stop over a hundred years ago, and it hasn't changed much.

When me and Jake went north to fish for trout in a cold February week, we decided to spend a couple of nights there—right in the middle of our fishing area. It was certainly too cold to camp out, anyway.

We thoroughly enjoyed the warmth, hospitality, food and especially the rathskeller underneath it in the evening. Even the fact that the fire escape was outside our room, and in such an emergency, the guests would have broken our glass door and trooped across Jake's bed to get out, didn't bother us too much.

But Jake who owned newspapers, didn't have to write what he did about me in his sports columns!

"Here he was," he wrote, "a man who has traveled all over the world, walking through the lobby of the best hotel in northeast Iowa carrying on his shoulder an extremely large cardboard toilet tissue box full of clothes. You would think that such a man would be able to afford better luggage!"

Well, it's the only thing I could find that would hold a pair of chest waders, insulated coveralls, thermo underwear, storm coat and hat, a wicker creel, a fishing vest and assorted canteens and coffee thermoses!

BOOT BASS ON THE VOLGA

Me and Jake were camped on the Volga River near Fayette. Our former pasture field campsite is a golf course now, darn it! The world is just becoming too civilized. But back then it was a great place to camp, near that big spring and all. And the smallmouth bass were just waiting for your lure.

We had acquired hammock tents to simplify our camping—you know, the kind that is to be slung between two trees. It has a rainproof top and mosquito netting sides, with a zipper clear down one side so you can get in and out easily. Comfortable, but cold on a chilly night.

Now Jake didn't like to sleep between two trees, so he always put his hammock on the ground with his sleeping bag inside, and the top propped up on sticks. This particular night we had our tents about fifteen feet apart with a fire between us—it was cold!

I woke up to a cold foggy dawn lying on my side facing Jake's tent. I opened my eyes to see the face of a cow about six inches from mine. It startled me so that I jumped slightly. This frightened the cow so that she snorted, then wheeled, and ran right through the still sleeping Jake and off down the embankment towards the river.

Moose wasn't hurt, but he was so startled that he stood upright in his sleeping bag and tent.

So there he was, jumping all around the campsite like a big caterpillar in a cocoon having a one-man sack race shouting, "Whoa—whoa—what happened?"

And I was laughing so hard I couldn't tell him!

But the day doesn't end there. Later, after we cooked breakfast and filled our canteens from the greatest spring in northeast Iowa, we split up and hit the river. By ten o'clock I had caught a couple of nice smallmouth, and had seen a real lunker break water in a large pool. I slowly edged my way out into the head of the pool, which was surrounded by trees and brush on one side and a high cliff on the other. Soon I was in almost to the tops of my hip boots.

I heard someone coming through the brush, and then Jake's voice saying, "Any luck?"

"Mine ain't luck, Old Buddy," I said. "You know that. It's skill. I'm about to demonstrate it by catching a big lunker I spotted here in this pool."

"I'll catch him for you, then," he said, laughing.

I looked around to see him try a backhand horizontal cast with his fly rod, loaded with a Super Duper lure, from under the trees. The move resulted in a horrible miscast, and the lure, instead of dropping in the deeper part of the pool about twenty feet away from me, struck the water about six inches from my right boot. Moose recognized that he had tossed a baddy, so he retrieved the line right away. The retrieving action set the hook in the largest smallmouth either of us had ever seen on the Volga! The bass had taken the lure just as it hit the water, and Jake caught my lunker just six inches from my leg!

The bass jumped, I jumped, my right boot filled with water, and with Moose yelling at me to grab my net, I sat down in about two feet of cold water.

Later, back at the spring, with me dried out before the fire, Jake said, "Bear, I'm going to have that bass mounted."

"The hell you are!" I said. "That's my bass, after what he put me through, I'm going to clean him and fry him for lunch."

And I did, too!

BRIDGE TROUT

Like I said, everything happened to me and Jake—only this time it happened to just him. He was on a combination hunting and fishing trip to Wyoming—without me, dangit—and one morning he woke up real early and couldn't get back to sleep. He just sneaked out quietly to the edge of the cabin camp where he was staying, taking his fly rod. A small wooden bridge crossed a trout stream there, so he proceeded to cast around on both sides of it. Noticing that the best hole seemed to be right under the bridge, Moose, without thinking, dropped his lure right down through a large crack in the floor of the bridge. You guessed it, hooked a very large rainbow!

Then frustration set in. The whole camp was still asleep, and he was too far away to shout loud enough for someone to hear his cries for help. As a last resort, he tied the line to the bridge, then waded up under it in the cold water and grabbed the fish. Luckily it was still on the hook. Jake said it wasn't the biggest trout he had ever caught, by any means —but he had it mounted anyway!

FISHERMAN'S WINE

We were camped on Crane Creek that Labor Day weekend, and had a goodly number of smallmouth and rock bass to our credit. Set up near the truck was our umbrella tent with a canopy, plus a chuck box with a white gas stove to cook on—all the comforts of home for a couple of old fishermen.

We had made camp on Friday evening, then after a good night's sleep and a hearty breakfast, split up and went our separate ways on the stream on Saturday. I came back to the campsite for lunch, as we had agreed to do. While relaxing with a cup of coffee, I spotted Jake coming up the creek bank—and it looked like something was wrong. He wasn't walking too straight, and occasionally he would stumble—falling all the way down once.

He looked at me kind of funny when I offered him a cup of coffee, and without saying a word, entered the tent and flopped down on his sleeping bag, and by the time I made myself some lunch, was snoring loudly.

After I ate my lunch, I picked up my fly rod and trudged off downstream, occasionally flicking a lure into a pool and hooking a nice bass.

About a half mile down, I came to a small washed-out dam, and sitting on it was an older man in bib overalls still-fishing in the pool below it. I joined him.

"Want a drink of wine? I made it myself from rhubarb," he said. "We call it piestengel."

I knew about piestengel, made some myself.

As I lifted the gallon jug and took a swig, I noticed that it was about half empty.

"Is that big guy with you?" he asked.

When I told him yes, he said, "That guy sure liked my wine. He drank almost all that's gone out of that jug. Nice guy. Hope to see him again."

"Hide the jug, next time!" I said.

BEAR'S HOLE

There is a place on Bear Creek which Jake named "Bear's Hole." Why? Because I can walk up to it almost any day, anytime of the year, and pull out my limit of trout.

I used to like to think that they named the stream after me, but it's much older than I am.

About "Bear's Hole," it happened years ago, before we knew this particular stream too well.

Now, Jake is an avid trout fisherman, and a good one, much better than me—although I'll never admit it to him. He always seems to have a sensitive touch, and can see or feel the slightest hit on his fly line. He used to always limit out first.

Bear Creek is never too heavily fished because of the difficulty of getting to it. You can walk a half-mile over a bluff that is as steep as a cow's face, or down a logging road for a mile that is too rough for a mule—or you can walk in level for two miles and wade the creek several times at the lower end where it is deep and cold. This eliminates the lazy type of trout fishermen.

Moose had stopped at the first likely looking hole, and I told him I was going further. Arriving at a good-looking spot with a big rock overhang, and other large rocks out in the creek, I made a cast and immediately caught a fifteen inch rainbow. Then another, and another, and so it went.

Jake showed up a little later empty handed, unusual for him.

Seeing my stringer, which I had not as yet put in my creel, he said, "Those look a little better than the usual, Bear."

"Not bad," I said, as I hauled in another.

I followed him up the creek, and soon found myself one over the limit. As we headed back, him with an empty creel, I asked him to carry my extra.

As we hiked down past my lucrative hole, I told him he ought to throw in there.

He said, "No, I won't fish in Bear's Hole."

And he never has!

Nearing my pickup truck, I said, "Well, Moose, for a highly competitive fisherman, you are taking this remarkably well."

"That's just on the outside!" he growled.

FISHERMAN FOOD

Trout fishermen will eat anything—anything that doesn't try to eat them first—and even some of those things!

There are two kinds of hunters and fishermen—those whose work is primarily inside and who just like to get out, and those who have a definite taste for wild game and fish, and who are meat hunters. Sometimes one is a combination of both.

In winter the hunting and fishing can sort of bog down, but it doesn't need to. Rabbit and coon seasons run late, and some seasons, like coyote, last all year long—depending on where you are.

Ice fishing is getting to be more and more of a popular wintertime sport. It's tougher nowadays, since you can't abandon your tip-up, retire to shore and check it occasionally with binoculars, as you once could. Now you have to stay right with it.

I still like to get out in winter. But, even though when a nice spring day rolls around and I wish I was back on the farm or working as a telephone lineman or something, when the freezing rain and snow arrives I'm glad to be shuffling papers, writing articles and books, and conducting a lot of business by telephone or internet—inside, where I can control the climate.

As for winter fishing, I still like to go after trout in cold weather—where the streams run too fast to freeze.

Not too long ago me and Jake were "enjoying" the fishing of Bloody Run. It rained overnight, the ground thawed, my panel truck, in which we had slept, had sunk to the axles. We built a fire under an overhanging cliff and proceeded to cook up a couple of messes of our "fisherman's spe-cials"—ham chunks, onions, potatoes and eggs, all scrambled and fried up together. There we stood, eating out of our mess kits, as the freezing rain ran off the cliff and fell into our food, making little spewing sounds as it hit the hot pans.

"Boy, that sure goes down good!" I said.

"Yeah," the Moose said, "but if Bettie ever served me up anything like this, I'd beat hell out of her!"

Yes, sir, there is a lot of enjoyment in wintertime fishing!

TROUT, SQUIRRELS AND CATFISH

But it wasn't winter when we had the next set of adventures. It was September, on the Turkey River.

We were tent camping again, and the trout fishing had been reasonably good, when we met The Couple. They were wearing the latest, not to mention the ultimate, in waders, vests, hats and shirts—and were carrying the most expensive looking flyrods we had ever seen, plus nets and bait boxes. They looked like they had just stepped out of Abercrombie and Fitch. Our conversation with them revealed that they had gone on a guided trout fishing expedition in the Rockies, and decided it was their sport—so were trying it here.

"But there are no fish in this stream," she said. "We haven't even had one bite. You men are wasting your time."

Me and Jake looked at each other and grinned. We didn't have the heart to tell them about the five trout we had between us so far, and expected five more—a limit for each of us.

We went up to our tent and tried to take a nap, but kept being interrupted by a large, noisy gray squirrel chattering in a nearby tree. Jake finally got enough of his incessant screeching, and stepped out of the tent and threw a rock at him to chase him away.

We were both surprised when the little timber rodent fell out of the tree, dead, from a blow to the head.

"What are you going to do now?" I asked.

"Let's eat him for supper," said Moose. "Squirrel season is open, and I do have a hunting license. My methods might be a little old fashioned, but I'm legal."

So we did—stewed squirrel and fried trout made a wonderful supper for two tired and hungry outdoorsmen.

Later, at one of our favorite holes, Jake hooked onto something big. It didn't fight like a trout, and besides, there wouldn't be one that big in that river anyway.

When he finally got it up near shore, at the risk of breaking his flyrod, it turned out to be a channel cat—a big one!

"It'll go five pounds, Bear," he said.

"Naw," I said. "You're dreaming."

"Betcha five bucks!"

"You're on!" I said. "Be prepared to pay up."

We stopped at a grocery store in Elkader, and while the clerk was weighing the fish, a lead sinker fell out of its mouth!

"Well, I'll be darned," said the Moose. "It looks like somebody else caught him before me!"

I took the fish away from the clerk, held it up by its tail and shook it. A half- pound of lead fell out on the scale!

"Why, that old cat must like to eat sinkers," said Jake.

"Yeah, sure."

And you know what? That catfish weighed five and a half pounds without the lead—and the Moose was miffed at me because I wouldn't pay off the bet!

GIFTS

Me and Jake figured out how to get what we want for Christmas, and we are more than willing to pass the information on to you as good advice,

When Christmas comes up, some of you woods and waters types are sure to receive sporting goods as gifts. Then again, maybe you won't. Have you tried dropping hints to your wife about that new Remington automatic, or that fiberglass bow? It doesn't work—believe me! She won't know what you are talking about, anyway.

No, that's not the way to do it—never try hinting at your wife, kids or other family members.

Try hinting at your sportsmen friends instead!

Now, those friends aren't going to get you anything for Christmas—especially not a Remington automatic. (Well, one of them might, especially if you give him a twenty-five horse outboard for his birthday.) But they will get the message to your wife.

I first found out about this several years ago when my son and I lost all our fishing gear in a whitewater canoe accident. I just about quit fishing. (And if you believe that, I've got some land down in Florida I'd like to talk to you about!)

Then one spring (the first week in May) I had to address a group of engineers in Rochester, Minnesota.

Old Moose said that he had to go to Minneapolis on business so, "Why don't we meet in Rochester and go down into northern Iowa trout fishing for a few days."

I finally agreed to go, after he convinced me I could use his son's fly-rod, plus some of Jake's lures.

Then, on my birthday, April 29, what should I get as a gift from Rosemary and the kids but a beautiful fly rod and a carrying case!

Next day at the office, Moose said, "Hey, how do you like the new fly rod?"

How did he know? He picked it out! Rosemary had asked him what I needed in sports equipment, and knowing nothing about fly rods, she had asked him to select it.

"Oh, I didn't really select it," he said. "I picked the one I knew you would want, then I picked one that cost a lot more and one that was much cheaper—knowing that when she went to the store she would get the one in the middle. And she did."

Of course, there are other ways to get sporting goods for Christmas. There is blackmail, there is horsetrading, there is buying it yourself.

Take the latter. I know one guy who bought his wife a size forty-six hunting coat for Christmas. (She weighs 109.) But, then, she bought him an eight-speed blender for the kitchen.

Then I have a very good friend who received the most beautiful gun cabinet I have ever seen. But his wife got a piano! There is an inequity there somewhere—but horsetrading is horsetrading.

As for blackmail, let me tell you how my son obtained his first shotgun.

He was ten years old. Lots of rabbits in a wood patch behind our place. He had been shooting an air rifle for years and was really very good. In my collection of shotguns I had a sixteen gauge bolt action which he really had his eye on. Before Christmas he started in asking for it as a gift. He had fired it a few times before, so one morning I suggested we stroll through the woods and see if he could hit a rabbit.

To make a long story short, he bagged six rabbits in about an hour, and even though I fired three shots, I didn't hit any. Of course, my excuse was that I had to keep an eye on him and his shooting.

On the way back to the house he said, "Hey, Dad, I know you've taught me to tell the truth, but I could say WE got six rabbits without lying, couldn't I?"

He got the shotgun for Christmas!

But the best way is still to let your friends know. (Lately I've seen Rosemary in close conversations with several friends of mine—so I hope everyone got the message.)

I think I made one mistake, though. I suggested that I would never get anyone anything for Christmas that they might buy themselves.

She said, "There isn't anything you wouldn't get for yourself!"

So I might wind up with an empty sock.

Don't forget I told you how to get what you want, but if your friends are too stupid to pass the word along, that's your problem.

HISTORY

Me and Jake used to sit in our old flat bottomed skiff on one of our favorite rivers, when we were young, and watch the airliners fly overhead, and saying how we would like to be in one of them, going somewhere— anywhere, for business or pleasure.

Then three or four decades later, after we had been flying well over a hundred thousand miles each year, and doing business all over the world—and combining hunting and fishing with the business trips—we found ourselves in an airliner looking down on that very same stretch of river.

As we were pointing out the landmarks visible to us at six miles up, I started laughing.

"You thinking what I'm thinking, Bear?" he asked.

"Yeah, Moose," I answered. "History doesn't repeat itself—it reverses itself!"

OUTDOOR PHRASES

Statement: I got it!

Meaning: I know that seven people shot at it but it's really my bird.

Statement: He went behind an obstruction just as I shot.

Meaning: I missed him by a mile, anyway.

Statement: I never bring game home, because my wife doesn't like to fix it.

Meaning: I didn't get anything.

Statement: I raised three big ones to the top of the water.

Meaning: I didn't catch any fish.

Statement: My stringer broke and I lost them all.

Meaning: I didn't catch any fish.

Statement: They just weren't biting today.

Meaning: Everyone was catching fish but me.

Statement: You are fishing in the best spot, that's why you are catching the most fish.

Meaning: But don't ask me to change with you, because you might start catching them here.

Statement: I have decided to become a catch-and-release fisherman.

Meaning: I never catch anything anyway, and this way I won't be expected to bring anything home.

PART THREE

OUTSIDER IN A SMALL TOWN

So you think you would like to live in a small town? No matter how long you live in one, unless you were born there, you will always be considered an outsider!

There is an awful lot of encouragement to move to a small town in today's world, especially by people who have never been there. The writers, the musicians, even the politicians, are all singing the praises of small town America, saying that's where the true values lie, and we should all seek them out. Baloney!

My wife and I don't exactly consider ourselves to be small town people, although we both grew up in small towns. Well, we didn't really live in town. Actually, each of us was born and raised in the country about five miles outside of a small town. But all of our activities were in the towns—school, shopping, sports, entertainment and most of our friends, as well as a few enemies.

And these two towns were over a thousand miles apart, but we were amazed at the similarities, when we compared information. Of course, after having lived in metropolitan areas for a number of years, we tended to remember only the good things—and even then only those things that were prominent, and affected our lives extensively.

So, after over a quarter of a century of marriage, and three grown children away from home, we decided to go back to small town living—trying to find a small town to live in, and a business in which to engage. We were seeking that elusive dream of the real America as sung about by country/western singers, and written about by poets. What we found, of course, were all the problems of the cities just rearranged, as well as lots of unexpected joys—but very little of what we remembered from our younger days, when things happened which we did not know about, or we were just too young to remember. We weren't exactly seeking our roots, since we didn't want to return to either of the towns from which we came, so we deliberately selected one in between—then another, and another. We actually lived in three small towns over the next few years, each offering distinct advantages—and, I must add, distinct disadvantages as well. The first one had a population of eleven hundred, although the parochial school system served three other smaller ones within a few miles. There were no public schools closer than the county seat, population twelve thousand, fifteen miles away.

The second one boasted all of twenty-seven people, but was only five miles from a county seat of one thousand.

The third one was a county seat town of four thousand, but the whole county had only eight thousand residents.

There was a reason, of course, for us to choose each of them in succession, and these reasons will become obvious as you read through this section of this book.

The author has deliberately chosen to identify the towns, even though it might cause a mass immigration to them, or a mass emigration out!

The characters are not identified, except for giving them titles, for a different reason. Those people who live there would soon identify themselves, as well as other residents. Some of them might get swelled heads, and others might try to find out where the author now resides and come after him with pitchforks, tar and feathers—or whatever small town people use on such occasions nowadays! Those people who don't live there won't really care who the others are.

During these years in the small towns, we kept up a running correspondence with two friends in the suburbs. This consists of copies of some of the letters, as our experiences in the towns unfold.

What's that expression? "It was fun while it lasted!"

PREFACE

As an outsider moving to a small town, your biggest problem will be that everyone knows who you are and why you are there right away, but it will take you some time to sort all of them out.

Then, too, you will immediately run into trouble making a living. I learned all this the hard way.

If you come to the town and take a job that is open, you will be accused of stealing it from a native—although there might not be another qualified applicant within fifty miles. This can put you at the mercy of one local resident—your boss—and in some situations, of everybody in town, too.

If you buy a local business, which depends on the community for its income, the residents can refuse to patronize an "outsider," and you will fail.

If you do buy, or even start new, a local business, you are competing with a local who might have done that.

If you develop a business with no local customers, you might still have to hire local people as employees. This causes you to come under pressure because of where you get supplies and services—as well as whom you hire, or don't hire, and especially, whom you fire!

But, if you are smart enough to gain employment elsewhere, and commute to your small town residence, you can be as independent as you want to—shop where you please, make friends with whomever you wish, and tell everybody in town to go to hell!

I have done all five, and believe me the last one is the best.

Since we came from small towns, we swore we would never go back. The educational, social and business advantages were few, and the ones we came from, although they were over a thousand miles apart, had caste systems worse than that of India.

But after we had the rug jerked out from under us a couple of times there, we decided we had to do something—and our own business seemed to be the answer.

We figured you have two choices in selecting a new home town; you can go back where you came from, which is out of the question for us, even if we still liked it there, since we didn't come from the same place; or you can just pick one you think you might like, based on location, job or business possibilities, as well as social and recreational activities.

The trouble with returning to your old hometown is acceptance. No matter how far you have gone, or how famous you might be, you are still looked upon as what you were when you left. We know a man and wife in a town of five hundred people who, after several years away from home, became very proficient in the restaurant business. When they decided to start their own restaurant, they ultimately determined that their hometown was the place to be. No matter how many jobs they provided, or how many tourist dollars they brought to other businesses in the town, he is still that little ragged, dirty kid whose dad ran a service station. And his wife, a strikingly glamorous outgoing woman involved in many community betterment projects, is still that pudgy little girl from down beside the tracks.

And even our case, when we returned to my home area for my father's funeral, one guy kept asking us what we did for a living. Knowing what it would be like, we simply told him we worked for a publishing company.

When he kept asking, "But what do you actually do?" the bragging almost set in.

"Well, we are Vice President and General Manager and Secretary/Treasurer, respectively, of a company that publishes six engineering magazines and four directories," we told him.

Without even hesitating, he replied, "Boy, you always were lucky."

We couldn't tell him about all the years of working for idiot bosses who were not engineers, or who knew nothing about finances, the years of going to school and getting no sleep because of working several jobs, because he would never have understood.

You see, since only successful people return to their roots, all you have to do is leave and you automatically become rich and famous. That's all there is to it. "Boy, you sure are lucky!"

Would we ever go back home? Naw!

WEST POINT, A TOWN FULL OF CHARACTERS

Dear Elmer and Jody,

Remember when you use to talk about moving to a small town—well, guess who's doing it? Us! That's right. We are about to become residents of a town of eleven hundred people. We're going to be owners of a weekly newspaper that serves this town and three others, which are even smaller, and the total of which make up a school district.

What do we know about newspapers? Very little—but we can learn. We almost bought one as an investment back when we were making the big bucks in the Suburbs, and always thought we would like the business, although we didn't relish living in a small town again.

Can you just pick a small town? We did. After tiring of more heavily populated areas, and after getting into many phases of publishing, we were almost forced to make a change, but we didn't really pick a town. It was more like it picked us.

We ran an ad in the state's largest newspaper looking for a weekly newspaper to buy, and the owner, or rather, his wife, called us. So we drove all Sunday morning to get to West Point, about three hundred miles away.

Our first view of the town was impressive enough, as we drove in across the open country from the north. We could see two tall church steeples rising out of tree-lined streets in the late winter sun. Then we had our first meeting with a resident.

It was in the form of a dark blue two-door car coming at us head-on, on our side of the narrow blacktop road! Obviously this was to be a game of "chicken." Having no place to go except into a deep ditch, we just stopped dead in the road. We could see the consternation in the looks of the two young men in the front seat as the car swerved over and passed us. We were starting to have second thoughts about West Point.

We arrived in town to see a large grassy square containing playground equipment, park benches and a tall two-story building. Going around the square were dozens of automobiles, bumper to bumper, and each with one or more young people as occupants. Going nowhere, just around the square. We wondered if there was some sort of festival going on in the town.

On the opposite side of the four streets from the grassy area were business buildings, all of which seemed to be occupied, but none of which seemed to be open. Getting out of our car at the building labeled "Newspaper" for a prearranged meeting with the owners, we were hailed by the driver of the dark blue car.

"Sorry, folks. I thought you were someone else."

We wondered just how many four-door beige Cadillacs there might be in a town of that size.

The Old Editor and his wife were waiting for us, and soon we were looking at his ancient typesetting and printing equipment. We already had the facts and figures on the business end of the operation, having gotten them on the phone and in the mail from his wife.

Later, as we sat in the living room of their spacious home, just around the corner from the office, we begin to realize that The Old Editor wasn't being very friendly—his wife had done most of the talking. He even sat with his back turned about halfway toward us. Maybe he didn't want to sell—perhaps it was all her idea. After all, she was the one who answered our ad. Or maybe he was just hard of hearing. But, we decided to get down to business anyway.

When we asked him for a price, she gave us one, for the paper, the machinery, the building—everything.

Our next statement threw the whole meeting in a different direction, and immediately drove an obvious wedge between them.

Together we told them, "Folks, you don't have one piece of equipment that we know how to run, and we're not interested in any real estate. We'd like to procure the rights to the newspaper and circulation list only. You keep the rest. We plan to take camera-ready copy to a central printing plant about fifty miles away where we have already visited and worked out all the details. Now, will you give us a different price?"

The Old Editor's face lit up like a Christmas tree, and hers became crestfallen. We agreed on a price, and when we offered to have our lawyer draw up a simple contract, with a covenant not to compete included, he laughed and said his lawyer would do it a lot cheaper.

We spent the rest of the day visiting with them and learning a lot more about them and the area. The Old Editor had gone to work for the paper while still in grade school (he never attended high school), and had now owned it for forty-one years. It was over a hundred years old and he was just the third owner. He loved printing, but didn't care much for the newspaper business, so he just took in whatever news and advertising came in—didn't work at it.

His wife was fifteen years younger than him, and since a newspaper ties its owners down so much, she had wanted to sell out and hit the road. We had just screwed her plans all up, by letting him stay in the printing business. We gathered he didn't want to go anywhere anyway.

When we inquired about the traffic, and if there was something going on in town, they said no. It was like that every weekend, as well as lots of evenings. And they told us to look at the faces of the drivers—they all had a lost-in-space expression!

We're coming back next week to sign the contract and look for a place to live. We don't believe we're doing this, either!

Allan and Rosemary

Dear Elmer and Jody,

Well, we just got back from West Point. We signed the deal on the newspaper, we take over in two weeks. And we bought a house!

When we asked The Old Editor and his wife about renting office space and a place to live, they insisted that they could make room for us in their business building, rent free, at least for now. For a place to live, The Old Editor said, "Let's go see the Big Guy."

The Big Guy turns out to be a man who owns a farm implement company, a furniture store, a lumber company, a building contracting firm and lord knows what else. He said he didn't know of anything to rent, but he had built a brick ranch-type house, a little nicer than most, which he would be happy to sell us.

When we told him we couldn't afford to buy until we sold our suburban property, he said, "Sure you can!"

And that same afternoon he took us to a savings and loan company in another town, and he and we told them our story. He had built the house nine months before for someone who couldn't swing it, and had been paying on a construction loan on it ever since, with no buyer in sight. The house was all done except for a little wiring and plumbing. The savings and loan company told us what they would loan us, so we signed up.

So there we were, with no money and no income yet, buying a new house. When we got back to The Big Guy's place, he made out a statement like he would for the purchaser of a farm implement repair part, stating what the balance was that we owed.

"Don't you want us to sign a note, or something?" we asked.

"Why?" he said. "You aren't going anywhere. You just bought a newspaper. Pay me when you sell your other place."

We enjoyed visiting with him. He told us he tried farming as a young man, on rented property, but lost his shirt. He had started the implement company with a small amount of money borrowed from his mother, and it had prospered, but he was in the process of selling it to his brother and three others who worked there. He was afraid they might go broke by taking more out of it than they put in. He doubted their management ability.

He had gotten good financing and broken up his mother's farm on the edge of town and starting building houses. (Ours is one of them.) Then he sort of backed into the lumber business. When he started building, he went to the only lumber company in town and tried to make a deal. He wanted them to deliver lumber to his job sites in large quantities, and at a discount. Typical small town merchants, they told him that if he wanted to buy lumber from them, he could come in and order it and pay for it like everybody else. He started his own lumber company!

He said he got into furniture the same way. People would come in to get remodeling materials and express a desire for furnishings they couldn't find. So he started getting it for them—by special order at first, then he started stocking it. By now it is a full-blown furniture and floor-covering store.

He even set up one of the three insurance agencies in town. One of them does most of his business out of town, and just lives here. When The Big Guy tried to make deals with the other one, he was laughed at. (He said the agent was so twisted he even ran an ad once bragging about the fact that his agency had paid out fewer claims than any other in the area during a certain period of time!) So The Big Guy set up one of his employees in the insurance game, giving him all his business—enough to get him started.

He served as mayor for a few years and, over the objections of many, shoved curb and gutter down their throats. Now he says the ones who objected are bragging the most about these improvements to West Point.

His wife is very nice, too. We think we could become good friends. They are very down to earth people, like most who start out with nothing and pull themselves up by their bootstraps. They say they actually own or have built over half the taxable property in West Point. Besides, three of his companies advertise in the newspaper!

Afterwards, we visited both of the insurance agencies. The first one laughed at us, too, when we told him we wanted to pay by the month, since that would be how we billed the newspaper advertisers, so our income would be monthly. He told us we would have to pay annually, just like his other customers, who are mostly farmers.

The Big Guy sponsored Insurance Man, now on his own, said, "However you want to pay it! We want your business."

We're back home in the Suburbs, listing our house, which we hope will sell quickly. It's been quite an experience, and we are looking forward to the next ones!

Allan and Rosemary

Dear Elmer,

Rosemary is still straightening up our new house after our move, and I'm here at the office waiting for a visitor.

By working day and night we got out our first few papers, and they went fairly well. The Old Editor took me around on the first Friday we were here to meet all the advertisers. They really came in with lots of business. It seems that their biggest fear had been that The Old Editor would just quit, and they would be without a paper to hold their community together. My little study of newspapers over the past couple of years has shown this to be a problem.

It's happening all over the country. If the newspaper dies, then the town dies, and there are ghost towns by the thousands to bear this out. Without a newspaper there is no local news, so the town starts to become a bedroom town. Since the grocery stores can't afford to advertise in the big city papers that cover the area, or on television, soon they close, and more and more people have to shop in the city. Soon the bank shuts down, because if people have to go elsewhere to shop, they will do other things there, too.

Then you start to see the schools absorbed into the larger ones, and the town just becomes a distant suburb. And all because the only means of tying the community together by means of communications, the newspaper, is gone.

It is obvious that the business people of West Point don't want that to happen—which is to my benefit.

While visiting with The Insurance Man that first Friday, he mentioned that he and his wife were chaperoning the Senior Prom, which was that same evening. We had been trying to think of a way to make a big impression with our first paper, and here it was!

I went home and told Rosemary to get her glad rags on, we were going to the prom! She wondered if they would let us in, and I said they couldn't possibly refuse, after they saw my camera. The Old Editor hardly ever ran pictures, because nobody brought him any, and his production methods made it too expensive. I intended to change all that.

I had also always heard that, in a small town, everybody knows already what's going on—they just read the paper to find out who got caught! I had hopes of changing that, too.

I know it was that way where I grew up.

When I got out of the Navy, I went up to another town about twenty miles away to visit the widowed mother of a guy I had spent some time with overseas, and who wouldn't be home for a while yet. Lo and behold, unbeknownst to me, he had a younger sister!

To make a long story short, we wound up at a movie in another town even farther away. I got her home at one o'clock in the morning, and while I was eating breakfast just five hours later, my mother came in and said, "I understand you were out with a girl from up the country last night," and she even named her name! I decided to trace the information to see how it traveled so far so fast.

The girl's mother had a sister, whose husband farmed out the road from us, and to whom she had talked early that morning, and who had told her husband about the date. He in turn had told our neighbor across the road from us when he went up to do chores for the farmer. The neighbor had come home for breakfast and told his wife, who had seen my mother outside and came over to tell her. And all before six o'clock in the morning!

The mayor of our town once told me that he believed that if he went to Paris and went down the deepest, darkest, most obscure alley he could find and went into a house of ill repute, the girl he would get would be from his high school graduating class, and the whole home town would know about it before morning!

We were met at the door of the gymnasium, at the Prom by The Insurance Man and his wife, and when I complimented her on her dress, they both laughed. I couldn't believe this extremely attractive young lady, in the very short green dress, was the mother of six children. Then she explained why they were laughing.

"When his mother came over to baby sit this evening, the first thing she said was, 'Dear, your dress is too short. Why, I can see right up to where you divide!' and we've been laughing ever since!"

It was a cute dress, and her panty girdle matched the color, so she was covered. She really could have been taken for one of the senior girls.

I asked who the big guns were in sports, and zeroed in on them and their dates with my camera, although I took lots of photos of other couples, too. With Rosemary taking notes as I shot, we came away with an abundance of material. Our first paper, the following week, had a full page spread of pictures from the Prom.

We upped our print order to twenty five percent over circulation, and people came to the office and bought them all. Our regular subscriber list gained fifteen percent. They liked what we did!

Then this past week was the regular monthly meeting of the Community Club, which functions in lieu of a chamber of commerce, and I got to meet more residents and learn more about them and the town. Of course, three fourths of the meeting was devoted to bringing

The Twisted Insurance Agent up to date, since he hardly ever goes to meetings, so never knows what's going on.

With a couple of papers behind us, it's getting to be a little touchy working in the same building with the former owner. People keep coming, in and telling us how much they like the new paper, compared to the old. The Old Editor doesn't seem to mind, but it is obviously upsetting to his wife. We might have to move soon. We could use more space, anyway. But there just isn't any rental property in town.

I joined the Community Club, and have been asked to join the volunteer fire department. I'm not sure I want to—I saw enough burns in the Navy, and enough blood in the big city police department as a Saturday Night Cop, to last a lifetime. And this area seems to have an awful lot of fires, and even more fatal automobile accidents, to which the fire department has to respond. I think it's the drinking. This area is rife with beer drinkers, and they start young.

Allan

Dear Elmer,

I'm starting to realize just what a town full of characters this is.

The other night I was working late when the Local Politician stopped in the office.

"I hope you're going to give the Party just as much coverage as your predecessor did," he announced.

"You bet," I said, "and I have no idea which party you are referring to." (I am very apolitical!)

He left in a huff. Later, when I told The Insurance Man about it, he filled me in. The Politician has been representing this area in the State House of Representatives

for several terms, but was defeated last election and is now home and running for the school board. In the legislature he was famous for doing controversial things. For example, several times he was thrown out of the

Senate chamber for going over there without a coat, which was strictly forbidden by that august body.

His point was, and a good one, too, that people who didn't have sense enough to take their coats off when they got hot were not intelligent enough to run the State's business.

"Well, he shouldn't have any trouble getting on the school board," I volunteered.

"Oh, no," exclaimed The Insurance Man, "people won't vote for him for that, it would keep him here. They used to elect him to the legislature just to keep him out of town."

One night I was uptown with The Old Editor when he suddenly exclaimed, "Oh, my god, the old Timber Beast is in town! Let's go talk to him."

I wasn't sure I even wanted to meet someone called The Timber Beast, much less talk to him. Turns out he was a real nice old guy, looked down on by most because he dressed in rough, heavy, ragged clothes, and lived out in the woods where he eked out a precarious living cutting fence posts and firewood which he sold in town.

He told us that he had just acquired some milk goats because one of his grandchildren, who lived elsewhere, had been diagnosed as having a rare disease, which required goat's milk instead of cow's milk in his diet. Such a gentle, compassionate man—despite his looks! I'm sure the townspeople had a different opinion of him after I went out to his place with my camera, and did a poignant news story on his project.

Then came the Firemen's Ball!

We had to go, right? And while Rosemary was knocking them dead in her cheong-sam, with the high-necked collar and slit skirt, which I had bought for her while on a business trip to Japan, I was trying to avoid The Doctor and The Undertaker all night. No, I wasn't afraid of getting sick or dying, right there. They just started following me around.

You see, in our business everybody gets to know who you are real quick, even though you might not know who they are. Wherever I would be, there they were. When I finally confronted them about what they wanted, they said, "We're The Doctor and The Undertaker, and one of us is going to get you before the night is over."

After we had had enough fun for one night, met many new people and I hadn't gotten sick or died, since we had to work the next day, we announced our departure.

"You can't go yet," some of them almost shouted, "the party isn't over."

When we reiterated that we had to, The Fire Chief leaned over and told us, quietly, "You don't understand—whoever is first to leave a party around here, everybody comes to their house when the party is over."

"Sure they do," I said. "Some of these people are ready for bed right now."

Our clock said two A.M. when the telephone woke us up.

"Better get dressed," came the voice in my ear, "there are a couple dozen of us, but don't worry, we have plenty of food and drink."

We believed him, and we had twenty-two people in our basement rec room until sunup!

I finally had to go to that doctor the other day. I had a little irritating growth, like a wart, right under my belt in back. When he looked at it, he said he would cut it out. I asked him when, and he told me to lie down on the table.

When his cute little nurse, who was one of our neighbors, asked him what that thing was, preparatory to filling out a form, that goofy doctor said, "Well, that little thing is a so-and-so (here he gave her the medical term for the growth), and that big thing is Allan's ass!"

I discovered a remarkable phenomenon in the game of advertising, which I have been able to work to our advantage—that is, most of the time. In the case of a dealer for a national chain of products, such as feed, fertilizer or implements—and sometimes even hardware or cars, they have cooperative advertising.

This means that the national operation will send to the local newspaper a schedule of ads for which they will pay half, if I can sell the local business on paying the other half. Since most local outfits can't afford that heavy an ad schedule, if they will approve them, we run them for whatever the national company will pay, and pretend that the local ones paid their half. It works very well for all of us—the local merchant gets his name on a national ad, the national company gets what it pays for, and we get half the rate. Larger newspapers could not afford to do this, but we'd rather have half of something than all of nothing.

Then I met The Barge Terminal Man! I went to a local seed, feed and fertilizer company and made my sales pitch. He thought it was great. But he said it would have to be approved by the owner of the company, or her son. They had inherited it from her deceased husband, and they actively managed a grain elevator and barge terminal down on the big river. He agreed to accompany me there that same afternoon.

No sooner had I said the words "cooperative advertising" than The Barge Terminal Man came apart. His face absolutely livid, he literally shouted at me, "Don't come in here talking to me about the Co-op! I don't want anything to do with any Co-op."

The more his manager and I tried to explain that we weren't talking about the Farmers Cooperative, one of his competitors, but were talking about a shared advertising plan much to his advantage, the madder he got.

He finally ordered me out of his office, and threatened the manager with his job for even listening to such a thing in the first place. As the manager and I headed back, he said to me, almost plaintively, "You only had to listen to him once. I have that to contend with every day."

We now have an office of our own. I spoke to The Big Guy about it, and he owned the now defunct skating rink, which he rented out to an auto body repairman, but who didn't use the office. The area was completely remodeled to suit our needs, with a new rest room, even.

We dreaded telling The Old Editor about it, but it didn't seem to bother him any. I cemented our friendship by writing my very first editorial after our move all about how he and his wife had been so good to us, even bringing us fried chicken one night when we were working late, and that we would value their friendship forever.

It brought an immediate reaction from all their friends, and ours, in the way of nice comments about him and his wife and how the community had always thought the world of them.

Allan

Dear Jody,

Allan's out running around somewhere with a bunch of guys distributing tickets for the Sweet Corn Festival, which the town holds every year, and I'm minding the office.

I'm starting to adjust to this area pretty well. Allan says we live in a town full of characters, and he might even be one—or at least he is fast becoming one.

Some of the women are also characters, some nice, some not so nice.

One woman came in and really ripped me up for not attending her son's advancement ceremonies to Eagle Scout—and I asked her how I was supposed to know about it. She had no answer, and then she asked what was I going to do about getting her husband a better job. I told her I never met her husband and had no idea what he did for a living.

Then another came in whose son was graduating from college and she wanted me to write something about it. She stood there at the front desk for over an hour trying to think of enough to say to make it a long article, even wanting to name several professors who taught him. I was really busy, but I tried to be nice to her. I don't think Allan would have been that patient.

Let me tell you about him and The Rich Woman, (although "woman" is not the word he uses!). I had heard about her from some of the other women, but found the tales hard to believe. Then one day I was in the town's only beauty shop, which is run by a wonderful lady whom every body seems to like. (Unfortunately, her husband, who worked with welfare recipients, started helping one of them above and beyond the call of duty, so The Beautician kicked him out! But that's another story.)

Everyone in the beauty shop had appointments that day, including me, and The Beautician was a few minutes behind—not enough to disturb anyone, but still behind, nevertheless. In comes The Rich Woman, just as one of the chairs got empty, and plopped down in it, saying to the bewildered woman who was next, and who had actually gotten up and started for the empty chair, "You'll have to wait, I'm in a hurry," and, to The Beautician, "I need my hair fixed, now!"

As the young woman who should have been next sheepishly took her seat, the others were looking at each other and muttering something about her always doing things like that. I was fuming, and I couldn't believe what I had just seen.

A few days later her husband died suddenly—the wags around town said he was probably glad to go!

Now, when Allan and I bought the newspaper, we knew we would be together twenty-four hours a day—something we had never done before, and we weren't sure we could work like that. So we agreed, at my recommendation, that we would divide up the duties, and try to stay out of each other's territory.

I took the book keeping and finance, because of my background in that, and also I took the social news—weddings, engagements, meetings and funerals. I didn't want to supervise any employees, or solicit any advertising. So far the system has worked out fine.

A few days after The Rich Woman's husband died, she came boiling into the office, screaming about how screwed up the obituary was. Now we just take what the mortuary gives us, and that's usually over the phone.

The obituary wasn't incorrect, she just thought that her husband deserved more space. Apparently she wanted a eulogy right in the newspaper.

After I tried to reason with her in a nice way, while she became more and more demanding, Allan walked over. He knew we had agreed not to interfere in each other's territory, but this had gotten out of hand. In his usual diplomatic way, he said, rather loud and clear, "Ma'am, I know that to you, your husband's death is a major tragedy and a great loss—but to us it's just another damn obituary. Now, get the hell out of this office!"

She almost ran for the door.

Turning to me, Allan said, "Sorry. Didn't mean to interfere."

"Thanks," I said.

The Rich Woman has been back in the office several times since, to bring news items on her family. She always looks around to see if Allan is here first, but she keeps her voice down whether he is or not.

The Assistant Postmistress, who is probably in line for the top job when The Postmaster retires, took it on herself to tell me, (one of my duties is also to pick up the mail), that we had to start getting the papers to the post office by three o'clock each mailing day. I asked her why, since they don't go out until after five, and they don't have to do anything to them—we do all the paperwork. She said no matter, that is when she wants them.

Since we can't possibly get them done by then, I called the post office in Fort Madison, the next big town, just fifteen miles away, and asked about their schedule. They told me anytime before eight, and as late as eleven if they know in advance. And subscribers will still get their newspapers the next day.

When the local postmaster learned that I had moved our mailing permit to the other town, both he and his assistant came rushing to see us. The amount of help they get is based on the amount of mail they handle.

She tried to tell me that we couldn't mail from somewhere else, since we were located here in West Point—until The Postmaster shut her up. I think we will soon be back mailing from here again, with the full cooperation of the local post office.

I hadn't much more than gotten set up in our new office, and we had hired a couple of part time girls to help us, when The Old Gossip showed up. She proceeded to apprise me of who was sleeping with whom, who had been married to whom and to criticize the way all the women in town dressed, including me and our office girls. After her third visit in as many days, I was getting a little tired of it. When I mentioned it to The Beautician later, she started laughing.

"The Old Gossip's two daughters were the girls little boys learned from around here," she said, "and some of the big boys and men, too. Even when they were in grade school they would go in the little boys' room and remove their clothes for money, and if none of the boys had money, they would take off their clothes, anyway. One is a known prostitute in the city, and maybe the other one is, too."

The next time the old gal came in I couldn't resist innocently asking her about her family, especially her two daughters, and pumping her for details. I don't think she will be back, at least not to gossip.

With the local elections not too far off, the politicians are streaming in to talk to Allan. He laughs about it, but they tell so many lies, even about things that we attended, and know better, that I can't stand to see or listen to them anymore. I go in one of the other offices when one shows up. You have to want a job awful bad to go through that. I wonder how they can live with themselves. Most of them are men, but some of their wives are just as bad.

Hope you and your family are O.K. We miss you, more and more each day. It would be nice to have a couple of sane people to talk to!

Stay in touch,

Rosemary

Dear Folks,

It is true that most of the people here are natives, inbred since the first ones arrived from overseas in the last century. You can't get married beyond your fourth cousin—there isn't anyone else.

But I guess I'm starting to be accepted around here now, as the summer goes by. At least they are including me in their humor, even playing jokes on me, sometimes. The Fire Chief, The Insurance Man, The Assistant Coach and The Civil Engineer came in the other day and wanted me to accompany them on making the rounds of the business establishments, mostly taverns, to distribute tickets to the annual Sweet Corn Festival. What they really wanted was to take my old white convertible, since The Engineer is a convertible nut, and mine is the only one around.

With him driving, we hit all the places—me with my camera recording the event for posterity. At the very last place, and we had sampled food and drink at all of them, I had the camera up to my face when The Chief stuck something in my mouth and said, "Have a pickle!"

I like all kinds of pickles, so I bit down, hard, and started chewing. I thought I was going to die! That was the world's hottest pickle. I found out later the boys sometimes took bets on whether or not somebody could eat a whole one. I sure couldn't. They laughed at me all the way home.

Then on Friday Rosemary and I were invited to a "Moon Party." What is a "Moon Party" you ask? Well, we did, too, having visions of everybody going out somewhere and baring their behinds, "mooning" everyone. But, no, it's a boating party. Most of the friends we've made have boats, so the Friday closest to the full moon, three times each summer, they all gather for an adults-only party on an island in the big river and eat, drink, sing and tell jokes around a big bonfire—all in good clean fun.

The highlight of the evening, of course, is "Everybody's Uncle." He loves to tell jokes, and they love to have him tell them. When he gets started on one, and they are usually pretty dumb in the first place, as soon as he realizes he has a captive audience, he starts to drag it out, thinking of all the innuendos he can use to enhance the story. Instead of becoming bored and irritated at him, they encourage him by interrupting him to ask questions, to get clarification and for repeats of certain portions of the story. The crowd continually laughs at him, not at his story, and, since he doesn't know the difference, he enjoys his celebrity status immensely. Some times one of his stories takes up most of the evening.

On this, our first time, after Uncle finally got his story told, The Chief asked us if we would like to play "Cheeky Cheeky." We told him we had never heard of it, but we were game for anything as long as it was clean and decent. He said that even the kids play that game.

The whole crowd was asked to kneel on the sand in a great big circle— boy girl, boy girl. The woman next to me reached up and pinched my cheek, saying "Cheeky Cheeky." When I asked what was the object of such a game, The Chief told me to just wait, it builds to a climax. I was directed to pinch the cheek of the woman on the other side of me and repeat the phrase "Cheeky Cheeky," so, feeling silly, I complied. And so it went, all around the circle—people pinching each other's cheeks and saying, "Cheeky Cheeky."

When it got back to me again, the lady next to me, who had to be the shyest one in town, reached up and pinched my nose, saying, "Nosey Nosey," and so we went around the circle again. And then it was "Chinny Chinny," and so on until we had covered almost all the parts of the face. Everyone in the circle was laughing uncontrollably, even Rosemary, who was kneeling across from me, but I couldn't see what was so darn funny.

Soon I found out. It was me! I happen to notice something I wasn't supposed to see. The Shy One next to me had something black on her fingers, and while everyone was simply pinching each other's cheeks, she was smearing that stuff all over my face! The Chief had deliberately asked her to get next to me.

What could I do but laugh. You wouldn't dare try to get revenge on a bunch like that. To try to make the best of the situation, I just left the gunk on my face for the rest of the evening.

Then, to add insult to injury, on the way home The Chief and his wife, with whom we were riding, pulled into the most popular tavern in town, as did the rest of the moon party crews.

So there we were, in dirty swim suits, with sand all over our legs, our hair looking like that of Australian Aborigines, and me with dark gunk all over my face, being introduced to people we had never seen before, and some we had. I told The Chief and The Insurance Man, "You guys, in just one night, have destroyed all the dignity it has taken me three months to build."

They, and the whole crowd, roared. What can you do?

That white convertible almost got me in trouble a couple of times. I was taking pictures at the pancake supper, which preceded the corn festival by a week, when I heard a voice calling me by name. I looked around and saw The Church Girl. She was an unmarried teacher, about thirty, and who was very active at church, playing the music, I had been told. She was working at the pancake supper.

When I walked toward her to see what she wanted, she said, "I understand you have a convertible. Can we go for a ride?"

"I'm not driving it," I said. "I don't drive it much, I drive my pickup."

A week later, I was driving it up to the corn festival parade assembly area with the festival queen's float behind it, since I had been asked to pull it in the parade. The float was a beautifully decorated farm wagon, festooned with all kinds of crepe paper, silk flowers and flags—made up by several festival workers. It was easily the best float in the parade.

Following a sketch of the locations for the parade entries, I pulled my rig in its designated spot, right behind the parade marshal's car and the dignitaries. Suddenly some one was yelling at me to get the hell out of there. I looked around and saw a rather red faced man approaching, screaming his head off. I actually looked behind me to see if it was really me he was talking to. It was The Grain Shoveler.

"You get that thing out of there and put it at the end, behind the tractors and horses," he demanded.

"No, I won't. This is the designated place for it," I said.

"That isn't even supposed to be in the parade. Get it to the back, or take it home. And if you don't, I will!" he threatened.

Then I realized that he didn't know that this was the queen's float, so I calmed down and tried to reason with him, but he just got madder. By now some flunky who was helping him line up the parade had joined in, and he was just as bad.

I decided I would do what these two ignoramuses requested, just to show them up, so I towed the float to the back of the line. I knew that some of the festival chairmen would be checking the lineup before the parade started. I removed my keys from the convertible and disappeared.

At about five minutes before parade time, I made myself visible again. Someone came running up saying that The Grain Shoveler was desperately looking all over for me. So I casually wandered off towards the tail end of the parade lineup to find a very irate queen and the six members of her court.

"Don't ask me what you are doing back here in the tractor fumes and horse manure," I said. "Ask that guy over there, the one wringing his hands with a worried look on his face."

A very docile, but still confused Grain Shoveler said they would hold up the parade until I moved the queen's float to the right place.

After the parade, when I had returned the float to its storage barn, The Church Girl, in a revealing peasant blouse, (I suppose she wanted to show the boys a thing or two), came up to me. She had two of her girlfriends in tow.

"I know you have the convertible," she said. "I saw it in the parade. Let's go for a ride."

"The keys are in it," I replied. "Park it in front of the newspaper office when you get back."

I'll see how The Grain Shoveler and I get along in the future. He looks like trouble.

Allan

NO RUTS FOR ME!

Dear Jody,

Allan is out on another fire call. They seem to have a lot of them since we've been here. He doesn't mind the fires so much, says he can run up and down ladders with the best of them. But he really hates the accidents.

Maybe we just didn't know about it in the Suburbs, and maybe not even as kids back home, but there seems to be more fatal accidents here than anywhere we've ever been or even heard about. It's been so sad since the sweet corn festival.

During the festival a local young father parked his motorcycle on his front walk and his three-year-old son managed somehow to pull it over on himself and was crushed to death.

The following week, two young men, one a worker for The Big Guy and the other The Big Guy's nephew, a college student, drove off the road and hit a utility pole, right on a straight stretch of road, and the college student was killed.

Then, the tragedy of all tragedies, six high school boys, ages fourteen to seventeen, lost control of their car between here and Fort Madison, the first week of school, and all were burned to death. One was the brother of one of our employees.

And there was Allan, who never wanted to get involved with the new rescue van, putting out the fire while the charred bodies were being removed from the wreck. He came home sick, as did most of the firemen.

A multiple funeral, in the high school gymnasium. The Undertaker's wife told me that she and her husband had scheduled a vacation trip to Alaska over a year ago for sometime soon, but were canceling it because it might look bad, as if they were taking advantage of this sudden requirement for their services.

I know that appearances mean everything in a small town. We have been criticized for not having the office open on Thursdays. The paper is mailed on Wednesday, the subscribers get it on Thursday, so nothing happens for us on that day. It's too early to solicit either advertising or news, so we just close up and do our cleaning, maintenance and bookwork. We are open on Saturday morning.

The Supermarket Man and his wife live in a very modest house not too far from us. When she invited me for a visit I was amazed at the elegance of the inside, including the basement rec room.

Noting my expression, she said, "Appearances, you know. We'd like to build a new house, but we don't dare. If our customers think we are doing too well, they won't trade with us."

Allan just came back. It was another fatal accident. A farmer was up in a tree with a chain saw doing some trimming. His wife could see him from the house, and begin to think he looked funny. Upon investigation, she saw that he had cut his thigh with the saw, got his leg wedged in the tree and hung there until he bled to death. The fire department had to go retrieve the body. I don't know how they can stand it.

The last accident, before this one, just a couple of nights ago, was fatal to the seventeen-year-old son of some new friends of ours. A new highway is being built about eight miles from West Point, and he took off down the unfinished pavement in his car, on his way home in the middle of the night, and hit a paving machine.

I didn't mean to get so morbid with this letter, but sometimes things just get to you, and it's hard to be impersonal about it, especially when you have to print it in your own newspaper.

I did have an interesting experience the other day. Two men came in and said they were from the state revenue department—a young guy and a middle-aged one.

"I want to see your sales tax records for the past five years," said the younger one. "And where is your sales tax permit? The rules say specifically that it must be prominently displayed."

"We don't have one," I said.

"You're in trouble," he said. "Let's see your tax records."

"We don't have any," I replied.

At this, the older man elbowed the younger one out of the way, saying, "I'll take over, now. What do you mean, you have no sales tax records, and no permit?"

"In the first place, we've only been here a few months, not five years," I said. "And the only thing we sell is advertising, and there is no sales tax on that in this state."

"What about printing?"

"Don't do any."

"What about wedding invitations and things like that?"

"Don't sell any," I said. "Look, I know how frustrating this must be for you fellows, but last spring we bought the rights to the newspaper, and that's all. The former owner kept the rest. You should have done a little more homework."

Of course I had set up our entire book keeping system, expenses, billing and tax system with a CPA used by The Big Guy, back when we first bought the paper.

Remember what we told you about The Big Guy's bill for the remainder of the purchase price of our house? Well, when the Suburbs house sold, I went in to pay him and he had no idea what I was talking about. Could find no record of it. It was a good thing I had made my own note. His wife indicated later that he didn't keep the bill, because he never intended to try to collect it, he was so glad to be out from under the construction loan on the house.

The other night we had come home from the office "dead dog tired," as Allan puts it, and were just considering what to fix for supper, when the doorbell rang. It was The Fire Chief. Parked in front of our house was a school bus, freshly painted light green.

"That's my new limousine," he announced, "we're all going for a ride in it, including you two."

When we protested that we were too tired and hungry to do anything like that, he grabbed us both by the arms and practically dragged us towards the bus, saying that we would eat somewhere. That somewhere came to be a pizza place in Fort Madison, where we and a dozen other couples spent the evening, after touring the countryside in the bus— singing, telling jokes and laughing.

Before returning to West Point, the Chief pulled into the grounds of the Prairie Hunters' Club, a more or less sportsman's club out in the country. Since no one was there, we were whooping it up like a bunch of kids, swinging on the swings, sliding down the slides and playing hide and seek in the dark.

Allan came over to me and said that he had run into a tree in the dark and hurt his head. We sought out The Chief, who got a flashlight from the bus and we looked at Allan's head. There was a large laceration at the front showing through his hair, and bleeding profusely. After we stopped the bleeding and got him home, he came out of the shower saying it looked liked it needed stitches. So we headed for the hospital at Fort Madison.

The nurse in the emergency room told him there was no doctor on duty, so they would have to call one. Then she said, "No, there is an obstetrician here waiting to deliver a baby, as soon as the mother is ready. He could sew it up, if you don't mind."

"Why should I mind?" asked Allan. "This guy should certainly know how to make a neat stitch!"

As the old nurse shaved the front part of his head around the wound, she asked, "You fell out of a tree?"

"No ma'am," answered Allan, "I fell into a tree!"

"Well, at least you are not drunk. Most people we get in here this time of night are drunk."

"Maybe if I had been drunk I would have missed the tree," laughed Allan.

I guess we'll just have to quit doing stupid things, but in this town and with this crowd it's hard not to.

Hope you are O.K.

Love,

Rosemary

Dear Elmer,

I had to take on the town bully the other night, and I don't know if I won or not, but it was an enlightening experience.

As Rosemary said in her letter, I hurt myself out at the Prairie Hunters Club, and had to have stitches in my head. (I kept thinking—there was no need for the stitches, since there is nothing in there to run out, anyway!) I looked so bad that I had to wear my cowboy hat to keep from making people sick. Since it didn't fit too well with hair in back but none in the front, I went to the barber and told him to go ahead and shave it all off.

Well, let me tell you about small town barbershops—within an hour everybody within thirty miles not only knew about my accident, but my shaved head as well. Now for the bully.

I had heard about Too Slim ever since we moved here—about how even back in grade school he had everybody buffaloed, and you shouldn't cross him. (I guess there's one like that in every town.)

A couple of nights after my accident, the Social Club held a fund-raising pig roast. Of course we had to go. I was subjected to a lot of good-natured ribbing by everyone, men and women alike. Things like, "I didn't know you could hurt an editor by hitting him on the head!" and, "The Prairie Hunters say they are going to sue you for damaging their tree!" and, to Rosemary, "You sure he didn't get that against the headboard of the bed?"

Then Too Slim walked up behind me and knocked my hat off. I was embarrassed that everyone saw my affliction, but I didn't say anything— just picked it up and put it back on.

A little later, in the chow line, he came up and knocked it off again. This time I got a little perturbed, so I asked him not to do that, it was not funny anymore, just embarrassing. I no more than got my hat back on my head, but what the dumb idiot knocked it off again, and just stood there with a silly grin on his face.

I didn't even bother to put it back on, or even to pick it up. Seething, I sat my tray down on the nearest table, grabbed Too Slim by his shirtfront with both my hands, pulling him close to my face. The whole room was dead silent as I said, "Slim, if you do that again I'm going to knock you on your butt, right here in front of all these people."

His eyes got real big, and mine probably did, too. I have to admit that I probably looked pretty formidable, what with a shaved head revealing a stitched up gash about two inches long, and a mad as hell expression. Slim didn't say a word, just bent down and picked up my hat and handed it to me, then lifted my tray off the table and put it in my outstretched hands. The rest of the evening he kept filling my glass, or my coffee cup, while I kept waiting for the explosion when he realized what I had done to him. It never came.

I found out later that Slim is a 4-H leader, and that his club of boys met at his home the very next night. I invited myself to attend. I have never seen a man with better rapport with teenage boys that Too Slim, and I said so in my editorial in last week's newspaper. I think I have made a friend for life. I'm sure that all he ever wanted was for other people's approval after he grew up, but didn't know how to go about getting it.

Of course, my reaction to everyone isn't always that positive. The Insurance Man took me quail hunting on several places where we had permission to hunt, the best being one of the farms of his brother-in-law. A couple of days later, I went back out there by myself, when he couldn't go. I hadn't fired any shots yet, just making my way past some old abandoned farm buildings, when I was accosted by a total stranger, who stepped out from behind one of the structures.

"Just what do you think you are doing?" he growled at me.

"Well, I'm trying to find some quail," I said, as friendly as possible.

"Get off my property, and right now!" he barked. "You city people think you can run all over anybody's place like it was your own."

When I told him I wasn't a city person, and that I thought I had permission to hunt there, and who gave me that permission, he told me that guy just rented the place. I headed back to my pickup, but on my way home I stopped at the renter's place to tell him what happened.

"Oh, is he back?" he asked. "I don't see him from one year to the next. He uses all his income from the farm to do some kind of missionary work in India, where he spends most of his time. He thinks he is saving the world, I guess. When I pointed out to him that there are kids within ten miles of him that don't have adequate food, shoes or clothing to wear to school, he got madder than hell at me, and told me to mind my own business. Don't worry, he'll be gone in a couple of days, so you guys can go back to hunting there again."

And you won't believe this, but just two days later that idiot came into the newspaper office, not knowing, of course, that it had a new owner. He had a long written dissertation about his work among the poor in India, with an appeal for support, which he wanted us to publish—said it would help spread the milk of human kindness to other parts of the world.

I took his write-up, tore it into little pieces, threw it in the nearest wastebasket, and said to him, "Mister, if what you dispense is the milk of human kindness, I'll get my milk from a cow!"

Looking at me in disbelief, he stammered, "Haven't we met before?"

"Yep," I said. "Two days ago you told me to get off your property. Now I'm telling you, get the hell off mine!"

He stood there in consternation as I wheeled and walked back to the composition room. I could hear him telling Rosemary that he was leaving in a few days and would like to straighten this all out.

Knowing how I think, she told him to forget it, that he had just given me material for my next editorial. And she was right!

I came into the office one afternoon, and Rosemary told me that the nicest young farm boy had been in and told her he had heard that I was an avid duck hunter, and he was, too. To make a long story short, I joined him and some others the very next day, down on the big river. I never saw so many ducks in my life!

Dear Elmer and Jody,

We had a nice Christmas. Christmas in West Point is a different experience. In the first place, they have a unique custom, which we had never run into before. It's called "looking at your tree".

The first time we heard it was when a neighbor said, "You are going to come look at our tree, aren't you?"

Naively we said, "Why, what's different about your tree?" or something like that.

But we were to learn that "looking at our tree" is just an expression. It means that for about a week before Christmas there is a continuous open house, night and day, in all the homes around here. Sometimes people gang up and go from house to house. Of course, you are only expected to show up at each place one time. And no one really cares whether you have a tree or not—they are just there for the refreshments and good cheer. What a custom! The whole world should adopt it.

We were asked to be judges of the Christmas lighting contest for homes and businesses. That was fun. The American Legion sponsors the awards.

Then came the parties! The Legion had one, the fire department had one, and several other groups. But the best one we went to was at the home of The Fire Chief. Right in the middle of the festivities in came a jolly old Santa Claus, totally unexpected by our host and hostess, driving, of all things, a goat! Just as Santa stopped him in the middle of the living room, the excitement must have gotten to the "goatdeer," because he raised up his tail and let go. Seeing what was about to happen, one of the guests stuck his hand under the goat's tail and caught the discharge.

Looking around for some place to put it, he spotted a pocket in Santa's jacket, and in it went!

On the afternoon before Christmas, the Community Club had arranged for some skydivers, dressed like Santa and his elves, to jump near The Fire Chief's house. The plan was for Old Santa to go into the house then reappear to lead a parade through town on the fire truck. Of course, in the house the skydiver would be replaced by a waiting substitute Santa. The Chief's teenage brother, slightly overweight and very shy, was asked to play this role. What poor Santa didn't know, when he sat down to hold court in the Social Club with the little kids, was that two very sexy class-mates of his, as prearranged by me, would come in and sit on his lap and melt his beard for him! Santa didn't need a fire that day!

Following Christmas, then, was the homecoming dance, since in this community, most people who have gone away return at that time. By now we know enough people to mingle and have a good time wherever we are, and the dance was no exception.

Then there were New Year's parties galore, and we went to three differ-ent ones. On New Year's Day came the clincher! All the taverns and clubs are open from six to eight in the morning, serving free Tom and Jerrys and raw oysters. And you are nobody if you don't get up and participate, no matter what you did the night before!

We survived, but just barely.

With the holidays behind us we are looking forward to spring, but the characters keep coming out of the woodwork—making more grist for our editorial mill.

For example, the owner of the #2 grocery store. He seems to be a nice guy, but a lousy businessman. I think he was forced into the business by his father, who founded it as a young man. We bill for advertising at the end of the month, but he hadn't paid us anything for several months. In order to avoid a confrontation, I wrote him a note with his invoice, telling him we wouldn't solicit any more of his business until something was done about what he owed us. The next morning when I opened the office door, there was a large envelope, pushed through the mail slot, containing the full amount—in cash! What a trusting soul. We could have kept the money and claimed we never saw it, but that's the difference between small and large towns.

One of the mail carriers stopped in the other day and asked for a free subscription. Said he might not do as good a job of delivering the papers, since they are all mailed, if he had to pay for a renewal. I refused, of course, and when I mentioned it in my editorial, the postmaster jumped me. Said the man might lose his job. I told him I didn't care—extortion is not right, no matter if it is tried by a government employee.

When I discussed it with a part time carrier later, he laughed and told me that the first thing he was told when he got the job was to not tell anyone how high his pay was.

The mayor is a nice enough person, when he remembers. He runs a photo studio, and shoots most of the weddings hereabouts. They usually occur on Saturday, so Rosemary makes the write-up and waits for the photo on Tuesday, so the wedding news will appear in the paper of the week following the wedding. Last week an upset mother of the bride came in on Monday to tell us that the photographer had shot the whole wedding ceremony with no film in his camera! They were going to get all dressed up and do it again the next Saturday.

I don't go to town council meetings, because they send me the clerk's notes from which the minutes are developed anyway. Recently they stopped doing that, telling me that I could come and take my own notes. So I went. Most of the meeting was devoted to discussing the town's only full time employee, who had asked for a raise. They said he didn't do much to earn what he was currently getting, which was about twenty percent of what I was netting with the newspaper.

It wasn't much, but maybe he didn't do much, either. Yet, he was the town marshal, water and sewer superintendent, streets maintainer and maintenance man for all town facilities. Some of the people in the audience complained that his police car, which the town had just bought, was parked in front of one of the taverns every morning. (Until recently he had driven his own pickup, with no remuneration for expenses.)

This started me thinking, because my pickup is also parked in front of that tavern every morning, as are the cars of most of the businessmen in town. That's where we go for coffee—no one is drinking anything else that early in the morning. The coffee, milk and sweet rolls are laid out so that you can help yourself.

I invited myself to join the town's employee on a typical day, fully expecting to be bored. The temperature was in the teens when we met at his house. Getting into his pickup, we drove to the sewage plant where he tested the discharge, checked all equipment to see if anything was about to break. Then we went to all three water wells and made the necessary checks and tests. Then we went back and traded the pickup for the police car, went to city hall to see if anything needed his attention, and to complete his reports for the previous night's police work and this morning's sewer and water tests. Then we joined the others for coffee at the tavern.

After coffee, we went back to the sewer plant where he pumped out the sludge into an old tank truck and spread it on some adjoining fields. On our way back, we drove into the town dump (landfill) to look for any illegal dumping, such as dead animals, or fire. We both went home for lunch.

After lunch we climbed into a paving tar truck and put a layer on two blocks of streets he was repaving. Then added gravel, then more tar. This is an ongoing task.

By now it was suppertime. After supper he picked me up to accompany him on his nightly checks of businesses, and speed control, with radar, of the main drag.

I really don't know what he would have done if some of the equipment had been broken, since he also has to maintain it, or if there had been something in the landfill for him to remove, or a fire, or a crime committed, or if some of the tests hadn't been positive, or if he had had to plow snow!

I got a lot of comments when I wrote this up, with no editorializing, under the headline "The Coldest Job in Town." And he got a twenty percent raise!

One of the school board members chewed me out for not attending their meetings. They too, send me the meeting minutes. So I decided to go to one. The school board president is a tractor mechanic who barely finished the eighth grade. (I remember what dad used to say? "Go ahead and get your degrees, boys. So you can go to work for some guy who went through the third grade and owns the company, or was elected to some position that controls your life.")

At the meeting, one member tried his best to get them to upgrade some office course equipment, since the supplier would give them what they paid for the original in a trade-in. Didn't even get a second to the motion. Then they spent forty minutes discussing what wattage light bulb should be put in the hall to the gymnasium. I never should have written that one up, but I did—without editorial comment.

And speaking of the school, the other day I received a letter from a first year journalism student at the state university, who is from West Point. In it he told me I didn't know anything about newspapering, a newspaper is an art, not a business, and that my paper carried too much advertising. Of course, I could see the hand of a professor of journalism, who has never had to work for a living, knows nothing about economics or business, and who has probably tried to get some little crappy articles published, but was rejected.

The letter contained twenty-six grammatical and typographical errors in its two pages. I marked them all in red, gave him a C-minus, and mailed it back to him!

Allan

Dear Elmer and Jody,

There's a little bank here that is a branch of one in a bigger town, and the banker is a local boy who is related to everyone here (but who isn't?), and that is why he got the job. When we first arrived in town we opened our business account there, but our personal account away from here.

When he discovered this he wanted to know why he didn't have them both. I told him I didn't want them mixed up. He assured me that would never happen, so, to pacify him, since he is an advertiser, we opened a small personal account with him. And guess what, the first check we wrote to our printer (the biggest one we write), bounced! They took it out of the wrong account.

He is in the habit of coming in the office and walking right back to where the girls are composing the pages of the paper, but I think he might have gotten broken from that last week. He picked up a small electric hand waxer, and before anyone could warn him, said, "What in the world is this?" and turned it upside down, letting the cap fall off and dumping hot wax all over his wrist. He yelled pretty loud! I told The Insurance Man, who is The Banker's nephew, about it, and he just shook his head.

At least he was interested in what we were doing, which is rare around here. Since this is a farming community, not only are they not interested in anything else, but they act perturbed if you are not a farming expert. I was at one of their houses one night when in the middle of a conversation about farming, one of them turned to me and said, "We are discussing farming here. Shouldn't you be participating?"

To which I replied, "Are you going to discuss publishing when you come to my house?

Laughing, he said, "I see what you mean!"

I came into the office the other afternoon and was told that The Fat Farmer from the Knights of Columbus had been in to tell me what he thought of me, and was up at the tavern building up a head of steam to take me on. I knew he had a reputation for a high temper and pig head-edness, but I didn't care.

It had all started the previous week when someone called to chew me out about not running an article on the new K.C. building. I tried to explain to him that I had already talked to the Grand Knight about it, and he had asked me to wait until spring so we could get pictures after the landscaping is done. That didn't pacify The Fat Farmer in the least. He went on to accuse me of being a lousy newspaperman, citizen and other things.

My editorial last week said that someone who had identified himself as The Fat Farmer, whom I had never met, said some unkind things to me on the phone. Then I went on to tell what he said, and what I told him. Now apparently he had come to beard the lion in his den.

A little later my staff scattered when a short, but portly man entered through the front door. "You the editor?" he growled.

"Yeah," I said. "You the stupid idiot who's been bragging to everybody in town about what you're going to do to me?"

He was so mad he didn't even see the tape recorder lying right on the counter in front of him. When he finished his tirade, he asked, "Just what are you going to do about it?"

I quickly rewound the tape and pushed the play button. As he listened to himself, his face became redder and redder. I thought he was going to blow a gasket right there in my office, but he turned and stalked out. I heard later he went back to the tavern and announced that you better not fool with that editor.

Soliciting advertising gets to be fun, sometimes, too. There is a small department store here that spends a very small amount in advertising. He doesn't feel like he has to, and he is not alone. There is a laundry and dry cleaner who doesn't advertise at all. They flank, on either side, our biggest advertiser, the super market, so they just ride on his coat tails. He brings the people to town, and they get the business, too. (That's one thing about the big town malls. They won't let anyone do that—all must share in the advertising, or it will be added to your rent if you don't advertise.)

The department store manager really criticized me in front of all The Community Club members one night for taking advertising from an out of town store that rents formal wear. There are so many weddings here that

that is a big business. He told me that he rented formal wear, too. I asked him how was I supposed to know, he never advertised it, or much of anything else. I could see the wry look on the face of The Supermarket Man!

There is a new hardware store whose owner keeps complaining that advertising doesn't help him. But he doesn't advertise things, just the store. And institutional advertising doesn't work in a small town. Nobody cares who you are, just what you have to sell.

Don't get me wrong, we are really enjoying this, even the idiots. There are lots of humorists in a small town, also. The other day we got in the mail, with cash, a classified ad from someone who wanted to sell a "mushroom" dog. It was obviously a joke on someone, because the telephone number to call yielded a laugh at the other end. So at the end of my editorial I asked that the owner get in touch with me, since I had a female of like breed, and would like to get some puppies!

Some guy stopped in the other day and said he was an auctioneer, would be placing some ads from time to time, since most farm sales are in the spring. Wanted to know about an auctioneer's discount. I told him it was the same as an editor's discount given by auctioneers. Said he never heard of such a thing—so I told him now we are even!

Had another case similar to the #2 Groceryman. This guy erects grain bins for farmers. His ad invoices piled up until Rosemary called his company to talk to the purchasing agent, and got the owner instead. He proceeded to lay into her like she was too stupid to be talking to someone as high up as the president of such a large company. When he got all done, she simply said in a quiet voice, "And you, Sir, are without a doubt the rudest man I ever talked to."

The very next day he was in our office to apologize. She was out, and he was hoping I wouldn't write one of my famous editorials about this. I told him I wasn't the one he owed the apology to. He has been trying ever since to be nice to her, after church, when we eat breakfast out, anywhere he sees her car. But she won't have anything to do with him. I almost feel sorry for the guy—and he has such a nice wife, too!

Speaking of eating breakfast out, there is a great small restaurant here. It used to be a drive-in, but was expanded. It is run by the nicest couple. They have a whole flock of kids, so they ought to know how to prepare food. The guy makes the best strawberry milkshakes in the universe, and, as you know, I've tried them all! I just about split the other day when I was there and two out of town ladies were eating. When the wife, who does most of that marvelous cooking, asked them about dessert, one of the women asked if their pies were homemade. When she said, "We make them here," the customer got up to leave, saying, "Well, if they're not homemade, I don't want any."

Back to the school. Saturday afternoon I was washing my truck when Rosemary called me to the phone. It was the Coach and the school Principal. They started complaining about something I had written that was derogatory to them. I probably did, but I had no idea what they were talking about. I finally got them to shut up long enough to ask them. That unsigned letter in the school paper, they said, it looked like something I would write.

I blew up! I pointed out to them that everything I write has my name on it, in real big letters. I hadn't read the school paper. And besides, the first rule of journalism is that you never print anything where the author won't identify himself. Their staff adviser to the paper should know that.

Some of my best "letters to the editor" are unsigned, so I won't publish them. Even then I mention them in my editorials, sometimes, and beg the writer to identify himself, so I can print it.

"Well, we just wondered if maybe you didn't like our school," moaned the Principal.

"Don't wonder anymore," I told them. "I think the school has a lot of possibilities, full of great kids and dedicated teachers. It is you two idiots that I don't think are doing your jobs. I don't think you even can do your jobs. But, just because I don't like the current president doesn't mean I hate the United States. The same thing applies to you two. Just because I don't like you stumblebums doesn't mean I dislike the whole school."

"You're sure not going to make a lot of friends around here," griped the Coach.

"I didn't come here to make friends," I told them. "I came here to run a newspaper."

But I'll bet my friends, my real friends, outnumber theirs five to one.
Allan

Dear Elmer,

We publish the items from the police blotter exactly as they are listed at headquarters in the town hall. The other day one of our biggest advertisers threw a fit because of what we printed about his nephew. Said that the policeman was getting too big for his britches, and that we shouldn't be publishing such harmful information. When we looked it up, it said, in one line, that the kid had been fined for underage drinking!

We bought a boat. Yep, with most of our friends being boaters, and after enjoying our trips to the island in the big river last year, we decided to join them.

There is a marina in the county seat on the river where most of these people do business. They all have families, so they keep pretty big boats. When we started looking, The Marina Man misread our desires, and tried to sell us some smaller boats, since there is just the two of us. Finally we got him convinced that we wanted something similar to what most of our friends have, a large eight-passenger tri-hull. We thought his price was too high, so we asked The Fire Chief and The Insurance Man about it. They told us to get The Marina Man aside when no one else is around. We did and the price dropped ten percent.

When it came time for our first moon party of the season, we invited the man in the electric company that serves this area, and who is a big advertiser, if he and his wife would like to join us. They couldn't, but he asked us why don't we lease that island. When we told him we didn't even know who owned it, he said his company did. So, he put us in touch with their real estate office, and they sent us a lease, for just a token amount per year. The lease stipulated that the island was to be used for recreational purposes only, and the real estate man, jokingly but serious, said that this didn't mean we could build a tavern on it!

We called a meeting of the thirteen couples who have boats and use the island, at our house, to tell them what we had done, and that we wanted the lease to be for all of us.

They decided to form a boat club, limited to people from that area, and to leave the lease in our name to avoid confusion. I guess they trust us. We didn't want it to become like the Prairie Hunters Club, which was formed by local people, but since they let everybody in, now it is controlled by people who live far away.

We voted not to charge dues, just to take up a collection whenever we needed money for rent. The Civil Engineer said the worst thing we could do would be to get

organized! We elected an Admiral (me), a Rear Admiral (The Insurance Man, who watches all the rears, anyway), a Sexetary (The Supermarket Man's wife, for obvious reasons, her swimsuit!), and a Treasurer (The Civil Engineer's wife, who has a good figure—no, that's who is good with figures).

Every time we go up to the island on weekends, we rope off a section of the beach for the little kids, so they don't get near the boats. We have put up a welcome sign, asking visitors not to litter—otherwise anyone can use the island. The Boat Club is not greedy.

Rosemary and I learned that several of the teachers at the local grade school run by a religious order had expressed interest in going to the river sometime. No one could take them, since the others have their boats full of family members. We called the principal, a middle aged, very conservative woman, as were all the younger ones, too. She was really pleased to be asked, and accepted the invitation for four of them.

Teasingly, I said, "I must warn you, I don't allow anyone in my boat unless they are wearing a bikini."

There was dead silence on the phone for about thirty seconds, then she said, "Allan, would a red pants suit be all right?"

When they showed up, two of the younger ones wore swim suits under shorts and tops, and the latter were removed when we were away from the beach and the other boaters, and one wore a simple cotton dress, which was up to her armpits most of the time in the wind, since she liked to drive the boat. They all seemed to enjoy themselves immensely, and we will take them again.

I have started playing a little golf again. One of the fairways runs along the fence of a prison farm—barbed wire, close together.

"What if I hook one over there?" I asked.

"Oh, it's O.K. to go get it," said my companions. "Just don't try to come back!"

I've been playing in a foursome every Thursday, when our office is closed, which is made up of The Insurance Man, The Supermarket Man and the local Clergyman. When I told them about my old rule of not discussing business on the golf course, or be penalized by having to buy drinks back at the clubhouse, they liked the idea.

On the fourth hole, on a drive across a pond, The Insurance Man hit the opposite bank and his ball rolled back in the water. "Oh, God," he exclaimed.

"You're talking business," said The Clergyman. And guess who had to buy drinks?

This is the same Clergyman who appointed himself chaplain of the fire department. I think it was so he could drink beer with the boys, but I wouldn't say that out loud. One night at the fire hall he was needling me about being the only one in town who doesn't belong to a church. I told him I had known only two clergymen real well in my whole life. The other one had me closer to joining than I had ever been, but now this one has me farther away.

"Good," he said. "We get just as much credit for keeping you bad ones out as for getting the good ones in!"

I thought Rosemary would split when I told her.

Of course there are some things I haven't told her. Like The Blond Widow that manages the golf course. When I was out taking pictures for the paper of the course, she came riding up on a golf car, and asked me to join her. She was a little too friendly. Finally, she stated that if she didn't know my wife so well, she'd be all over me. I ran for cover!

The Farm Boy's Black Lab had puppies sometime back, and since neither she nor the father were registered dogs, although they are both purebreds, he gave away the puppies to his friends. He asked me if I wanted one when they were born, and I told him yes, I would take the pick of the litter. He said I couldn't have her, he was keeping her for himself.

Every few days he, or one of the other guys, would ask me when I was going to get a pup. Then one day The Insurance Man stopped in to tell me that I was too late, all the dogs were gone. I just smiled.

Now the pups are four months old, and The Farm Boy was cussing his two dogs, saying he couldn't teach the young one a thing, and they were eating him out of house and home.

"Are you ready to give me that pup, now?" I asked.

"Yeah, but I'm not going to haul her down to you. You can come and get her!"

So now the other guys are saying, "You knew that all along, didn't you?"

Yep, I tell them. That is the way you get the pick of the litter. Almost everyone who has his first litter of anything, wants to keep one. But after awhile, they realize their mistake, and want to dispose of it. By then it's too late for some people to take it—it's not little and cute anymore. So I just lay back in the weeds and wait, as I did this time. I named her Dixie, after one of my aunts, and she looks like she will be a great retriever.

I'm looking forward to hunting with her this fall. But for now, the sweet corn festival is coming up, and we have to work on that.

Allan

Dear Folks,

Well, the Sweet Corn Festival came and went, and although it was probably considered a success by the town, it was a disaster for me. In the first place, I was stupid enough to volunteer to be a chairman. You see, there are four chairmen each year—two incumbents and two newcomers. Unfortunately the other three serving with me like their beer, so I can never find them. Even when they scheduled meetings at their homes, their wives wound up conducting them, because the husbands couldn't get away from the taverns.

The last night of the Festival, when the four of us met to settle up with the carnival ride operator, one of my co-chairmen announced that there would be no Corn Festival next year, so we would not be signing a contract for the rides. I said we could not decide that, and that there were no four men in West Point that could decide that. Since the Festival is run by the Community Club, they were the only one to make that decision—and we just represented them.

With that, another chairman jumped up, threw his cowboy hat on the floor, and berated me loudly for trying to take over the town. Said I would eventually be gone, and that the rest were stuck trying to make sense of what I did. I told him that what he said might be true, but that while I am here I intend to do everything I can for the town. By now I was bearing the brunt of the wrath of all three drunks. The carnival operator said to me that we could mail the contract later, so we left.

At a meeting of the Community Club the following week, at which we wrapped up the Festival, I was again criticized for "trying to take over." About the only thing I had done to make them think that way was to suggest that the talent show, which is part of the Festival, be broken up into several categories. Participation in it has slacked off, since the judges always pick as the winner some two or three-year-old in a cute costume, who is trying to dance, but can hardly get one foot in front of the other, while very good talented people are passed over. When I pointed out that somebody had to take over, since the others were usually drunk and unavailable, I was told that they preferred that "outsiders" remain more in the background, serving only as helpers to the residents. Of course, I immediately resigned as chairman of the Festival—over the objections of the Club president.

As I walked out with another member, he said, "It's tough for us outsiders to get accepted."

"I haven't been here very long," I said, "but I thought you were a native."

"Oh no," he said. "I've only been here twenty-nine years!"

Then, to hang it all, the last night of the Festival, a ride had collapsed, breaking both legs of a young college student—who had worked part time for us, but had quit to go to school. Later, I received a notice from the state job service that he had filed for unemployment compensation, which would be charged to me. I went to the office and objected, stating that one of the criteria for drawing the funds was that the filer must be available for work, and none was available. I told them also that I had a job for him, which he could sit down and do, even with two broken legs.

They gave him the money, anyway. I suspected that the hearing officer was related to him. Heck, everybody around here is related, except us!

So much for the Sweet Corn Festival! One thing I learned—don't get involved with community celebrations.

More banking problems. One of our employees insisted on a large raise, and when I refused, she told me that with our business income, we could well afford it, according to her husband's aunt, who worked at the bank. I should have attacked the Banker, but knew it would do no good. When I mentioned it to the Insurance Man, he told me that was why the bigger businesses in town, including him, kept only token accounts at the local bank—with their main accounts elsewhere.

We started another publication. We have a feature in the newspaper, which lists happenings in the area over the life of the publication. Of course, that gets us in trouble sometimes. Like when we copied a birth notice from an edition seventy-five years ago. The old gal listed is still alive is mad as a wet hen, because she has been telling everyone that she was a lot younger! Anyway, we get so much material of this type—school pictures, local glamour girls in their basketball bloomers, old farming shots, stories of traveling—that we decided to put much of it into a monthly magazine. So far it is doing well.

My business, like any other, depends more on ideas than anything. Sometimes I run a "signature page," on which I feature some particular event, and ask local businesses to make a token contribution to it, in return for having their names listed on the page. We don't make any money on it—it's more like a service to the community. One advertiser, a feed mill, adamantly refuses to participate, saying that it is a ripoff.

The County Fair came up last fall. All newspapers run stories after the fairs, telling about the winners. We decided to run a Fair Supplement to the paper, featuring the upcoming entries—kids, mostly. We went all over the county, taking pictures, interviewing parents, writing about livestock and crafts. I solicited advertising from every merchant and business in the area, including a few feed mills—except one.

When that week's paper with the supplement came out, the feed mill operator stormed into my office and gave me "what for" for several minutes. After he calmed down, I pointed out to him that the supplement was just one of my ripoffs, in which he had said he would not participate. He left, after telling me to put him on everything like that in the future.

The Farm Boy and I have spent a little time together in the woods and on the water. When I told him of my idea for starting a "shopper," a free circulation paper containing only advertising, he said he would be interested in calling on advertisers for it part time. My plan is to offer free want-ads to individuals to get readership.

But I needed several thousand dollars start-up money. Big idea!

The second biggest implement dealer in the state is located in one of the towns our newspaper serves. So big they own several farms, whose tenants buy their equipment from them. So big they have their own bank to finance implement purchases and repairs. And they had announced an open house!

I took my camera to the event, and spent the day talking to satisfied customers and staff members. Found out they sold over a million dollars worth of combines alone at the open house. I made up a two-page spread story in the following week's edition of the newspaper. Then I went to their bank, with my business proposal for the shopper, and a request for a loan—with no collateral.

The Young Banker said, "I know exactly what you are doing, but I don't dare turn you down!"

Allan

Dear Elmer

Had a little trouble with the school paper. Once a month the school newspaper staff makes up the content and we give them a full page of the paper—which, of course, we compose. I don't usually read it until it comes out. They have faculty advisor, and that is his job. It is usually full of typical high school news—activities, that sort of thing. We cover sports separately.

Last month the girl who sets our type called me over to her machine and suggested I read the school's contribution. The whole collection was nothing but opinions of the new editor, and mostly about the local newspaper—how bad it was, how could the residents put up with it, and how the editor, an outsider, would never fit in.

I called the advisor and told him I would not include it in my newspaper. Made him mad. Said he wanted to encourage students to speak out. Told him to choose another way to do it, then. Sid they would put out their own newspaper. And they did, a little mimeographed sheet of opinions. Later the editor's mother came into my office and berated me about freedom of the press, and other stuff.

"After all," she said, "he is the editor."

"Yes ma'am," I replied, "and I am the publisher. And in any publication, including the Chicago Tribune, the editors do what the publisher wants."

About my shopper—I just keep getting in trouble. It has been very well received by advertisers and readers alike, as an extension of the newspaper. But......

There is an enormous furniture story in one of our towns, whose owner-manager would never talk to me. Called me up, asked me to come over.

"I want to advertise in your shopper ever week," he said, "on the front page."

I immediately lost the enthusiasm his opening words had generated, and I told him I would not sell the front page—it would not be fair to the other advertisers.

"I spent thousands and thousands of dollars on advertising," he said, to impress me, I guess.

"But you have never spent one cent with me," I reiterated.

When he insisted on the front page or nothing, I told him where to go, and left. No sense in having the headaches of being in business for yourself if you can tell at least somebody that!

Back to the school. I got lucky. I was shooting pictures at a basketball game when I noticed a student, slight-of-build boy with glasses, following me around.

I started showing him my camera, and let him shoot a couple of shots, after he told me he was interested in photography, in response to my query. I invited him to come down to the office next day, and bring his camera.

He didn't have much of a camera, but seemed knowledgeable. I learned he was the son of the local department store owner, and a freshman. I hadn't met him, but I knew his older brother was a big gun in school sports, and his sister was very popular as well. I made him a deal: I would pay him a small stipend for every school picture he took that we used, put his byline on it, and he could use my camera, film furnished. Later we would teach him to use the darkroom. The kid's a whiz!

Then I sought out the brilliant, popular, student daughter of a friend of mine, and lined her up to write a school column weekly. The school news is now more than covered.

The young man's father collared me the other day, and asked me what I had done with his youngest son. "He's always been surly and standoff-ish," he said, "so whatever he's doing, I hope he keeps it up."

"Every kid needs his own thing," I said. "He has found his."

The Farm Boy and I were preparing for our first duck on opening day, and were discussing it with the Insurance Man and the Fire Chief, when they said they would like to join us. I pointed out that it was ten o'clock at night, and they needed hunting licenses and a duck stamp. No problem, they told me, grinning. They went and got the manager of the hardware store to open up and sell them licenses, then woke up the postmaster to get their duck stamps. You can't do that in the suburbs!

Allan

SECTION 2

BENTONSPORT AND BONAPARTE, TOWNS FULL OF NOTHING

Dear Elmer and Jody,

I think I just stumbled into a possibility of business expansion.

What with the lack of privacy of the local bank, I started snooping around others in other towns. Met one bank president at a Lions Club meeting, at which I was a speaker, and he asked me why I didn't buy the two newspapers in two nearby towns, which were for sale. I told him I didn't have any money. He said they did. So now we own three papers, a shopper and a nostalgia magazine! Hired the Farm Boy full time.

One of our new possessions came with a large new cement block building in Bonaparte, a town of about five hundred, thirteen miles away, so we will move our main office and composition operation there. That one also came with several employees, since it is an old letterpress operation. We don't need all the people, so I interviewed each of them to determine whom to keep. One guy, a press operator, came on strong, saying that since I was not a printer, I couldn't get along without him—so he wanted much more money. He was much chagrined to learn that I plan to sell the equipment to a junk dealer, and don't need him at all.

An inherited columnist in the county seat notified me that she wanted a two hundred percent raise. I told her she made Frank and Jesse James look like two Sunday School teachers—that I had bought a newspaper, not inherited a bank. I will replace her, of course.

The Soak-the-Newcomer syndrome has really kicked in. The guy I hired to install central air in the building asked for a partial payment when he was about half done. After I gave it to him, he disappeared until the money ran out. Came back and finished up, but I refused to pay him because of the problems with it. He's mad, but I'm stubborn.

I gave one of my inherited employees permission to come to work an hour earlier than the rest, because her husband went at that time. After I realized she wasn't typing copy, but talking to her friends on the phone for that hour, I rescinded the privilege. Another one's husband is a policeman in a town about four miles away. Since we usually work late on Tuesdays, making up the papers, he started coming in the composition room, in his uniform, and standing behind her while she worked. I asked him not to, since it is distracting. He glared at me, and came right back the following week. When I dismissed his wife, he threatened me over the telephone, not knowing that my phone has a tape recorder attached. I played the tape at a town council meeting in his town. I don't think he will bother me anymore.

Having the new papers printed at a different printing plant than the one we used before. Had a little trouble with their "back room" employees ignoring my requests the other day. Got a call from the business manager when he arrived at his office.

"Just who do you think you are, upsetting my people like that?" he asked.

"I'm the guy who wrote you a check for several thousand dollars last month," I told him, "but no more!"

I hung up and left the office for about three hours. When I returned, he was sitting in our reception area. I was told he had been there since shortly after I left. No more problems with his back room!

Got a call from the IRS office for this area. The voice said, "We'll be out there Friday to shut you down. Might as well go ahead and let all your employees go."

When I tried to get some questions across, I was ignored—told again that they would be at my new office on Friday. Since Rosemary had set up our bookkeeping system with a Fort Madison CPA, we called him. When the two IRS agents, one old, one young, showed up, the CPA was there, too. They were shocked to see us! They were looking for the former owner. We pointed out that we had purchased the assets of his corporation, not the corporation itself. Much chagrined, they left.

We subsequently learned that the younger one, who hadn't had the job very long, was the son of a local farmer, who had a grudge against our predecessor—so the son was out for revenge. We heard later he had gone back to school—jobless, I suppose.

Small towns!

Allan

Dear Jody,

We moved again—please note our new home address. And you won't believe this place we moved to!

Just four miles from our central newspaper operation in Bonaparte is a small historical river town, Bentonsport. Old houses, dam across the river, a few sorry-looking cabins and trailers squatting in the mud of the riverbank.

Allan and I were driving through here one day, when he remarked that this house, out in the edge of the town, and the surrounding land, was for sale. He had seen it listed in the state historical society's bulletin, since it is in the National Register of Historic Places.

We drove up and were looking through the windows, when he remarked that he knew who had the key. Once inside, he was shocked when I suggested we buy it. So we did—sold our place in West Point and moved. It is much closer to our new office.

It was fully furnished, so we had to dispose of much furniture, mostly antiques—but we kept the baby grand piano in the music room. The house is all brick, walnut beams in the attic, twelve-foot ceilings, twenty rooms, three working fireplaces, three wells, basement under half of it, and a large barn. It was built over a century ago, by Mormon craftsmen, for the founder of the town, the man who built the dam and put in grist and textile mills. Over three thousand people lived here then, and a similar number in Vernon, across the river. Today Bentonsport boasts twenty-seven inhabitants, and Vernon four!

We can run our boat on the river—there is a launching ramp near us—but our timing was poor. Our daughter is in the process of moving from Wyoming to New Mexico, and, wanting to keep her four horses, shipped them to us. All of a sudden we have a barn full of horses, cats and Allan's black Labrador retrievers!

We have a lot of remodeling we want to do, and some just plain maintenance to do, in order for it to be where we want it. The former owner, a retired Air Force officer, just used it as a weekend place, but after he became ill, it wasn't very well maintained. I'll send you pictures.

Love,

Rosemary

Dear Elmer,

I've been learning what it's like to try to get something done in a very small town. I lined up a guy to install a new furnace and air conditioner in our office building. He got it about half done and asked for a partial payment. Didn't come back for a month—until the money ran out, I guess. Now he is almost finished, and when he asked for more money, I told him not until it is done. Haven't seen him for a week. Learned through the grapevine that he took a job as maintenance man at a religious college in another state. His wife is bugging me for the money—says she has someone lined up to finish the job. I'm doing it myself. Don't ever intend to pay him anymore until he adjusts the amount—if at all.

Told Rosemary if I ever get out of a job I'll become a handyman in this county and get rich. I can see why it is one of the poorest counties in the state—nobody wants to work. Tried to hire someone at one and one-half the minimum wage to just come to the house and look after the animals. No takers, yet people are sitting on their front porches and complaining about how poor they are.

Been meeting some of the local residents who are ambitious. Man and wife own a small river hotel, which they have turned into a museum. She's tough, but all right, and he is hilarious. We like them both. He has one arm off at the elbow. I don't know how, and will never ask. The other day he was cutting some glass for a window, when his arm slipped and he cut a small gash in the stub of his missing arm. He wrapped a towel around it and I drove him to the hospital, about five miles away. Lots of excitement when he walks in with a missing arm, and the stub wrapped in a bloody towel! He milked it for all he could, before his doctor showed up and laughing told everybody the truth.

He has been a great help to us. I came home the other day and, noticing his truck in the driveway, I called out to Rosemary, asking where she was.

His voice came back, saying, "We are upstairs, in a closet upstairs, getting plastered!"

She had decided to try to put new plaster in it, and he had volunteered to show her how.

There is an old lady here who runs a combination bookstore and museum, guarded by a mean dog, which is always lying out front. I was riding our biggest and meanest horse, Old Brutus, along the road there the other day, when the dog decided to attack. As he nipped at the heels of the horse, I could feel Brutus tighten up under me. I grabbed the saddle horn with both hands as the horse kicked the dog, sending him sprawling clear back to the front of the building. The old lady came storming out, telling me I might have killed her dog. Told her I hoped so. But I didn't. He runs away now when we ride down there.

I was fishing down along the riverbank the other day with a couple of West Point friends, when a very pretty, but obvious slow thinking girl showed up. About eighteen or twenty, I guessed. She was wearing a dirty, tight-fitting short dress, but not much else.

One of my friends said, noticing bruises on her legs, "You look like you hurt yourself. Did you fall down?"

"My husband did that," she answered, "he hits me with stick sometimes."

Later I asked One Arm about her, and he told me the town's resident Dirty Old Man, had agreed to keep her after her family rejected her because if her mental condition, and supposedly had married her when she got old enough.

"He wasn't doing anybody any favors," he said. "I think he just wanted a woman, and this was an easy way to get one."

I have since seen her and her husband, and he is something else—dirty, mean looking, unfriendly. Probably in his sixties. Don't know what they live on, in a dirty old shack down by the river.

It's hard to believe the number of elegant old and new houses perched on the hills, looking down on shacks, trailers, and hovels crowded along the muddy river banks. Mostly weekend or summer places, but some permanent.

Allan

Dear Elmer,

It's difficult to get anybody excited around here, including my doctor. I woke up early the other morning with a feeling that someone was sticking a knife in my chest. Jumped into my pickup and raced to the hospital. They did an EKG while waiting for the doctor—who is also a farmer.

Eventually I spotted him strolling casually along in front of the building, listening to the birds sing, watching the animals, while I'm lying there dying!

"You certainly took your time," I said.

"Nothing wrong with you," he said. "When they called, I thought this must be my week for coronaries—I've got two in here now. But not you. The EKG said no."

With that, he poked me in the chest with his finger, and I almost went through the ceiling. Turns out a little muscle had slipped. He gave me a shot of something, then worked it back in place. He accused me of doing something stupid to cause it.

After denying it, I remembered that I had moved my boat in the yard under human power the night before—too lazy to fire up the tractor or pickup.

"That'll do it," he said, laughing. "And quit being a nuisance. I don't like to get up this early, except to do my chores."

I have a feeling his cattle get better attention that his human patients!

Met the tax assessor. Wish I hadn't! We received a notice of a drastic increase in our real estate taxes, so I drove over to the county seat to inquire as to why.

"Increased value of the place," he said, aiming on of those 'I got you, fella' grins at me. "Obviously you have done a lot to it."

"Just because I mowed the grass, cut some weeds, and added a few flowers and paint shouldn't make it worth that much more."

Of course I knew he was right—I had stolen the place anyway. I just didn't like his attitude.

Don't know how much longer we will be here. Some outfit wants to buy the papers. We're getting tired of deadlines. Might just sell.

Since we acquired the rural magazines last year, that just might be enough. We can run them from the Bentonsport house, so we won't need office space. Are you getting your copies? You are on the mailing lists.

Allan

Dear Elmer and Jody,

Sold the newspapers, kept the magazines. Interesting when one of the new owners arrived in Bonaparte, with his wife, guess what she said?

"This place is really grim—and no way would I live here!"

Looks like he is staying without her, and commuting on weekends back "home."

Bentonsport is not a bad place to run the magazines from, except it is too far to an airport—and they take us all around the country. But it is nice to have a business that is more or less world wide, not dependent on local customers.

Since this place is in the National Register of Historic Places, the State Historical Society asked us if we would let them have an open house on a Sunday. Said they would do everything—serve, as guides, close off the bedrooms with ropes, put down runners for the traffic, and no children would be allowed. We could expect about three hundred people. We reluctantly said O.K.

After I my count went past three thousand, I gave up!

The following Saturday a couple showed up, who said they were on the tour, and asked if we would consider selling the place. We told them no. They said they had four kids, teenagers and younger, who were active in 4-H, and our place would be ideal for their activities. They left, disappointed.

Then one Saturday we were discussing the fact that our son lives in a Chicago suburb, one daughter in New Mexico, and the other is in the Peace Corps in Africa. Why are we still living in the country? Right in the middle of this conversation, that couple showed up again. We shot them a price, and they bought it. We wish them luck—hope they either have plenty of money for gas, or plan to cut a lot of firewood!

We have already found a place from where we want to publish magazines.

Allan

SECTION 3

ALBIA, A TOWN FULL OF ITSELF

D̲ear Elmer and Jody,

The house has seventeen rooms, including three full baths, plus a full basement and a very large attic—and it is on the "cruise strip," just five blocks from the courthouse square. We think the location might discourage vandalism, with all the cars going by, since we have to be gone quite a bit. Two of the rooms have become offices, but we have rented space in an insurance office as well.

Our first problem is "soak the newcomer," of course. The first thing we did was to have all the plumbing replaced, by a very reasonable and professional plumber. He called me at our old location to tell me that the local gas company wanted a large deposit before they would turn the gas on, even though we had been customers of theirs for some time. I told him to replace the furnace with an electric one. I guess he told them that, because suddenly we had gas, he said.

The house needs a lot of remodeling. The local electrical firm gave us a quote on rewiring it, to be done in stages. After they had a new service connected, and put in a new circuit breaker box, they wanted a partial payment of half. Then the head honcho came back to tell us that he had underestimated, and the rest of the job would cost us more that the total original quoted price. I told him to go to hell, of course, and hired a guy fro a neighboring town to finish. More about the stupid electrician later.

All four of our rural and horse magazines are printed in Waverley, and they do a very good job—but, trying to be a good citizen, when the local newspaper asked to quote on printing one of them, I decided to give them a try. I even let them see a copy of the other printer's itemized invoice.

Proofreading the copy from the other printer usually took less than an hour, because they were conscientious. After eighteen hours of making corrections on the new copy, I finally got it back to the local outfit. Then they expected me to come in and finish up preparing the magazine and getting it to the post office, which was all done by the previous printer.

The last straw was the post office. When the postmaster told me the mailing cost was three times what it had been, I tried to tell him that the rate had been dictated to us by the central office to which he reported. He said they were wrong! When I reported this to the central office, the director asked me to fill out some forms and take them to the local post office, telling them to send them to her in their mailing with regular reports. The assistant postmaster blew up!

"The only way you can mail anything from here, Fella," he screamed, "is with stamps on it, in your own envelope!"

Something else to report to the central office. Of course that ended us trying to do business locally—no more printing, no more mailing.

Then one of our employees took a large mailing up to send to Canada, since we do business all over the world. A postal employee sold her the stamps, then later the assistant postmaster told her they were the wrong stamps for a foreign country. When she tried to tell him what happened, he told her she was just "shit out of luck," and would have to buy the other stamps. I took the complaint on that one all the way to Washington, and the postmaster came down to my house to apologize. But the assistant still did not see where he had done anything wrong. More about him, and the screwed up post office in Albia, later.

Allan

Dear El,

Now I've been offered a job, back in manufacturing. A company in Dubuque wants to take over an old abandoned building here and start a new branch plant in it. I have been offered the position of General Manager, the Head Honcho. I have reservations, but I'm going to do it anyway. I have started several manufacturing plants, and served as chief engineer—but I've never actually run one.

My first entanglement is with the general contractor. He has his own ideas, some good, some bad—won't listen to anybody. He won't be here long. About to break with his father, who actually owns the business.

Remember the electrician who more than tripled the price for wiring my house? He wanted to do the wiring for the plant. Guess what I told him!

And the assistant postmaster? He and his brother are in the telephone installation business—him part time, his brother full time. Guess what I told him!

Planning on about 150 jobs, fifty to start with. Got 1500 applications. Everybody in the county grabbing me to discuss some relative's application. Fortunately I don't do all the picking personally.

Just what in hell have I gotten myself into?
Allan

Dear El,

Got the plant, all 51,000 square feet of it, with millions of dollars in equipment up and running. Reasonably good crew, but troubles haven't ended. Never will.

Driving back from home, where I had been for lunch, the other day. Pulled out of a long line of traffic by two cops in a cruiser. (Don't know why it takes two to man one patrol car.) Gave me a ticket for speeding. If I was, so were a dozen other vehicles. When I told my secretary about it, she told me I had fired the daughter of one of the cops. I told her I didn't know him or his daughter, and I hadn't fired anybody. She told me that our production manager let her go because she had worked only thirty days of a 180-day work period. I heard this same cop, when off duty went to the jail and beat up a black man his daughter had been dating. When I went to the mayor with my complaint, he said the cop and his wife both were in the law enforcement department, and that everybody wanted to get rid of them, but they were experts in union affairs, and job litigation.

Soon I had to release the husband of the court clerk for failure to do his job. I was called for jury duty the next day. Simple case. Man arrested for being intoxicated—he was walking down an alley to his home. Found not guilty on that charge, so the sheriff's deputy and policeman who had arrested him charged him with assault. They just couldn't stand the guy, so had to get him on something. You should have seen him—mild mannered, about 130 pounds, couldn't assault anything! The jury foreman suggested that we spank everybody and send them home. I suggested we spank the defense attorney and county prosecutor as well. He said that if the arresting officers had been mature none of this would have to be considered.

We found the guy not guilty, much to the chagrin of the local magistrate—whose only qualification for being appointed to the job was that she was the widow of a highway patrolman. Before that she worked at the local weekly newspaper.

Allan

Dear Elmer and Jody,

Back to the post office. My first secretary, who was very good at her job, developed a lingering illness and had to quit work. I had her final check mailed to her home, out on a rural route in the country. Her first name was "Gene," spelled that way. The post office decided that was an error, so they sent her check to a man by that name in town. He was away at the time, so we had a lot of trouble getting her paid. I wish the postal employees would stop thinking.

The next boondoggle was everybody's paychecks. Until we got everything on line between the parent company and the Albia plant, the checks were mailed to us from Dubuque. One week they didn't show up. Postmaster was away, and assistant postmaster said they had not arrived.

Friday (payday) came and went, and still no checks. I told everybody that if they wanted me to I would write checks out of my maintenance account to cover them temporarily. Some did. The following Wednesday evening the postmaster came to my house, again very much chagrined, to tell me that the checks had been there all along. Since they were in a cardboard box, it was assumed that it was junk mail, so nobody had bothered to give them to my secretary, who picked up the mail on her way to the office every morning!

Now for the country club. I was approached by a banker and another businessman about joining the local club and running for president, since no one else would. The statement was made that maybe I could get it straightened out. When I inquired about what was wrong, they said that it had at one time 120 members, but since just anybody could charge expenses to its accounts, it had gotten into a six-figure debt. Then when they arbitrarily solicited enough from each member to pay it off, they lost half their members. I declined

But I did get elected to the vice presidency of the Chamber of Commerce. This would automatically make me president next year, if the railroad runs right, and it always does.

Allan

Dear Folks,

Well, they elected me vice president of the Chamber of Commerce, as I predicted—and it brought about the last straw of small town living. The Chamber has one full time employee, a secretary. I stopped in the office the other day, to try to get up to date on activities, and she appeared to be mad about something.

"I suppose you are going to get rid of me," she said, "and put some friend of yours in here."

I told her I did not understand, that all my friends had good jobs.

Turns out she thought I was there to do an audit of the books, so she confessed that many things were not quite right—especially with the IRS.

Of course, the other officers of the Chamber supported her, and I resigned. This old Outsider couldn't convince them that all I wanted was to get it straightened out.

And guess what? Some outfit in Tennessee wants to buy the magazines! They can have them.

We listed our house on Thursday and accepted an offer on Tuesday.

More banking problems, though, to mar our return to the anonymity of a bigger community. Closed out all our accounts in one bank—no problems. Other bank had computer problems, said we couldn't close out for several days. Manager got mad when I suggested that maybe they had a manual backup system. They didn't know how to use it! I waited, while they learned.

The movers are loading as I write this. Next town, 140,000 people— where we can pick our contacts, and the whole population won't treat us as outsiders! Small town living—phooey!

We'll write you from there.

Allan

Well, we tried! After three towns—one dinky, one small, one a little bigger—we still felt like outsiders, and were treated accordingly. Now we can sympathize with that old guy in West Point who said, "I've only been here twenty-nine years!"

PART FOUR

OUT TO GET RICH AS A WRITER

"He does not write at all whose writings no one reads."—Martial, A.D. 40–102.

ANYBODY CAN WRITE—good, mediocre or bad material.

But EVERYBODY can't expect to get PUBLISHED.

Some good material falls by the wayside, while being passed by worse material, simply because the writer doesn't know the necessary procedures of HOW to get it published.

This was written to REMEDY THAT, especially as related to periodical publications such as magazines.

This gives you many pointers on WHAT to write, and, even more important, for WHOM to write it.

It then tells you the importance of HOW you PRESENT it to publishers, and gives you advice on doing it correctly.

It even tells you how to get it published, by knowing where and how to SUBMIT IT, and when and how to FOLLOW UP.

It also explains PAYMENT methods and the pleasant, satisfying PROFITABILITY of Freelance Writing.

It will make you a better, more informed Freelance Writer, and, most important, a PUBLISHED WRITER.

Writing for periodicals is fun and profitable, if you are good.

INTRODUCTION:

Dear Writer:

My name is Allan Young, and my principal source of income is as a freelance writer, and I have been writing as long as I can remember. I have written thousands of technical articles, and have authored seven non-fiction books from them. This treatise is my way of attempting to pass on to you what knowledge I have been able to glean from my experiences in getting my material published.

Now you are probably asking yourself, "Who is this clown, and why does he think that he can give me advice on how to get my material published? After all, I am a writer, I am a pro, and I know that the world can't wait to read all of the material that I write." (I once felt that way myself.)

Well, let me tell you a little bit about myself, and my own long, successful career as a freelance writer, editor and publisher of several publications which used freelance writers as their main source of material.

I have been editor and publisher of a series of engineering magazines, owner/editor/publisher of a group of rural and horse magazines, as well as a group of newspapers. I have held executive positions in large manufacturing companies—ranging from chief engineer to vice president and general manager to president. But I always wrote—and still do—many technical articles and books.

I think everyone should write. Write the way you talk—don't try to be Ernest Hemingway, don't try to copy the style of others—be yourself—but write something every day.

As early as the sixth grade I was writing poems and essays. By my junior year in high school I was editor of the school newspaper.

Now, before you start thinking that only a bookworm who buries himself in that sort of thing can get published, I'd like to state that I was a pitcher on both the high school baseball team and the one sponsored by the town in summer. I worked part time on a horse farm and for the Forest Service, as well as running the projector at the movie theater. I served in the South Pacific in the Navy.

Today, besides being a registered professional engineer and a certified manufacturing engineer, I am a horse show judge, a licensed pilot, a licensed marine pilot and engineer, and I hold a master's license for inland lakes and rivers—many subjects for writing.

Early in my career as a young engineer I was on the staff of one division of a world wide manufacturing company. The vice president of engineering called his entire staff together one day, and pointed out to us that some of our competitors were beating us out of many contracts, simply because they had better publicity and public relations than we did. We might even have the better equipment, but they had a better press. He encouraged us to begin writing for the technical magazines in our field., as well as speaking before various technical groups, on the premise that this would not only enhance our company's image, but would make us a few bucks on the side as individuals as well.

I thought to myself, "I should be able to do that." Since not only had I been interested in all kinds of writing as a youngster, and had produced what I considered to be well written pieces, but I felt that if I could communicate as well on paper as I could verbally, then I could certainly get my material published. So to make a long story short, I started writing short pieces describing manufacturing processes and tooling and machinery applications, and submitting them to the technical magazines of the day – and they began to be accepted. If one magazine turned one down for some reason or another, usually because they had published something similar recently, I would send it to another.

Within a few years I was writing for seven different technical magazines on a regular basis and adding about fifty percent to my regular income in doing so. That is how my family was able to live in a better house, keep two cars and a boat, my wife had a better wardrobe, my kids had new bicycles and skates, and I had new sports equipment.

It required very little effort to do, because I was writing about the things I knew. Eventually I was asked to write a regular column on manufacturing processes by one of those technical magazines, and this led me to accepting employment with them as Engineering Editor, from which position I was promoted to Editor, then Publisher. Then I became Division Manager. During those years I used mostly freelance technical writers on all those publications. But I didn't stop there. I continued to do freelance writing myself on other subjects, mostly my hobbies, which I knew best.

After tiring of flying hundreds of thousands of miles per year over an extended period of time, I decided to bail out of that type of position and stay closer to home. So I acquired a company, which owned five weekly newspapers, a shopper, a monthly farm magazine, a monthly nostalgia magazine, and one technical magazine devoted to factory maintenance. Then I took over a company, which produced a rural heritage publication, a horse care magazine, a horse directory and another nostalgia magazine. Also, I had a book publishing company. Again, I used many freelance writers in these publications.

Eventually I became tired of running a publishing business, where I couldn't do much writing myself, so, over time, I disposed of most of the publications, including the newspapers. Now I have more time to write.

What I would like to do is pass on to you some of my experiences as a fifty-year freelancer, starting in sixth grade, who is still active. I can do this by offering advice on how to get your material published in publications of the type with which I am familiar—which includes just about all of them.

I believe that I have learned the do's and don'ts, and I am certainly willing to share them with you.

Allan Ishmael Young

CHAPTER 1

WHAT TO WRITE ABOUT, AND FOR WHOM TO WRITE IT

Write What You Know

Choosing subject matter about which to write is very simple. You write what you know. Now, that doesn't mean you have to have learned it through osmosis. It can be a subject with which you have taken the time and effort to become knowledgeable. But you must know the subject matter.

As a youngster, I wrote poems, short stories and essays of a true nature about the woods, rivers and mountains of Virginia where I was growing up and going to school. Later, as an engineer, I wrote technical material, and felt that I had the ability to describe a machine or a process so that someone who had never seen one could understand it.

Then, with my many interests, I started writing on a variety of subjects. I have written, had published (and been paid for) articles, for periodicals, on subjects ranging from duck hunting to nuclear welding and laser measurements, automotive design to raising pumpkins, international machine tool shows to trout fishing, building experimental aircraft to baling hay, maintaining outboard motors to hunting mushrooms—and many others.

This doesn't mean that you have to have that many subjects to write about. It just means that you shouldn't attempt to invade a new territory and write about subjects with which you are not familiar unless you intend to take plenty of time to make yourself familiar with them first.

Publishers are forevermore plagued by people who discover something that is new to them and who just can't wait to tell the rest of the world about it—when just a minimum amount of research would show them that the rest of the world has already known about it for some time.

Just as there are associations devoted to every conceivable subject (there is even an Association of Association Managers), there is a publication which includes any subject on which you might have expertise—be it gathering wild rice or nuclear physics. A little research at your local library's directory department can steer you in the right direction, as well as enhance your knowledge.

Leave Yourself Out Of It

Do not write about yourself unless you really have a captive audience, and have an interesting story to tell. Nobody cares what you do or what happens to you personally, unless you are already a celebrity. It is a lot more interesting when you can write about happenings, places, other people and things.

One time, I had a young lady propose to me a story about Haflinger horses. Her idea was to visit with a well-known breeder of these animals and tell our readers about them. But when she produced the article, it was not about Haflinger horses, it was not about breeding Haflinger horses, it was not even about a person who was raising Haflinger horses. The article was about her visiting a man who raised Haflinger horses, and as I told her, I didn't really think anybody cared. I know I didn't. I wanted to learn about Haflingers.

Later, when she sent me a story about a gelding that was going to have a colt in the spring, I realized why she had to write about herself. She had invaded a new territory in which she had little, if any, knowledge. She should never have tried to write for a horse magazine.

Besides, writing about yourself for a periodical becomes too slanted and opinionated for most editors to use. I'm sure you are saying to yourself by now that this guy is referring to himself all through this text. But keep in mind that this is not a technical treatise for a periodical. It is written for the purpose of giving you the benefit of my experience, so, naturally, in order to do so I must inject myself into the text continuously, so please forgive me.

Your Opinions Aren't Interesting, Either

When you are trying to get your foot in the door as a freelance writer, don't expect the editors to be the least bit interested in your opinions. That's worse than writing about yourself, unless, of course, you are already famous.

Be aware that most periodical publications are basically "how to," and that's the kind of material they expect.

I have had people submit to me their opinionated write-ups on events, people or subjects. And, as a publisher, I simply was not interested in letting somebody else vent their spleen in my publication, which was devoted to informing the readers about a particular field of endeavor.

As an example, while publishing engineering magazines, I received a treatise on how one particular manufacturing operation was not effective the way companies were performing it, and why didn't "they" come up with something better. Later, when he asked me what I did with his article, the author was much chagrined to learn that I had "round filed" it, and was even more so when I suggested that as soon as he developed a replacement manufacturing method, he could write it up and I would publish it.

Write For The Readership

When you select a subject to write about, and an approach to take in writing it, make sure you gear it for the readership involved. Do not ever attempt to write to please your friends, relatives or whomever you consider to be critics. Most of these people will be jealous of the fact that you even attempt to write in the first place, and very few of them will support or encourage you.

A remarkable exception to this statement is my wife, who is my best and most positive critic. I have dedicated all of my books to her. There have been times when she was proofreading a manuscript and would tell me that something didn't make sense, to which I would reply that it wasn't supposed to make sense to her, it was written for a different audience. Then I would reread it, and it didn't make sense! I hope you have someone like that, too.

Once, while writing one of my regular columns for an engineering magazine, one of my cohorts in the engineering department saw it and asked if the editor of a competitive publication might not be critical of it. I told him he might, but it wasn't written for him. It was written for engineers and manufacturing managers like us.

Another co-worker told me that I was writing "old Stuff." I told him that just because we did it every day didn't mean it was common knowledge. My research had shown me that just the opposite was true.

It has been said that in writing fiction the key word is "audacity." You have to give the publisher, and reader, something he has never had, and can't get anywhere else.

The key word in writing for the reader of periodicals has to be "accuracy." If it isn't right, somebody will catch it, much to the detriment of both you and the publisher, if it even gets that far. (A gelding, being a castrated male, can't even father a colt, much less give birth to one!)

So, you have your material checked by someone knowledgeable in the subject, for accuracy, before the editor, or worse yet, the reader, does it for you. Sometimes, of course, this can be a problem. You have to give instructions that they are to check for technical accuracy, only, and not to edit or rewrite it to suit themselves.

Once I produced a rather lengthy article on a technical training school and sent it to the head of the school to be checked for accuracy. He butchered the material—rewrote the article, filled it full of puff and a sales pitch to recruit new students, rather than a technical article on the equipment and processes used there, as I had written. After he called later to ask why it hadn't appeared in the magazine for which it was scheduled, and learned that it was cancelled, he came right out to see me, lunch invitation and all. I guess he decided any publicity was better than no publicity. The article was never published, in any form.

Even if the editor had caved in and published it, I'm sure it would have been at the bottom of the readers' survey.

Always make sure that you do your writing for the readers of a particular publication, and the editor will most certainly consider your material.

Are You A Writer, Or A Reporter?

If you intend to thrive and prosper as a freelance writer, don't ever take on writing assignments. If you begin to let editors and publishers dictate to you what you write and the schedule for writing it, then you become a reporter, not a writer—simply being sent out to cover a happening or a subject to fill a space in their publication. Consequently, you become just one of their arms instead of a freelancer. You become a staff member under their control, without the benefits of a regular employee, and your own independent activities are limited.

Such an arrangement might look good on the surface, with some guarantee of stability—but the loss of freedom to write for anyone anywhere isn't worth it.

Chapter 2
HOW TO WRITE IT AND PRESENT IT

H ow To Grab The Editor Or Reader And Keep Him

As a freelancer, you not only want to write an article so that it will be understood and enjoyed by the reader, and will entertain and inform him as well—but it must also be written so that it will grab the attention of the editor who reviews the article in the first place. Editors do not have time to read in detail each item they receive in order to make a decision on whether or not to use it. So consequently, everything about a magazine article written by a freelance writer must be attention getting. The ideal type of article for a periodical publication is one consisting of headlines, sub-heads, captions and text.

The same things hold true for the reader. In order for good readership to occur, the headlines must get his attention, then the sub-heads must tell him more of the story, then the captions give him enough details so that if he doesn't have much time to read at that particular moment, at least there is enough to this point to let him know if he wants to read the rest later.

Headlines As Attention Getters

When the editor first opens the envelope, and looks at the article, the headline had better grab him immediately, and I'm not talking about the subject matter. The subject matter itself might be wonderfully interesting to the editor and to his readers, but the headline itself had better grab him—even though he might change it at his discretion later. The ideal headline is the type that the newspapers produce—one that says, "Joe Blow was killed, and the butler did it." Now that is a real attention-getting headline, and it can apply to periodical publications, too. For another example, try one that says you can learn to do so-and-so in one lesson. That is a real grabber, because regardless of what the subject matter is—if I can learn to do anything in one lesson, I want to read on and find out how to do it, or find out how someone else did it.

Sub-heads As Story Enhancements

After the editor/reader sees the headline, then any sub-heads, which are built into the article, should tell the story in a little more detail. They should be sprinkled throughout the article, not just under the main head-line—and they should tell the whole story.

One publication with which I am familiar calls these "Express Stops," and they actually have a time established and printed on the cover as to how long it would take to read all of the Express Stops in each of their editions, so that the reader who skims through the magazine superficially in order to determine which articles to go back and read later should be able to know just how much time that skimming should take. And that's important in this busy world. Most of us don't have time to sit down and read through a complete magazine from cover to cover, even over a longer period.

Well Written Captions Also Tell The Story

If there are illustrations, and it's always nice if there are—whether they be pictures and drawings or charts and graphs—the captions and illustrations should tell the story, also. Then, if the editor/reader wants to know more details, he will go on and read the text.

The captions should be very descriptive of the illustrations, but should not be so long as to compete with the text, or to take too much time to read. One of the worst things that can be produced in a magazine article is a photograph or sketch or diagram of any kind that is not completely described in the caption. Have you ever seen one of those that shows a group of people at a dinner, and the caption says, "Here is a group from the such-and-such club enjoying themselves?" Well, we can tell that by looking at the picture! What we would like to know is who those people are. We would like them identified in the photograph itself.

Again, by reviewing the headlines, then the sub-heads, and then especially the illustrations and their captions, the reader/editor should have the story. Then, if this creates the desire to want to know the details, he can pursue it further by reading the entire text.

How To Present Hard Hitting, But Interesting, Text

Before even beginning your text you had better know where you are going, you should know what you want to say and have some idea as to how to say it—unlike most novelists, who say they start with a basic plot, then just see where it takes them. It's better to start with an outline and stick pretty close to it. I've written some of my best stuff with a pocket size tape recorder while driving long distances, with my outline in the seat beside me. I don't recommend this method for everyone, but it works for me.

Also, don't present it like a speaker, who tells his audience what he's going to tell them, then he tells them, then he tells them what he told them. In material for periodicals, just tell them once, then stop. There is no reason for the text material to go on and on interminably. It should say what it should say, then come to an end.

Flowery beginnings and endings are really not very interesting in a magazine article, either. I knew a freelance writer once who submitted a lot of good material to me, and I used most of it. But he had such lengthy lead-ins for his articles that I knew that every time I received one I could throw away the first two type written pages without even reading them, because they didn't have anything whatsoever to do with the subject matter of the article. He never changed, although he knew that I paid him less because of the hassle.

In my early years as a freelance writer, I asked a publisher for whom I had more respect than any other, before or since, how you end an article. He said, "Just quit. When you have said all you have to say, just stop."

And that has always worked for me.

In your material, never insult anybody, much less the advertisers—and you should know enough about the publication to know who they are before even considering writing an article for it. Once I received an article condemning all facets of the procurement of new manufacturing equipment and controls, and expounding on the virtues of getting used machinery instead. Just a swift perusal of any of my magazines would have shown the author that all of them contained advertising from new equipment builders and distributors—and none from used machinery people.

Then, too, keep all articles positive. We don't read to learn what not to do unless we can also learn what to do.

CHAPTER 3

HOW TO GET IT PUBLISHED

Publishing Is A Business, Not An Art

Back when I owned a string of newspapers, a first year journalism student from my hometown, who was at the state university, wrote me a letter telling me that I knew nothing whatsoever about publishing, and stating that my newspapers carried too much advertising, and that publishing is an art, not a business, as, unfortunately, I had been led to believe.

Of course, he had been in journalism school only three months, and I figured he was probably quoting some journalism professor who had always been on the university payroll, and who had never in his life had to make a living writing anything, or producing anything that was written.

I am here to tell you that publishing is a business, not an art! Writing might be considered an art, but getting it published, getting paid for it, and selling the publication in which it appears is all business. Don't get me wrong—it is a wonderfully enjoyable business, and that is why I have been in it most of my professional life. And that is why I am sharing my experiences with you, so you can do the same—at least to whatever degree you choose.

Even though I enjoy other careers as well, writing and publishing has always been a major interest, and has produced most of my income since I started doing it long ago.

(And the journalism student? His letter contained sixteen typographical and grammatical errors! I gave him a C-minus, marked in red, and mailed it back to him.)

There are many ways, of course, for the written material of freelancers to be used and to produce income for you. Television, for example, literally devours the written word, because it must be written before it can be seen and heard. Since the primary thrust of this text is getting material published, and of course, hopefully this can lead on to bigger and better things in other phases of creating material, we will concentrate on telling you how to get your material published in a variety of periodicals.

Of course, in order to get it published, you have to submit it to some publication in some manner.

What Are The Reasons For Publishing It?

Prior to doing this, you have to first consider why you want the material published, and why an editor would publish it. Your reasons for wanting it published, can be many-fold. You can be doing it strictly for the money. You can be doing it to satisfy your creative ego. You can be doing it because you hope to create a future as a writer, and you are looking for a foot in the door, or another stepping stone. But the reasons are very important.

When I was chief engineer for a machine tool company we used a unique method of torch cutting steel plates to save our customers money. In order to publicize this, I produced an article about it for a machine tool magazine. Payment for the article was immaterial, because I wrote it in order to get more business for my company. And it did.

Then you have to consider why a particular editor or publisher would want to publish your material in the first place. He, too, has to have a reason. Now, his primary reason will be that he must satisfy his readership.

There must be a portion of his subscribers who want to read the material that you are submitting. He may look at this from several sides.

First, it might enhance his overall publication from a long range standpoint to publish an article such as you produce. It might enhance the particular edition in which he is running it. It might be a new slant on an old subject, or completely new material which he would like to use, or he simply might be seeking a balance of material for this particular edition or series of editions, and yours happens to fit that mold.

What I'm saying is, the reasons why you want something published, and the reasons why an editor or publisher would publish it, might be one hundred and eighty degrees apart, but that is immaterial, as long as it helps you to understand why he might be publishing some material of yours.

Why You Should Shoot For Readership

The main thing that you have to do as a freelancer is to shoot for readership. If your articles are not read, you are not going to be published, and in order to shoot for readership, you have to get past the editor and publisher in the first place. Keep in mind that they will know their readership better than anybody will.

I once had a local school teacher approach me about allowing him to write a historical column for one of my publications. And I asked him, "Why do you think that I would want to publish that?" And he said, "Because this is what older people are interested in." I pointed out to him that over ninety-five percent of my readership was between the ages of twenty and fifty. I didn't really have many older people reading the publication and since I already had a column that reviewed past events, I couldn't see devoting a lot more space to nostalgia.

Obviously, he had not done any research at all on my publication to see whom the audience might be. His reason for wanting to publish such a column had to do with his own particular interest, rather than those of the readership.

Offering Previously Published Material Is A No-No

Most editors and publishers do not like pre-published material. I receive material quite often from people who send it in as a clipping from another publication, asking me to republish it, and pay them for it. There's an old adage that says that, "If I can't be the tablecloth, I sure don't want to be the dish rag." What we look for, as editors and publishers, is original material.

I have even had people say, "Well, such-and-such a publication which is much bigger and more popular than yours, published this, so I would think that you would want to, also." That doesn't make any sense at all. Even though the other publication might be bigger, or have a larger staff and higher income than mine, to me mine is still number one, and I expect to publish only the best material.

So there aren't too many people that want to be bothered with pre-published material. If they do, they will go directly to the publication that produced it. We have had several association publications republish articles from our magazines, with our permission, simply because it fit into their subject matter. They wanted to inform their membership about the subject. That works out very well.

Also, don't submit to the publisher repeated material. If you have written an article for a given publication on a given subject, and had it printed at one time, don't just follow up with more of the same, because magazines, within their given subject matter, prefer a variety of material.

Be Sure To Send It To The Right Place

For heaven's sake, when you submit something to a magazine, make sure that you have the right address for the publication! Publications, like you and me and other businesses, do change addresses once in awhile, so at least look far enough ahead to make sure that you send it to the right address so that the publishers will receive it.

And look at the magazine's staff. Pick the staff member to whom your material should be addressed. Otherwise it might never get past the receptionist, or the clerk who opens the mail. If they are aware of the fact that the publication is not looking for material on certain subjects, they might return it or dispose of it as it comes in, and the real decision-makers might never see it.

So at the very worst, you should pick a name from the masthead of the magazine, and direct the material to them.

CHAPTER 4

RESEARCHING THE PUBLICATION IN ADVANCE

How To Evaluate Current Publication Content

Make sure, when you do get a sample of the magazine, that you review the types of articles that are being published, so that you will not be sending irrelevant material to the publication. The editors don't have time to check out everything you send, so they will take one quick look to see if it is relevant, then they will let it go. We had one magazine devoted to draft horses. If somebody sent us an article about quarter horses, as soon as we saw the name, it was gone. We wouldn't even consider it, and all publishers operate the same way. When we published Factory Maintenance News magazine, if we received an article on the management of the materials section of a factory, we also ignored it, because it certainly did not pertain to what we were doing. Our Practical Horsecare magazine was devoted to the care of horses by laymen horse owners—it was not a veterinarian publication. And this is spelled out in many ways. So an article about the activities of a vet would be rejected with very little time devoted to reviewing it.

As a freelancer, I once wanted to do an article on the manufacture of classic horse drawn carriages by a company with which I was familiar. They refused to cooperate, telling me they didn't want to give away their secrets. Now, every time this has happened to me, once I found out what they were doing, I was in a position to tell them that their competition was way ahead of them already.

This time I approached an Amish buggy maker instead, thinking it might make an interesting story. The owner welcomed me with open arms, cooperated fully, and encouraged me to take all the pictures I wanted, as long as I did not photograph any of the personnel. I came away with an article on buggies for a rural magazine, one on their unique material handling for a magazine devoted to that subject and another for a quality control publication.

This is an example of writing what you know, and what you have learned—but giving it several different twists—several articles from one bit of research.

Use The Rifle Versus Shotgun Approach

The foregoing leads us into this subject. You should not only concern yourself with sticking to material with which you are familiar—again, write about that which you know—but you should also make sure that you direct it to a publication that uses that type of material. We received material all of the time for our magazines that was totally unrelated to our subject matter. We produced writer's guidelines, which were available free to anybody for a self addressed stamped envelope, and even people who had these guidelines in their possession still sent material which was totally unrelated to our subject matter. Such a waste!

This is what is known as the "shotgun approach". Generate a lot of articles, mail them off to as many publications as you can, and hope that you hit something. It is a lot more satisfying, and a lot more probable that you will have an item published, if you take the "rifle approach", where you research the magazine, find out what they do, and zero in on them as a target for particular articles. We have several freelancers who have done a magnificent job of this, and every article we receive from them is opened and read with anticipation. Now this doesn't mean that we accept and use all of the material that comes from these people, but we do look at it.

There are other freelancers whose material crosses our desk, and we don't even open it. As soon as we see their name, we either return it, or discard it—depending on whether or not it has an envelope in which we can send it back, because we know that those people have no idea what we are about, don't care, and have probably never even seen a copy of the magazine. They probably picked up on our name and address from a directory of some sort, and they are taking the scatter gun approach to sending us material.

Don't Let Your Ego Get You In Trouble

Of course then, there are other people who take the egotistical approach. They do ask for samples of the magazine, and the letters usually say something to the effect that, "I have some wonderful material for your magazine, and if you will send me a free one, I will consider sending it to you, and you will really be lucky to get it!" Well, since most publications that use freelancers look at literally hundreds of articles every day, most of us don't even bother replying to that kind of request.

It costs money to produce magazines. In our case we would send anybody a magazine for a given amount plus postage and handling. If the person wasn't any more interested than that in making a connection with us, then we weren't interested in them either, because their material can't be any better than their attitude in attempting to get it published.

Don't Duplicate Material Written By Others

Now after you have researched the magazine enough to find out what is being published, for heaven's sake, don't duplicate the articles in the magazine. One of our magazines did carry a section on "unique horses." We published an article one time on miniature horses, the little guys that only get to be about thirty inches high—and we were immediately flooded with articles about miniature horses. Once you've seen a miniature horse, you've seen them all! We weren't that interested in following up with other articles about miniature horses immediately.

After we published the article on miniature horses, we did have one of our freelancers come through with an article on "giant horses," and thought that was great! So don't duplicate the articles that are in the magazine, just research them for the types of things that are being done, and then do something different.

Respect Your Real Customers, The Readers

Now, as part of your research for the magazine, make sure that you develop a healthy respect for the type of readership that the magazine seeks. This is easy to tell from the types of articles that are being published. So whatever you do with your articles, don't poke fun at the readership. You can poke fun a little bit at the people or at the things you write about, be they animals, machines, events or whatever, but the readership itself has to be respected, or the editor and publisher won't consider your material.

They don't want to lose that readership!

CHAPTER 5

HOW TO SUBMIT YOUR MATERIAL

No Editor Wants A Hassle

Now that you know what to write about, and for whom to write it, and how to present it, and, to a degree, how to get it considered for publication because you have researched the particular magazine to which you are sending it, and have decided to take the rifle approach and send it to somebody—now comes the very important subject of how to actually submit material so the editor or publisher will consider it.

Rule #1:   No editor wants a hassle!

Rule #2:   If you think you can get away with hassling an editor, reread Rule #1.

When an editor goes through freelancer submitted material, he does it rather rapidly—again, because of the time element involved in doing so. He can't get involved in a one-on-one with any given writer.

We made it a point in our publications not to produce anything of a religious or political nature, since our publications were about people, places and things. We tried to avoid that type of controversy. I did receive a wonderful article from a woman in Tennessee who told her story very well, but threw in some religious sales pitches. I called her and told her that I liked the article, would like to publish it, but I would like to take those two paragraphs out. She told me no, that she thought they were very important to the content of the article, and to her status as a writer.

I neither agreed nor disagreed with her. I sent the article back, and we put her on our list of unwanteds.

Again, Rule #1: No editor wants a hassle.

Don't Let Quantity Of Material Frustrate The Editor

There are also a lot of little things that violate Rule #1. I have received material where each sheet was in a transparent folder, which meant, even if I used it, in order to send it to the printer to have the type set, I had to pull each of those sheets out of the transparent folder and put them in some kind of order. Again, it was a hassle.

There is also nothing worse than having to wade through unreadable writing, or faded computer type, in order to glean something from the material itself. And this can present a problem, one of time and frustration.

Variety Of Material Must Match Editorial Format

A variety of material, especially in short items like poems and essays, is really preferred by an editor and publisher, as long as it still fits the format and basic subject material of the magazine.

But try not to get so far off base with it that it doesn't fit the format. If there is a poetry page in a magazine that constantly runs poetry, don't try submitting prose—because chances are they're not going to publish it.

Publishers Are Not Running Schools

Don't ask for a critique of the material. We are forevermore getting articles from freelance writers who say, to a degree, "I am a new writer. If you don't want to publish this material, please tell me what's wrong with it." Or even more experienced writers who say, "I would like to see something like this published in your magazine. If you don't use it, please critique it for me so I will know what to submit in the future."

Well, just whom are we kidding? We editors and publishers are not running a school for amateur writers. We either get good material or we don't. If it's good we'll use it, if it isn't we'll send it back.

Sometimes even when it is good, we send it back because we simply don't have the space to include it in the publication, and this is usually explained to the author.

Your Biography Is Not Important

The other side of the coin is the people who load us up with biographical material. I have received six-line poems from people who sent me a two page biographical sketch, bragging about all of the places where they have had their poems published. Frankly, I couldn't care less.

Our magazines, like most, were devoted to the subject matter which the writers produced, not to the writers themselves. We had a lot of writers for whom we have the utmost respect. We really think the world of them, but we didn't even publish their addresses. If you want that, you can contact us, and we will be happy to give it to you, and we will brag them up 'til who laid the rail! But the publications themselves were not about the authors—they were about the subject matter written by the authors, and we can't emphasize that enough.

Container Size Must Be Adequate For Returns

Make sure, also, that the material you submit will fit into the return envelope if you want it back.

Our policy was that, after we published an article, we took the return envelope, and put the article, the author's check, all illustrations and everything else back in the envelope, and return it in that manner. We also send a copy of the publication, which contains the article.

I have received material, which I wanted to return because it was unusable, that would not fit into the return envelope, which the author sent me. And of course, I had this round file under my desk that caught stuff like that.

CHAPTER 6

HOW TO FOLLOW UP IN A POSITIVE WAY

Look At Publishing Schedule Before You Do

Whether or not you should follow up on material submitted to a specific publication is up to you. How soon you follow up, and how you follow up, is up to the magazine itself, and you have to do some more research in order to determine that. Again, keep in mind Rule #1: No editor wants a hassle! And this applies to all phases of submission.

Look at the publishing schedule first, and evaluate from that how long a period it should be before you follow up. Then make sure that the way you follow up is in such a manner that it won't automatically trigger a rejection for an article which they might be considering publishing in the very next edition. That has happened to us!

Be Patient, Publishing Considerations Take Time

Normally, when we receive copy for our publications (and most editors do this), if it is unusable, we return it immediately, regardless of why it is unusable. It might be excellent material, but if we have published something similar to it recently, then we will return it. If it is an eighty-six line poem, and we don't have room for it, we are going to send it back anyway.

If it is about a totally unrelated subject, we are going to send it back immediately.

Allow Long Enough For A Decision To Be Made

If we see even a faint glimmer of hope for the use of it, then we will hang onto it—but we will not reply to the author immediately. When magazines are published periodically—monthly, quarterly or whatever—a decision cannot be made, as soon as something arrives in the mail, as to whether or not to use it. We have to look ahead at the balance for the magazine—not just the next one, but future ones, too.

In our case, we accumulated the articles in a temporary file by subject matter, knowing full well that we had to keep a balance in the publications. We did not keep anything that we could not use, or that we did not intend to use. But if an author wrote us a letter after a couple of weeks, saying that he or she wants a decision because they have a possibility of publishing it somewhere else, or simply because they are impatient, then we automatically returned it, because we cannot make the decision as to when it will be used in that short a time.

So if you are going to follow up, be sure that you allow enough time for all publishing considerations to be made.

Evaluate Your Submissions Schedule

You are smart to submit one article at a time to a given magazine or publication, and have several of them in the mill at the same time to several magazines, so that you can wait them out. Now this doesn't mean that you can't turn right around and submit a different article to the same magazine at a different time span, but you must allow the editors enough time to make the decision.

Keep in mind that nobody wants to keep your material unless they are going to use it. Editors' files are cluttered enough as it is without them hanging on to unusable material. There are some cases where a magazine, such as one of ours which was published four times a year, might receive an article of a spring-like nature which we cannot use in this spring's edition, and we might sit on it until the next spring and use it. But, we might not know that for a few months yet.

Don't Expect A One-on-One With The Editor

Most of us writers, of course, are big egotists. Otherwise we wouldn't be out there laying our egos and personalities bare by trying to produce something in the way of an informative story or article. And most of us like to feel that we are personal friends of the editor or publisher or some staff member, but we cannot really expect a one-on-one relationship in a publishing operation that uses literally dozens of freelancers. It just doesn't happen. Not that it will become impersonal either, but you can't expect a reply and an evaluation on everything that you produce. You are probably going to wind up just getting a straight form letter like everybody else.

Yet like most publishing operations, we had dozens of freelancers for whom we have the utmost respect, and as I've said before, we looked over everything they produced whether we could use it or not. Yet we knew very little about them, and didn't even want to know. Don't take the self-centered egotistical approach of, "Hey, you can't get along without my material," because editors can.

CHAPTER 7

WHAT PAYMENT YOU CAN EXPECT

How Editorial Expenses Are Budgeted

There are several approaches to payment methods, of course. One is that you can negotiate payment on an accepted article, but there aren't too many editors that will do that. Again, Rule #1! When I was freelancing for technical magazines on a largescale basis, I always accepted whatever they sent me without question, and over half the time I was pleasantly surprised by the amount being larger than what I really expected to receive.

Almost all magazines, including ours, have an editorial budget. We looked at each edition, balanced the editorial content for it, evaluated each and every article, and established a price for it, based on that evaluation.

Don't Always Expect Payment On Volume

We do not pay a per page rate, because some authors take more space to describe something than others—not that they are any better or any worse. They just use more words. We do not negotiate values, because of our budgeting.

I had one article which I planned to produce, and I told the author in advance what we paid for such items, which we hardly ever do. He insisted on three times that amount, so I sent the article back to him. By return mail, I received five articles from him, and he told me that I could publish any or all of them, at the rate which I had offered him for the first one. I guess he decided that something was better than nothing, but I returned all of them to him. Again, Rule #1!

Some magazines pay on a page rate, simply because it's easier to calculate that way, but if you consider the value of the article to the reader, and then pay based on that, I think that you wind up with a much better quality magazine. There are some one-page articles that are of a lot more value than some two-page articles.

I had one lady who had written a number of articles for us on a regular basis, and we worked her into the budget. We did not underpay her. I guess she became enamored of her own writings, because suddenly she demanded a two hundred and fifty percent increase in payment! I told her that she made Frank and Jesse James look like a couple of Sunday School teachers, and I removed her name from my files.

Editors, by their very nature, are pretty hardheaded. Otherwise you could not produce a publication which would be self-supporting and self-perpetuating.

Payment For Assignments Should Be Known In Advance

Earlier on we discussed whether or not to take on assignments, and I personally discourage it for freelance writers, because then you become under the control of somebody else, and if the article that you produce is not published (even if you are paid a kill-fee), you cannot resubmit it to another magazine for publication. As a freelancer, I have always preferred to be in control of my own material, with the freedom to submit it in succession to several publications until somebody accepts it.

One of the problems from the publisher's standpoint in giving people assignments, is that in order to be fair, you are expected to pay their expenses for the assignment—plus paying them for producing the material. I have never liked to do that because I know how I would react to it if I were sent on a given assignment by a publication to produce material for them. I would try to work into that as many other articles for as many other publications as I could, since one of them was standing the cost. So consequently, for our publications, we very seldom put anybody on an assignment.

If there is an assignment that needs to be covered where expenses are involved, we would have it done by a staff member because they were already on the payroll. Then the only thing that we have to pay are the expenses.

Payment On Publication Is A Normal Procedure

We had many authors who would like to be paid upon acceptance, so they knew where they stood with the articles. Very few publications can afford to do that. There have been many articles that lay in the files for years after having been paid for and not used. I have done that with illustrations, but I wouldn't do it anymore.

As a freelancer, I always expected to share in what was going on, so consequently, I had to share the scheduling of the magazine as well, which meant that after the material appeared in the magazine, then I would share in the payment of it. Most publications pay upon publication because until it is published, they don't really know what to pay.

For most of us writers it is more important to get published than to get paid.

Even though publishers may evaluate the article, based on its value to the reader, until the article is actually laid out with heads, sub-heads, captions, photographs, illustrations or whatever—maybe the material even gets edited somewhat—it is difficult to make that kind of a judgment call. Your best bet is to gear your budget to receiving payment at a much later date than when you produce the material. But if you get enough material going, which we encourage very much, by submitting individual articles to several publications, and try your best to keep your articles current, while still being geared so as not to become obsolete, you can do that.

When reporting on events and happenings, in most fields, if you cover them correctly, your material can be timeless anyway.

For example, if you are writing about a specific event, you can produce an article about the most recent one of those events, while also covering the history and the usage and the people involved in the event in a general nature, so that your article now becomes timeless.

CHAPTER 8
WHERE TO SEND ARTICLES FOR PUBLICATION

Look beyond the publications on your coffee table—far beyond! There is another whole world of possibilities.

The Business Press—The recipients of these periodicals are those people and companies who produce manufactured products, such as machine tools and farm equipment, and professional services, such as consulting.

The American Business Press, an association of publishers, lists over 200 member companies, publishing over 1200 different periodicals, devoted to every subject imaginable.

The Trade Press—These publications go to those people who sell and service the products, and use the services, promoted in the business press, such as automobiles, farm equipment, hospitals, appliances and clothing.

There are over 700 publications in this field.

The Consumer Press—These are the publications which you and I might find on our coffee table or desk. They are designed to inform us on a variety of products and services, which we use in our daily lives.

There are literally thousands of magazines in this category, plus the many newspapers, daily and weekly.

The Organization Press—Pick almost any organization, and its members are receiving one or more publications devoted to it. The subjects range from retirement to engineering to gardening, to say nothing of the many veterans associations and educational groups.

There are hundreds of these periodicals, and all use freelance writers to a great degree.

An example of the way these publications are utilized is in the painting business.

There is a Business Magazine which goes to those who manufacture paint, featuring types of pigment and equipment to make paint, which they might use.

There is a Trade Magazine whose recipients sell paint and the devices used to apply it. They utilize the publication to learn what types of paint and equipment are available.

Then there are the myriad Consumer Magazines which tell you and me how to decorate and protect our houses, furniture, and other buildings and things with paint.

There is also a painting contractors association, which produces its own Organizational Magazine for its members.

If you are a person with knowledge of paint and painting, and you write, one or more of these publications will welcome your articles.

THE PROFITABILITY OF FREELANCE WRITING FOR PERIODICALS

There is a good income available from freelance writing for periodicals if you get enough volume going, and you go about it in a businesslike way. It is easier and more certain of publication than top-of-the-head fiction writing, such as novels, adventure or action stories. It can provide supplemental or even full time income. It can lead to regular columns in your areas of expertise, and to a well-known name for even greater success.

Some of the advantages are that you can have the opportunity to travel, if you wish, while still being based at home, and your expenses are deductible.

I still keep my hand in my other four professions—manufacturing (as a consultant to new plant start-up), horses (as a show judge), publishing (I own a small book publishing company), and as a relief captain of riverboats—and that gives me something to write about. My writing almost doubles my income. I think I could make a very good living by dropping all those things and just writing. But what would I write about? Pretty soon my professional knowledge would be obsolete—and you can't make a living writing about writing, anymore than you can by speaking about speaking!

Make sure that, with your writings, you make all the contacts that you possibly can with editors and publishers in the fields concerning subjects about which you are knowledgeable. And write something every day— anything at all. Just make sure you write something. Don't wait for inspiration. Just simply sit down and put something on paper, a disk or a tape. The tools you use are immaterial—it's the ideas that count, and for which you get paid. Again, make sure that you write only that which you know. Otherwise, you will look like an idiot. Determine your own writing style, and determine how to present it.

Then follow all of the rules about how to get something published— remembering that the only reason why a publisher will run your article is because it enhances his business.

Research, very carefully, any and all publications to which you intend to submit material, and make sure that your material is appropriate for that magazine.

In submitting your material, remember Rule #1: No editor wants a hassle!

The easier you can make it for him or her, the better chance you have of getting your material used.

Use your own judgment about following up on submitted material, but be careful about triggering an automatic rejection because of the way you follow up.

Keep in mind, when it comes to payment, that most publications are budgeted for contributed material, and payment is not negotiable. If you feel as if your article is of more value than you are being offered, be prepared to submit it other places—because nine times out of ten it will be rejected. And be prepared to wait for payment upon publication, because in most cases that is when you will receive it, and it will be non-negotiable.

My philosophy: everybody should write, whether they feel like they have the ability or not—everybody should write!

I'm here to wish you the best of luck in your writing career as a free-lancer for periodical publications. I hope that these experiences and suggestions help you to get your material published.

My suggestion is that you utilize this material best by highlighting those areas which can be of value to you, and keeping it handy as a reference whenever you plan to submit items to periodical publications. A minimum amount of research at your local public or educational institution library will yield names, addresses and subject matter to give you direction to find the periodical publications in your field.

GOOD LUCK!

About the Author

Allan Ishmael Young has a distinctive background in writing based on his own experiences in many fields of endeavor. His other books published by Writers Club Press, iUniverse.com, include an Appalachian Trilogy, consisting of KNOCKIN' THE BLACK OUT, A Novel of Coal Mining in the 1930's and 1940's, THE LEGEND OF THE HEAD ROCK, A Saga of the Northern Migration, and THE NEW REVEREND, Romance and Rancor in the Bible Belt—as well as FOUR NOVELLAS, The Nightingale of the Mountain Fold, The Angel of Camp Courageous, The Hostages of the Barren Hills, and The Victim of the Window Rock; plus THUNDER IN BRANSON, A Jake Tama Murder Mystery, Multiple Murders in the Music Mecca.

www.ingramcontent.com/pod-product-compliance
Lightning Source LLC
Chambersburg PA
CBHW061337280526
45784CB00001B/46